CONAN DOYLE

CONAN DOYLE

HIS LIFE AND ART

by

HESKETH PEARSON

'I am the man in the street'
CONAN DOYLE

TAPLINGER PUBLISHING COMPANY
NEW YORK

This edition published in the United States in 1977 by
TAPLINGER PUBLISHING CO., INC.
New York, New York

Library of Congress Catalog Card Number: 76–55906
ISBN 0–8008–1806–7

TO JAMES GALBRAITH MITCHELL

CONTENTS

LIST OF ILLUSTRATIONS

(between pages 114 and 115)

Dr. Doyle in the chair (*Mansell Collection*)
An artist's impression of Conan Doyle in Egypt (*Mansell Collection*)
Conan Doyle at Bloemfontein during the Boer War (*Private Collection*)
Wedding group taken on the occasion of his marriage to Miss Jean Leckie (*Dame Jean Conan Doyle*)
Brigadier Gerard salutes his emperor, from *The Strand* of 1895 (*Mary Evans Picture Library*)
Studio portrait of Conan Doyle's second wife (*Dame Jean Conan Doyle*)
Dr. George Budd (*Private Collection*)
George Meredith (*Mary Evans Picture Library*)
J. M. Barrie (*Popperfoto*)
Jerome K. Jerome (*Mary Evans Picture Library*)
An artist's impression of Doyle in the Langman hospital (*Mary Evans Picture Library*)
Sir Arthur Conan Doyle at home (*Mansell Collection*)
A visit to America: with Lady Doyle, Mary Pickford and Douglas Fairbanks (*Dame Jean Conan Doyle*)

CONAN DOYLE
In his study at Hindhead, 1904

INTRODUCTION by Graham Greene

THE POKER FACE

ONE has seen that face over a hundred bar counters – the lick of hair over the broad white brow, the heavy moustache with pointed ends, the firm, good-humoured eyes, the man who is a cause of conviviality in other men but knows exactly when the fun should cease. He is wearing a dark suit (the jacket has four buttons) and well-polished boots. Could Sherlock Holmes have deduced from this magnificently open appearance anything at all resembling the bizarre truth?

Mr Hesketh Pearson tells this far from ordinary story with his admirable accustomed forthrightness: Mr Pearson as a biographer has some of the qualities of Dr Johnson – a plainness, an honesty, a sense of ordinary life going on all the time. A dull biographer would never have got behind that poker-face; an excited biographer would have made us disbelieve the story, which wanders from whaling in the Arctic to fever on the West Coast of Africa, a practice in Portsea to ghost-hunting in Sussex. But from Mr Pearson we are able to accept it. Conan Doyle has too often been compared with Dr Watson: in this biography it is Mr Pearson who plays Watson to the odd enigmatic product of a Jesuit education, the Sherlock-hearted Doyle.

It is an exciting story admirably told, and it is one of Mr Pearson's virtues that he drives us to champion the subject against his biographer (Johnson has the same effect on the reader). For example, this reviewer would like to put in a word which Mr Pearson omits for the poetic quality in Doyle, the quality which gives life to his work far more surely than does his wit. Think of the sense of horror which hangs over the laurelled drive of Upper Norwood and behind the curtains of Lower Camberwell: the dead body of Bartholomew Sholto swinging to and fro in Pondicherri Lodge, the 'bristle of red hair', 'the ghastly inscrutable smile', and in contrast Watson and Miss Mortsan hand in hand like children among the strange rubbish heaps: he made Plumstead Marshes and the Barking Level as vivid and unfamiliar as a lesser writer would have made the mangrove swamps of the West Coast which he had also known and of which he did not bother to write.

And, unlike most great writers, he remained so honest and pleasant a man. The child who wrote with careful necessary economy to his mother from Stonyhurst: 'I have been to the Taylor, and I showed him your letter, explaining to him that you wanted something that would wear well and at the same time look well. He told me that the blue cloth he had was meant especially for Coats, but that none of it would suit well as Fresson. He showed me a dark sort of cloth which he said would suit a coat better than any other cloth he has and would wear well as trousers. On his recommendation I took this cloth. I think you will like it; it does not show dirt and looks very well; it is a sort of black and white very dark cloth'; this child had obviously the same character as the middle-aged man who wrote chivalrously and violently against Shaw in defence of the *Titanic* officers (he was probably wrong, but, as Mr Pearson nearly says, most of us would have preferred to be wrong with Doyle than right with Shaw).

It isn't easy for an author to remain a pleasant human being: both success and failure are usually of a crippling kind. There are so many opportunities for histrionics, hysterics, waywardness, self-importance; within very wide limits a writer can do what he likes and go where he likes, and a human being has seldom stood up so well to such a test of freedom as Doyle did. The eccentric figure of his partner, Dr Budd, may stride like a giant through the early pages of his biography, but in memory he dwindles into the far distance, and in the foreground we see the large, sturdy, working shoulders, a face so commonplace that it has the effect of a time-worn sculpture representing some abstract quality like Kindness or Patience, but never, one would mistakenly have said, Imagination or Poetry.

1943

AUTHOR'S ACKNOWLEDGMENTS

I AM especially grateful to Mr. Denis Conan Doyle and to Mr. Adrian Conan Doyle (executors of their father's estate) because, though I am not what is commonly called a 'spiritualist' and do not share their opinion of Sir Arthur's historical novels, they have nevertheless given me access to his private papers, with permission to quote from his published and unpublished writings, and indeed have helped me in every possible way with a courtesy to myself and a loyal enthusiasm for my subject which deserve a more whole-hearted agreement with their views and a more generous allowance for their sentiments than will be apparent in my work.

My sincere thanks to the following for their spoken or written contributions: Miss Mary Conan Doyle, Mr. Augustus Baker, the Rev. G. Maurice Elliott, Sir Philip Gibbs, Mr. John Gore, Mr. Francis Gribble, Mr. Lyn Harding, Mr. Robert Hichens, Mr. W. W. Jacobs, Mr. Hugh Kingsmill, Monsignor R. A. Knox, the Hon. George Lyttelton, Mr. A. E. W. Mason, Mr. Eille Norwood, Sir Bernard Partridge, Mr. Eden Phillpotts, Mr. Reginald Pound, Mr. Arthur Rose, Mr. Rafael Sabatini, Mr. Ernest Short, Mr. H. de Vere Stacpoole, Mr. Horace Annesley Vachell, Mr. Lacon Watson, Mr. A. S. Watt.

An article and a letter by Mr. Bernard Shaw are published by his kind permission.

The only considerable authority for Conan Doyle's life is himself, in *Memories and Adventures*, in *The Stark Munro Letters*, and in his four travel books. The Rev. John Lamond's 'Memoir' chiefly deals with its subject as a spiritualist.

CHAPTER I

A BRITISH CELT

CONAN DOYLE was Irish by descent, Scottish by birth, and English by adoption. Being of a plastic nature all three nations helped to mould his character, which included the chivalry and enthusiasm of the first, the pride and perseverance of the second, the stubbornness and humour of the third. Naturally he did not pass through life without having his chivalry described as absurdity, his pride as conceit, his stubbornness as stupidity. The truth will emerge as we proceed.

His grandfather, John Doyle, left Dublin for London in the year 1815 and soon (as 'H.B.') made a reputation as a caricaturist. A reaction against the ruthless drawings of Gillray and Rowlandson was setting in, and John Doyle's pleasing pencil led the fashion. 'My grandfather was a gentleman, drawing gentlemen for gentlemen,' wrote Conan Doyle. John's policy resulted in prosperity, and his four sons inherited his gift. The eldest, James, wrote and illustrated in colour *The Chronicles of England* and misspent thirteen years in compiling *The Official Baronage of England*. The second son, Henry, noted as a judge of old paintings, became manager of the National Gallery in Dublin. The third, Richard, illustrated *The Newcomes*, was famous as a contributor to *Punch*, and designed the cover of that periodical. We are primarily concerned with the youngest son, Charles, a civil servant, who spent his spare time painting. His whimsical moments brought forth fairies, but in darker moods his imagination grappled with 'wild and fearsome subjects', which displayed power, morbidity and humour in about equal proportions. At the age of nineteen Charles got a job in the Government Office of Works at Edinburgh, where, in 1855, he married Mary Foley, also of Irish parentage, who traced her descent, via the families of Pack and Percy, from the Plantagenets. They were living in a small flat at Picardy Place, Edinburgh, when their son, Arthur Conan Doyle, was born on May 22nd, 1859.

At first Charles and Mary could get along comfortably enough on his £240 a year. But when the family was increased by three girls and a boy life became difficult. Charles was not helpful. Though he sometimes managed, by the sale of a few pictures, to add another £50 to his income, he suffered from what is euphemistically termed the artistic temperament: that is, he took very little interest in his job and not much interest in his home; he lived in the clouds; and when his son writes that 'even his faults were in some ways the result of his developed spirituality', it is permissible to guess that the many paintings he gave away were exchanged for the sort of hospitality that engenders benevolence. He was, his son tells us, 'a tall man, long-bearded, and elegant; he had a charm of manner and a courtesy of bearing which I have seldom seen equalled. His wit was quick and playful. He possessed, also, a remarkable delicacy of mind which would give him moral courage enough to rise and leave any company which talked in a manner which was coarse. . . . He was unworldly and unpractical and his family suffered for it.'

Fortunately for their children his wife's temperament was not artistic. Though Irish and Catholic, like her husband, the climate of Scotland seems to have hardened her into one of those remarkable women, unremarked in North Britain, who feed, clothe, and educate a family on an income that the neediest government would not trouble to tax. She was also, like many Celts, proud of her lineage, a pride which was inherited by her first son; but

> They that on glorious ancestors enlarge
> Produce their debt instead of their discharge,

and Arthur discharged the debt to his with interest.

His childhood was Spartan, but he was sturdy. When seven years old he went to school and for two years endured laceration from a schoolmaster whose resemblance to a Dickensian character did not atone for the pain he inflicted. Arthur was, if anything, toughened by the treatment, and during out-of-school hours he engaged in many fights with his contemporaries. A love of battle was in his blood, and not even the experience of being knocked senseless by a heavy boot concealed in a bag, with which a bookmaker's assistant tried to brain him, lessened his desire to put up his fists on the least provocation, especially in defence of those who were being bullied by stronger boys than themselves.

Along with his warlike tendencies went a keen taste for

reading, and it was rumoured that 'a special meeting of a library committee was held in my honour, at which a byelaw was passed that no subscriber should be permitted to change his book more than three times a day'. He loved Mayne Reid, whose *Scalp Hunters* he read again and again. In after years he recalled how he had revelled in those tales of adventure: 'I do not think that life has any joy to offer so complete, so soul-filling as that which comes upon the imaginative lad, whose spare time is limited, but who is able to snuggle down into a corner with his book, knowing that the next hour is all his own. And how vivid and fresh it all is! Your very heart and soul are out on the prairies and the oceans with your hero. It is you who act and suffer and enjoy. You carry the long small-bore Kentucky rifle with which such egregious things are done, and you lie out upon the topsail yard, and get jerked by the flap of the sail into the Pacific, where you cling on to the leg of an albatross, and so keep afloat until the comic boatswain turns up with his crew of volunteers to handspike you into safety. What a magic it is, this stirring of the boyish heart and mind! Long ere I came to my teens I had traversed every sea, and knew the Rockies like my own back garden. How often had I sprung upon the back of the charging buffalo and so escaped him. It was an everyday emergency to have to set the prairie on fire in front of me in order to escape from the fire behind, or to run a mile down a brook to throw the blood-hounds off my trail. I had creased horses, I had shot down rapids, I had strapped on my moccasins hind-foremost to con-ceal my tracks, I had lain under water with a reed in my mouth, and I had feigned madness to escape the torture. As to the Indian braves whom I slew in single combats, I could have stocked a large graveyard, and, fortunately enough, though I was a good deal chipped about in these affairs, no real harm ever came of it, and I was always nursed back into health by a very fascinating young squaw. It was all more real than the reality. Since those days I have in very truth both shot bears and harpooned whales, but the performance was flat compared to the first time that I did it with Mr. Ballantyne or Captain Mayne Reid at my elbow.'

He displayed an early taste for verse by learning Macaulay's Lay of Horatius by heart, and such was its effect on his mind that he could reel it off almost verbatim when past fifty. Once he came into close touch with literature, but as he cannot have been more than four at the time he was unaffected by the contact. A chubby-looking, white-haired giant of a man called to see his father, and for several minutes the future creator of Sherlock Holmes sat poised on the knee of the famous author of *Vanity Fair*, who whiled away the time by making his gold repeater watch strike a hundred o'clock for the youngster's entertainment. Not content with reading the boy began to write, and there is a suggestion of the later romanticist in the theme of his first attempt: 'I was six at the time, and have a very distinct recollection of the achievement. It was written, I remember, upon foolscap paper, in what might be called a fine bold hand—four words to the line—and was illustrated by marginal pen-and-ink sketches by the author. There was a man in it, and there was a tiger. I forget which was the hero, but it didn't matter much, for they became blended into one about the time when the tiger met the man. I was a realist in the age of the Romanticists. I described at some length, both verbally and pictorially, the untimely end of that wayfarer. But when the tiger had absorbed him, I found myself slightly embarrassed as to how my story was to go on. "It is very easy to get people into scrapes, and very hard to get them out again," I remarked, and I have often had cause to repeat the precocious aphorism of my childhood. On this occasion the situation was beyond me, and my book, like my man, was engulfed in my tiger.'

At the age of nine he went to Hodder, preparatory school for Stonyhurst, where Roman Catholic boys imbibe as much truth as is thought good for them. On his journey to Preston, in Lancashire, he was overcome with homesickness and wept copiously. At Preston he joined a crowd of other boys and was driven the remaining twelve miles under the guardianship of a black-robed Jesuit. Except for the summer holidays of six weeks he remained for two years at Hodder, where he was fairly happy, his principal being 'more human than Jesuits usually are'. The outbreak of the Franco-German war during his incarceration at Hodder gave him an imaginative escape from the thraldom of lessons. Passing on to Stonyhurst he began to suffer in the cause of education. He wasted countless hours on Latin and Greek, which left him with a hatred of Greek only equalled by his loathing of Latin. He slaved away at Euclid and algebra, and finished up with an abhorrence of Euclid only equalled by his detestation of algebra. At the end of his life he wrote: 'I can say with truth that my Latin and Greek . . . have been little use to me in life, and that my mathematics have been no use at all. On the other hand, some things which I picked up almost by accident, the art of reading aloud, learned when my mother was knitting, or the reading of French books, learned by spelling out the captions of the Jules Verne illustrations, have been of the greatest possible service.' The bodily nourishment provided by the Jesuits was as uninteresting as the mental, their principle being that dry knowledge could only be absorbed with dry food. Breakfast consisted of bread and a mixture of hot water and milk. Butcher's meat for dinner, fish on Fridays, with pudding twice a week. For tea, a piece of bread and something called 'beer' but only resembling it in appearance. Supper brought a repetition of well-diluted milk, bread, butter, and quite often a sybaritic indulgence in potatoes. Perhaps the Jesuits felt that the effects of this diet might lead to disorder in the dormitories, which were always patrolled by a master at night-time. In fact the boys were never left to themselves for a moment, the priests taking part in their games, their walks, and their talks.

Even so the rigorous demands of religion were unsatisfied, and when good behaviour could not be secured by over-exercising the brain and under-exercising the belly, sterner measures were applied. The instrument of correction, Doyle had cause to remember, 'was a piece of india-rubber of the size and shape of a thick boot sole. . . . One blow of this instrument, delivered with intent, would cause the palm of the hand to swell up and change colour. When I say that the usual punishment of the larger boys was nine on each hand, and that nine on one hand was an absolute minimum, it will be understood that it was a severe ordeal, and that the sufferer could not, as a rule, turn the handle of the door to get out of the room in which he had suffered. To take twice nine upon a cold day was about the extremity of human endurance.' Young Doyle was constantly subjected to this barbarous punishment. He doubted whether any boys of his time endured more of it, the reason being that he had 'a nature which responded eagerly to affectionate kindness (which I never received), but which rebelled against threats and took a perverted pride in showing that it would not be cowed by violence. I went out of my way to do really mischievous and outrageous things simply to show that my spirit was unbroken. An appeal to my better nature and not to my fears would have found an answer at once.' His frequent penances were stamped in the memory of a schoolfellow, now Sir Bernard Partridge, who writes to me: 'I recall him at Stonyhurst College as a thick-set boy, with a quiet manner, and a curious furtive smile when he was visited with one of the school penalties, such as leaving his desk and kneeling in the middle of the classroom with his books. He was, I fancy, rather lazy in his studies, never taking a prominent place in his form: but his brain was very nimble, and he was constantly throwing off verses and parodies on college personalities and happenings —some of which I thought worth keeping.'

Doyle did not think much of his verses, though some stuff he turned out as a task on the crossing of the Red Sea by the Israelites was so far in advance of the average boy's efforts that it made him realise his literary bent. Among his comrades he became popular as a yarn-spinner, and this he turned to good account: 'There was my début as a story-teller. On a wet half-holiday I have been elevated on to a desk, and with an audience of little boys all squatting on the floor, with their chins upon their hands, I have talked myself husky over the misfortunes of my heroes. Week in and week out those unhappy men have battled and striven and groaned for the amusement of that little circle. I was bribed with pastry to continue these efforts, and I remember that I always stipulated for tarts down and strict business, which shows that I was born to be a member of the Authors' Society. Sometimes, too, I would stop dead in the very thrill of a crisis, and could only be set agoing again by apples. When I had got as far as "With his left hand in her glossy locks, he was waving the bloodstained knife above her head, when——" or "Slowly, slowly, the door turned upon its hinges, and with eyes which were dilated with horror the wicked Marquis saw——" I knew that I had my audience in my power.'

One letter he wrote while at Stonyhurst was preserved by his mother. The date is July 1873:

'MY OWN DEAR MAMA,

'I have been to the Taylor, and I showed him your letter, explaining to him that you wanted something that would wear well, and at the same time look well. He told me that the blue cloth he had was meant especially for Coats, but that none of it would suit well as Trousers. He showed me a dark sort of Cloth, which he said would suit a blue coat better than any other Cloth he has, and would wear well as trousers. On his recommendation I took this Cloth. I think you will like it, it does not show dirt, and looks very well, it is a sort of black and white very dark Cloth. You must write and tell me beforehand if you are going to meet me at the station. I know nothing about the train yet, but I will let you know when I learn. My Examen is finished, so I have finished all my work for the year, but of course it is kept profoundly secret who has got a prize. I trust I am among the Chosen few.

'I hope you and the bairns are making the best of your vacation, as I suppose you can scarcely call the time when I am at home vacation.

'I have never known a year pass so quickly as the last one, it seems not a month ago since I left you, and I can remember all the minutest Articles of furniture in the house, even to the stains on the wall. I suppose I will have to perform for Frank the office I have so often performed for Lottie and Cony, namely, that of rocking her to sleep. I suppose he is out of his Long Clothes now.

'We are going to have bathing during schools this evening, which is a nice prospect. This is the Golden time of one's life at Stonyhurst, the end of the year. Every Thursday is a holiday, and we are having Splendid weather.

'I will now say Good-bye and remain your Affec^e son

'A. C. DOYLE.'

In his last year he edited the College magazine, and at the end of his time amazed everyone by taking honours in the London Matric. He left Stonyhurst at the age of sixteen.

Long before he had managed to convince the authorities that he was not an ideal candidate for holy orders, his mother had been told that his schooling would cost her nothing if he were dedicated to the Church. As this would have saved her about £50 a year, no one could have blamed her for closing with the offer. But she may have remembered how often he had said to her, 'When you are old, Mammie, you shall have a velvet dress and gold glasses and sit in comfort by the fire'; or she may have been cooling towards the Roman faith; or, more probably, her conscience would not let her sell the soul of her boy. Anyhow she refused, and her son lived to bless her for the act and to make her later life comfortable.

While struggling with algebra and Greek and all the rest of the nonsense Doyle made a discovery, the joy of which more than counterbalanced the anguish of his lessons. This discovery, though he could not realize it at the time, settled his future career, decided the form of much of his literary work, and never ceased, through all the years of his life, to console and sustain him. The learning of history, like everything else at school, was repellent to him; but one day he dipped into a volume of Macaulay's Essays, and was enthralled. A new world was revealed to him, a vivid fascinating world quite unlike the grey and monotonous business that had bored him so much in class, and history suddenly became a living thrilling subject, 'an incursion into an enchanted land'. Then there were Scott's novels, the first books he had ever owned. For years they had remained unread; but at Stonyhurst they became his companions. He read them by 'surreptitious candle ends in the dead of night, when the sense of crime added a new zest to the story'. He always thought *Ivanhoe* the second greatest historical novel in the English language. We shall come to the first later on.

His last year with the Jesuits was spent at Feldkirch in Austria. Pausing in London on the way, the first thing he did was to visit Westminster Abbey in order to see Macaulay's grave. 'It was the one great object of interest which London held for me. And so it might well be, when I think of all I owe him.' At Feldkirch 'the conditions were much more humane and I met with far more human kindness than at Stonyhurst, with the immediate result that I ceased to be a resentful young rebel and became a pillar of law and order'. He did not, however, make a good impression on the first night of his arrival, because a master discovered him poking another fellow in the dormitory with a stick; and although he had the excuse that the boy's loud snoring prevented him from going to sleep, he was gravely admonished. It is possible, as he says, that he became more amenable to discipline at Feldkirch than at Stonyhurst, but a newspaper that he founded and edited had a brief career because it lived up to its motto, 'Fear not, and put it in print'.

On the whole he enjoyed his year in Austria. He did not

learn much German, because the score or so of English and Irish boys at the school got together and were as insular as their own countries; but he played football and went tobogganing and walked among the mountains and had real beer to drink and joined the school band, in which, being a hefty youth, he had to play a big brass bass instrument called the bombardon, which sounded 'like a hippopotamus doing a step dance'.

Leaving in the summer of 1876, he stopped at Paris on his way home. His godfather and grand-uncle, Michael Conan, who lived in Paris and whose name he had acquired at the font, wished to see him. Doyle had indulged in a rollicking farewell supper with a few other youths at Strasburg, and had exactly twopence left when he got to Paris. He did not fancy the prospect of driving to the Avenue Wagram and asking his uncle to pay for the cab, so left his luggage at the station and tramped. It was a sweltering August day and by the time the Arc de Triomphe came in sight he was exhausted. On seeing another pedestrian buying a penny drink from a man who carried a tin on his back, he halved his capital and did the same; and though the drink turned out to be liquorice and water it helped him on his way. After spending a few 'penurious weeks' with his 'dear old volcanic' uncle, he returned home, with nothing of value to show for his schooling except the encouraging valediction of a Stonyhurst master, who had called him up on the last day of term and addressed him thus: 'Doyle, I have known you now for seven years, and I know you thoroughly. I am going to say something which you will remember in after-life. Doyle, you will never come to any good.'

CHAPTER II

SOME ODD JOBS

HE returned to poverty in Edinburgh. His father was still painting, still in the clouds, still producing children, and still earning £240 a year. Another boy and another girl had arrived while Arthur had been laboriously wasting his time, and one more girl was on the way. Though his eldest sister was sending home her salary as a governess from Portugal, and two other sisters were shortly to follow suit, the domestic prospect was bleak, and the question arose: what was to be done with Arthur? A lesser woman might have insisted that he should begin to earn money at once, and Arthur's physique would have suggested a steady salary in the coal-heaving or furniture-removing line, but his mother was ambitious and took a longer view. Edinburgh having such a high reputation for medical learning, it was decided that he should be a doctor and take his degree at the University; and as examinations for several scholarships were to be held a month or so after his arrival, he swotted away at his classics, entered for one of them, and soon heard that he had gained the Grierson bursary, which meant £40 for two years. It seemed that Greek and Latin were about to justify the time he had spent on them, and jubilation reigned in the Doyle household, but on applying for the money he was told that there had been a clerical error, the Grierson bursary being open only to arts students. He naturally assumed that he would be granted the next-best possible prize for medical students, but was informed that 'the candidate to whom it was allotted has already drawn the money'. This placed him in a tricky position. He had a good case, but did not think it would forward his career if he began it by taking legal proceedings against his University; so he suppressed his rage and resentment and tried to assuage his disappointment by accepting a solatium of £7.

Entering the University in October 1876, he commenced the 'long weary grind at botany, chemistry, anatomy, physiology, and a whole list of compulsory subjects, many of which have a very indirect bearing upon the art of curing'. We need not follow him on his dreary course, which, however, was brightened by books that had nothing whatever to do with the tedious themes of his professional study, for the medical tomes on his shelves were not nearly so well thumbed as Thackeray's *Esmond*, Meredith's *Richard Feverel*, and Washington Irving's *Conquest of Granada*. He gradually collected a small library of his own, each volume of which stood for a sacrificed lunch. Every day, on the way to his classes, he gazed into one of those fascinating second-hand bookshops which no one with literary leanings can pass without a pause or a pang. Outside the door was a large tub crammed with tattered volumes at threepence apiece. Now threepence was the precise sum that Doyle was able to spend on his midday sandwich and glass of beer, so he had to choose between literature and lunch. Whenever he approached that tub a combat raged between the appetite of a youthful body and the hunger of a busy mind. The body won five times out of six, but when the mind was in the ascendant he spent a delightful five minutes choosing his volume from amongst a litter of almanacs, textbooks, and works of Scottish theology. In this way he picked up Gordon's translation of Tacitus, Pope's translation of Homer, Addison's works, Clarendon's *History*, Swift's *Tale of a Tub*, *Gil Blas*, Temple's essays, the poems of Churchill and Buckingham, and other stores for mental dissipation.

He made a new acquaintance in his student days: Oliver Wendell Holmes, whose *Autocrat, Poet,* and *Professor at the Breakfast Table* captivated him. 'Never have I so known and loved a man whom I had never seen. It was one of the ambitions of my lifetime to look upon his face, but by the irony of Fate I arrived in his native city just in time to lay a wreath upon his newly turned grave.' It was the leaven of science, especially medical science, which made the books so attractive to him, and he preferred Wendell Holmes to Charles Lamb because 'there is a flavour of actual knowledge and of practical acquaintance with the problems and affairs of life, which is lacking in the elfin Londoner'. It was perhaps not wholly chance that led him to name his most famous creation after the American essayist. The outstanding feature of Doyle's character was its simplicity and innocence, and he was deeply impressed, as only a simple man can be, by any display of knowledge, using that term not in its intuitive but in its instructive or informatory sense. Though he was but partly conscious of the fact, it was this aspect in the novels of Walter

Scott and Charles Reade that chiefly appealed to him and was
to influence his own historical romances. His obligations to
Macaulay and Edgar Allan Poe were of the same kind. If, he
once said, he had to name the few books which had really
influenced his own life, he would put Poe's stories second only
to Macaulay's essays. Macaulay seemed to know everything;
Poe seemed to deal with everything; and Doyle mistook the
memory of the first for profundity, the fancy of the second
for imagination.

It is hardly surprising that such a man should have been so
much impressed by the professors of Edinburgh University
that he popularised two of them in his books and attributed
vast intellectual powers to the dons who figure therein. To
any but the simplest and most easily gulled individual the
average professor is about as far from one's conception of a
superhuman or an electric force as it is possible for a man to
be. But if one of Doyle's professors is not a demi-god, then
he has to be a demi-devil. Of the two he was to portray at
length in several books, Doctor Bell (Sherlock Holmes) and
Professor Rutherford (Challenger), we shall speak later. Here
we may illustrate the point by reference to minor sketches of
the good don and the bad don. The first is Professor Maracot,
who appears in a story called *The Maracot Deep*, one of the
last Doyle ever wrote. We are told that he 'lives on some
mental mountain-top, out of reach of ordinary mortals'. From
this state of abstraction he is suddenly called upon to play
the man of action: 'I tell you he took hold of that ship and
everyone and everything in it, and bent it all to his will. The
dry, creaking, absent-minded scholar had suddenly vanished,
and instead there emerged a human electrical machine, crackling with vitality and quivering from the great driving force
within. His eyes gleamed behind his glasses like flames in a
lantern.' In a crisis which unnerves and prostrates everyone
else he again shows his metal: 'The quiet scholar has been
submerged, and here was a superman, a great leader, a domi-
nant soul who might mould mankind to his desires. . . . Upon
his face there was a look of such power as I have never seen
upon human features yet.' Our second example is the devil-
don, Professor Moriarty, who appears in *The Memoirs of
Sherlock Holmes*. Endowed by Nature 'with a phenomenal
mathematical faculty', at the age of twenty-one 'he wrote a
treatise upon the Binomial Theorem which has had a European

vogue'. Holmes calls him the cleverest rogue in Europe, the greatest schemer of all time, the possessor of a brain which might have made or marred the destiny of nations, and sums him up in this fashion: 'He is the Napoleon of crime . . . a genius, a philosopher, an abstract thinker. He has a brain of the first order. He sits motionless, like a spider in the centre of its web, but that web has a thousand radiations and he knows well every quiver of each of them.' Obviously the creator of Moriarty, Maracot, Challenger, and Holmes was greatly struck by the professors at Edinburgh University.

As one would expect, Doyle quickly followed the scientific drift of the period and became an agnostic. His nature demanded a belief in something, and as one usually obtains what is essential to one's nature he eventually got what he wanted, but his simple and susceptible mind was overwhelmed by the information recently poured out by Darwin, Huxley and others, all of which went to prove that the Bible had not given a very scientific account of Creation, and that the orthodox conception of Hell was humbug. This was a great relief after the Jesuits, one of whom had horrified him by declaring that everyone outside the Church of Rome was eternally damned, for he was much too kindly disposed towards his fellow-creatures to believe in a God with a diabolical nature. While ceasing to be a Catholic he did not become an atheist. His trusting, ingenuous, reverent nature favoured the idea of a beneficent power behind the universe, but under the influence of Huxley and the rest he reached a point where, before believing anything, he required proofs. 'The evils of religion,' he thought, 'have all come from accepting things which cannot be proved,' and he called himself a materialist for the odd and artless reason that he could not believe in personal survival after death.

Certainly there was nothing very spiritual in his appearance. At the age of twenty-one he was over six feet in height, brown-haired, grey-eyed, broad, and forty-three round the chest; he weighed 'over sixteen stone in the buff', and had the strength of a bullock. Not perhaps altogether aware that he was doing so, he described himself at this period in the first of his novels to survive, *The Firm of Girdlestone*: 'The long, fine curves of the limbs, and the easy pose of the round, strong head upon the thick, muscular neck, might have served as a model to an Athenian sculptor. There was nothing in the face, however, to recall the regular beauty of the East. It was Anglo-Saxon to the last feature, with its honest breadth between the eyes and its nascent moustache. . . . Shy, and yet strong; plain, and yet pleasing; it was the face of a type of man who has little to say for himself in this world, and says that little badly, but who has done more than all the talkers and the writers to ring this planet round with a crimson girdle of British possessions.' Naturally a man of this sort was a sportsman, and Doyle never missed an opportunity to box with anyone who cared to take him on, and at one time played as a forward in the University Rugby team. He must have studied a lot in his spare time, but one has the impression that he instantly dropped his medical books if there was the least chance of a bout with the gloves. 'I had an eager nature which missed nothing in the way of fun which could be gathered, and I had a great capacity for enjoyment. I read much. I played games all I could. I danced, and I sampled the drama whenever I had a sixpence to carry me to the gallery.' He became a great admirer of Henry Irving, whom he saw frequently in *Hamlet*, *The Lyons Mail* and other plays. But playgoing in those days was not unattended with danger, and once his strength and manliness were called upon. A dense crowd was waiting at the gallery door and a soldier made a girl scream by jamming her against the wall. Doyle remonstrated with him and was rewarded by a dig in the ribs. The soldier was about to follow this up when Doyle hit him clean in the face with both hands. The soldier drove him into an angle of the door and tried to kick him, but Doyle gripped him tightly. The situation was becoming unpleasant because the soldier's friends were showing hostility, one of them striking at Doyle's head with a cane and cracking his hat; but relief came with the opening of the door, through which Doyle flung his man; and then, feeling that his reception inside would be inhospitable, he saved his sixpence for another night and went home.

Meanwhile, those sixpences had to be earned, and he did his best to help the family as well by getting work as a medical assistant. For this purpose he compressed a year's classes into six months and advertised his services as a doctor's assistant for the time so saved. Knowing very little, and wishing to gain experience, he started by offering himself for nothing; but the first doctor who took him on valued his assistance at less than nothing, and after three weeks spent among the poorer classes of Sheffield in 1878 he left for London, where he stayed with some Doyle relations in Clifton Gardens, Maida Vale. He mooned about the metropolis for several weeks with empty pockets, often visiting the dock district where he watched the shipping and talked with the sailors who had roamed the world. He longed for adventure, and if it had not been for the thought of all that his mother had done for him he would have obliged the Trafalgar Square recruiting sergeants who liked the look of him, taken the Queen's shilling and joined the Army. For that matter he did 'volunteer as a dresser for the English ambulances sent to Turkey for the Russian war' late in '78, but the Turks did not hold out long enough for him to dress them. He felt humiliated by the lack of pence in his pocket. 'It affects me in so many petty ways,' he complained. 'A poor man may do me a kindness, and I have to seem mean in his eyes. I may want a flower for a girl, and must be content to appear ungallant. I don't know why I should be ashamed of this, since it is no fault of mine, and I hope that I don't show it to anyone else that I *am* ashamed of it; but I don't mind confessing that it hurts my self-respect terribly.' He was passing through that awkward phase common to so many young men whose bodily growth has outrun their spiritual development: 'The shrinking, horrible shyness, alternating with occasional absurd fits of audacity which represent the reaction against it, the longing for close friendship, the agonies over imaginary slights, the extraordinary sexual doubts, the deadly fears caused by non-existent diseases, the vague emotion produced by all women, and the half-frightened thrill by particular ones, the aggressiveness caused by fear of being afraid, the sudden blacknesses, the profound self-distrust.'

His next job was in a small Shropshire place called Ruyton-of-the-eleven-towns, where he stayed for four months, had little to do, and spent most of his time reading. It was here that his professional ability was first put to the test. During some festivities in a large country-house an old cannon burst and a bystander received a portion of it in his head. The doctor being out when the semi-demented messenger arrived, Doyle rushed to the scene, concealed his alarm at the sight, extracted the iron from the man's head, and was greatly relieved to find that the brain had not been injured, as he could see the clean white bone of the skull. 'I then pulled the gash together, staunched the bleeding, and finally bound it up, so that when the doctor did at last arrive he had little to add. This incident gave me confidence, and, what is more important still, gave others confidence.'

After that he got what he called 'a real money-making proposition'. Hard work, long hours, endless prescriptions to make up for the poorest classes of Aston, Birmingham; but he earned some £2 a month. 'On the whole I made few mistakes, though I have been known to send out ointment and pill boxes with elaborate directions on the lid and nothing inside.' The doctor and his wife liked their assistant, treated him as a son, and he returned to them on two later occasions, seeing a lot of low life, doing all the dispensing, and eventually taking on midwifery and the more serious cases in general practice.

While at Birmingham he began to write stories. The urge to do so was strong within him, and when a friend, struck by the vividness of his letters, advised him to try his hand at it, he knocked off an adventure yarn called *The Mystery of the Sassassa Valley*, sent it to *Chambers' Journal*, and to his amazement received £3 3s. He tried again for the same magazine, but though his next few attempts were not successful, he did not lose heart. 'I had done it once and I cheered myself by the thought that I could do it again.' *London Society* published his second story, *The American's Tale*, in '79. The small cheque was welcome, but it did not occur to him that he could ever be a success as a writer, and he never dreamed that he could himself 'produce decent prose'.

The financial situation at home, however, was not improving, and it looked as if prose of some sort had to be produced until he was authorised to prescribe pills. His father had subsided into a convalescent home, where he survived until 1893, and at the age of twenty Doyle found himself the head of a large and poverty-ridden family. Three of his sisters were sending home as much of their salaries as they could spare, and he was doing his best to provide for his own maintenance, but more was wanted to keep the home together, and it was early in 1880 that chance put something helpful in his way. One afternoon, while cramming for 'one of those examinations which blight the life of a medical student', an acquaintance named Currie walked into his room at Edinburgh and asked if he would care to go as a surgeon on a whaler at £2 10s. a month plus 3*s*. a ton oil money. Currie himself had got the job but found at the last moment that he could not fill it and wanted someone to take his place. Doyle did not hesitate, took over Currie's kit, was at Peterhead within a fortnight, and sailed in the *Hope*, a 200-ton whaler, on February 28th. He did very little surgery during the trip, which lasted seven months, and his chief occupations were to keep the captain company and supply him with cut tobacco. It was a free-and-easy life, for when the cook spoiled the dinner three times in succession by dosing himself too generously with rum, his habit was cured by one of the crew, who hit him so hard with a brass saucepan that his head appeared through the bottom and his neck was decorated by the sides of the pan like a ruff. Doyle's prowess as a boxer was useful and made him popular. On the first evening of the voyage he had several rounds with the steward, Jack Lamb, whose opinion was later delivered to the chief mate, Colin McLean: 'Doyle's the best sur-r-r-geon we've had, Colin—he's blacked my ee.' He did more for Lamb than that, for when the steward criticised the mate on his method of attacking a whale which had got away, both of them under the influence of rum, Doyle prevented bloodshed. Drink made the mate violent, the steward argumentative, and each time Jack referred to the whale's escape he was assaulted by Colin. After every bout Doyle tried to change the conversation, but the moment he had got his breath the steward began again: 'No offence, Colin, but all I says is that if you had been a bit quicker on the fush . . .' He never got further, the word 'fush' being the mate's cue for seizing him by the throat, and Doyle's cue for seizing the mate round the waist, after which they struggled until they fell apart from sheer exhaustion. The steward had a pleasing tenor voice and while cleaning the knives and dishes in his pantry used to sing sentimental ditties about women which filled Doyle 'with a vague sweet discontent'. Jack's later life ran in more tranquil channels: he became private baker to Queen Victoria and sometimes wrote letters to Doyle beginning 'My dear old Friend'.

Seal-killing began early in April, and Doyle did not like this part of the business. 'It is brutal work, though not more brutal than that which goes on to supply every dinner-table in the country. And yet those glaring crimson pools upon the dazzling white of the icefields, under the peaceful silence of a blue Arctic sky, did seem a horrible intrusion.' A strong sea-swell dashed the lumps of floating ice together, and Doyle, inexperienced at the game, was ordered by the captain to remain on board. In a furious temper he sat on the top of the bulwarks dangling his legs over the side, until the swell pitched the boat over to an acute angle and he shot overboard, disappearing between two blocks of ice. Coming to the surface he managed to scramble on board; whereupon the captain said that as he could not help falling into the sea he might 'just as well be on the ice as on the ship'. Doyle fell in twice again that day, which amused the captain so much that it more than made up for a bad day's sealing. On a later occasion Doyle's facility in falling off ice nearly ended in disaster. While skinning a seal he stepped backwards into the water, and as he was some distance from the others no one noticed the accident. 'The face of the ice was so even that I had no purchase by which to pull myself up, and my body was rapidly becoming numb in the freezing water. At last, however, I caught hold of the hind flipper of the dead seal, and there was a kind of nightmare tug-of-war, the question being whether I should pull the seal off or pull myself on. At last, however, I got my knee over the edge and rolled on to it. I remember that my clothes were as hard as a suit of armour by the time I reached the ship, and that I had to thaw my crackling garments before I could change them.'

In June they went farther north after whales, only obtaining four in three months, but Doyle showed such aptitude for the work that the captain offered him double pay, as harpooner and surgeon, if he would take a second voyage in the *Hope*. He relished the danger, and the lure of the Arctic with its 'peculiar other-world feeling' was upon him, but he had to refuse. The experience haunted him all his life, and he was never to forget the dazzling glare of the ice, the deep blue of the sea, the bright blue of the sky, the crisp exhilarating air, the perpetual daylight which made memorable the first glimpse of a star when they were back in the south, the sense of loneliness, the call of innumerable sea-birds, the half-human cries of the seals, the spectacle of a seal-pack scattered over the ice like grains of pepper as far as the eye could see, the lumbering bears, the glistening lead-coloured body of a whale as it jumped clear of the water, the thrilling moment when he saw suspended over him the huge side-flapper of a whale, one flick of which would have sent their boat to the bottom, the romance of

standing on the brink of the unknown, and the first sight after
six months of a woman at a lighthouse off the north of Scotland,
even though she was well over fifty and wore short skirts and
seaboots. He returned in a state of bursting good health, with
fifty golden sovereigns concealed in the various pockets of his
clothes, so that his mother 'might have the excitement of
hunting for them'.

During the last year of his study at Edinburgh he made the
acquaintance of a fellow whose influence on his literary career
was far greater than he ever knew. The student's name was
George Budd. He belonged to the athletic set in the University, played in the Rugby team, and was one of the fastest
and most determined forwards of his time, though the savage
fury of his game prevented him from receiving the international cap. Five feet nine inches in height, with broad
shoulders, an arching chest, and a quick jerky way of walking,
he had a well-built body and a strikingly ugly face. His hair,
yellowish and wiry, shot up from a square head and protruded
from his upper lip. A bull-dog jaw, overhanging brows, small,
deep-set, light-blue bloodshot eyes, set close together and either
radiating geniality or darting forth gleams of diabolical hatred,
a red, aggressive nose, strong yellow overlapping teeth, a throat
of the colour and texture of a fir-tree's bark and usually un-
protected by collar or necktie, a voice and a laugh like the
bellow of a bull—such were his physical characteristics. The
mental Budd was as peculiar. He was half-genius, half-maniac,
with a streak of charlatanism in his genius, and some sense in
his mania. Though he never appeared to work, he won the
anatomy prize from all the fellows who could not be torn
from their books. At a moment's notice he would take up
any subject with intense enthusiasm, weave the most amazing
theories around it, display a mind teeming with original inventions, carry his listeners away with him until they were gasping
with excitement, drop the subject suddenly, take up another,
and repeat the process. Torpedoes were once mentioned.
Torpedoes? Out came his pencil and he instantly began to
rough out a novel method of piercing a ship's netting. The
whole of the man was absorbed in the new idea; his enthusiasm
was infectious; practical objections were swept away by his
ingenuity; he had an answer for everything; and as he disposed of each difficulty he roared with triumph. The subject
exhausted, he turned to another. How had the Egyptian

workmen got the stones to the tops of the pyramids? Easy.
He explained how, and it seemed as if he had spent his life
studying the question. He was full of schemes for making
money, and he amassed imaginary fortunes on each and all of
the inventions which poured from his fertile brain. As he
jerked his way up and down the room he explained the new
contrivance, which was going to revolutionise something or
other, took out patents for it, included Doyle in the partnership, foretold its adoption throughout the civilised globe,
foresaw every conceivable application of it, estimated the
royalties they would make on it, planned out a dozen astonish-
ing ways of investing the money, and pictured their retirement
with fortunes beyond the dreams of millionaires; at the conclusion of which Doyle, who had been sailing through the air
on a magic carpet, found himself trudging home with nothing
in his pocket and a copy of Kirk's *Physiology* under his arm.

There was something both heroic and murderous about
Budd, whose fun could change to fury at a moment's notice.
He enjoyed horse-play, but no one played horse with him
twice, because it always began in good humour and sometimes
ended in the hospital. When in the mood he supported
authority; when in another mood he flouted it. A leading
London specialist was addressing the students, one of whom
in the front row kept interjecting facetious comments. The
specialist appealed for silence and Budd shouted, 'Hold your
tongue—you, sir, on the front bench.' The student ironically
suggested that Budd should make him hold his tongue.
Nothing loth, Budd picked his way among the inkpots along
the tops of the desks and dropped to the floor close to the
facetious student, who promptly hit him full in the face. Budd
seized him by the throat, rushed him backwards out of the
classroom, and 'there was a noise like the delivery of a ton of
coals'. Budd returned with a black eye and received three
cheers from three hundred spectators. Against this praise-
worthy performance must be recorded one that displays
another side of his nature. He did not drink much, but a little
alcohol had an immediate effect on him: he might want to
fight everyone he met, or collect a crowd and preach to it, or
play the fool in public. One quaint result was that, while he
could walk or run without deviating a step from his direction,
sooner or later he would unconsciously twist about and return
the way he had gone. Apparently sober, but really drunk, he

visited the station one night and courteously inquired of the ticket-clerk the distance to London. The clerk advanced his face to the hole in the glass in order to reply, and received Budd's fist slap on his nose. His yell brought the police, and Budd sprinted down Princes Street with some of the railway staff and constabulary in hot pursuit. But he soon out-distanced them, and after a while they paused to take breath and hold council. Suddenly they were amazed to see their quarry returning towards them and going as fast as ever, he of course being 'under the influence' and unaware that he had changed direction. They tripped him up, fell upon him, and after a violent struggle got him to the police station. Next morning he was brought before the magistrate and defended himself from the dock with such brilliance that he was let off with a nominal fine; after which he invited the police and everyone else who had witnessed against him to the nearest pub and entertained them with reminiscences and whisky.

His relations with women were of an equally incalculable order. Once he had to choose between compromising a woman or damaging himself. Without hesitating a second he chose the latter and hurled himself out of a third-floor window; but he was in luck, a laurel bush breaking his fall and the ground being soft. His marriage was just as precipitate. He fell in love with a girl who was under age, locked her governess in a room, disguised himself by dyeing his hair black, and decamped with the girl. Having consulted a Brad-shaw, and selected the most out-of-the-way place they could find, they spent their honeymoon in the village inn, where their sudden appearance and the weird yellow-and-black effect of his hair, the dye having failed to take in certain places, must have formed a topic of conversation among the natives for several years and made them far more conspicuous than they would have been in Piccadilly Circus. 'From this time forward,' wrote Doyle, 'there was added to his other peculiari-ties the fact that when the sunlight struck upon his hair at certain angles, it turned it all iridescent and shimmering.' They came to Edinburgh after the long vacation, took four small rooms over a grocer's shop, and furnished them sparsely. Budd met Doyle in the street shortly after this, thumped him heartily on the back, bellowed the details of the events just described, and carried him off to meet the lady. Doyle found a small, timid, gentle, sweet-faced, quiet-voiced girl, very likeable but utterly under the dominion of her husband, whom she obviously adored. Their flat consisted of a kitchen, a sitting-room, a bedroom, and a fourth room which Budd, convinced that it was a centre of disease, had not only locked up but had gummed paper over the door-cracks to prevent infection; though Doyle was equally convinced that the smell of cheeses from the grocer's shop below had put the idea into his friend's head.

Doyle became a frequent visitor; in fact he was almost the only visitor. There were never more than two chairs in the sitting-room, but he would sit on a pile of volumes of the *British Medical Journal*, dining off an apple dumpling, and listening to Budd as he strode about the room, shouting, gesticulating, talking. 'What did we care, any one of the three of us, where we sat or how we lived, when youth throbbed hot in our veins, and our souls were all aflame with the possibilities of life? I still look upon those Bohemian evenings, in the bare room amid the smell of cheese, as being among the happiest that I have known.' Doyle's simple, candid, modest disposition, his solidity and shrewd common sense, had a steadying effect on Budd, and when Dr. Watson explains his particular value to Sherlock Holmes we are reading Doyle's subconscious recollection of another quality in him that attracted Budd: 'I was a whetstone for his mind. I stimulated him. He liked to think aloud in my presence. His remarks could hardly be said to be made to me—many of them would have been as appropriately addressed to his bedstead—but none the less, having formed the habit, it had become in some way helpful that I should register and interject. If I irritated him by a certain methodical slowness in my mentality, that irritation served only to make his own flame-like intuitions and impressions flash up the more vividly and swiftly. Such was my humble rôle in our alliance.' It is as easy to perceive Budd's more spectacular rôle in the alliance. His mercurial and explosive temperament, his genius for improvisation, his quick inventive mind, his range and grasp of subjects, his outrageous behaviour, his buffoonery, the drama and comedy inseparable from his flamboyant personality, even the sinister and malignant qualities in his character, made an irresistible appeal to what was most durable in Doyle's nature: his boyish love of the unexpected, of the mysterious and the fantastic. 'His mind is so nimble and his thoughts so extravagant, that

your own break away from their usual grooves, and surprise
you by their activity,' wrote Doyle. 'You feel pleased at your
own inventiveness and originality, when you are really like the
wren when it took a lift on the eagle's shoulder.' Indeed, such
was the effect of Budd's bizarre character on Doyle's im-
pressionable and easily stimulated mind that we can find traces
of that impact all over his work. It is Budd, far more than
any original, who gives life to the professors in his books.
Some of his experiences with Budd are described in his stories,
many of which owe their inspiration to the same source. Budd
is in the energy of Holmes, the braggadocio of Gerard, the
malignity of Moriarty, the violence of Roylott, the fanaticism
of Maracot, and the more extravagant incidents and indi-
viduals who appear in his pages; while in the creation of
Challenger he is haunted by Budd, who, like the Professor,
has a device for deflecting a torpedo, a new and economical
method of separating nitrogen from the air, and so on. The
description of Challenger's personality is a description of
Budd's: 'If it is impossible to be at your ease, it is equally impossible to be dull in his company, for one is always in a state
of half-tremulous doubt as to what sudden turn his formidable
temper may take.' And when Challenger, in *The Land of Mist*,
goes to a séance in order to expose the proceedings, the medium
asks whether anyone present would own to a friend named
Budworth, which is a combination of Budd and 'Culling-
worth', the pseudonym invented by Doyle for Budd in *The
Stark Munro Letters* and retained by him in the story of his
own life. 'No,' reports the chronicler in *The Land of Mist*,
'no one would own to a friend named Budworth'—a casual
comment, the true significance of which was lost on Doyle,
who never recognised how much he owed as a story-teller to
Budd. His debt will be more apparent later on.

In due time Doyle underwent the horrors of examination
at the University, but in spite of his nervousness he noted the
comedy which preceded the viva voce. A crowd of students
were awaiting their turn to be called in: 'It was painful to
observe their attempts to appear confident and unconcerned
as they glanced round the heavens, as if to observe the state
of the weather, or examined with well-feigned archaeological
fervour the inscriptions upon the old University walls. Most
painful of all was it when someone, plucking up courage,
would venture upon a tiny joke, at which the whole company

would gibber in an ostentatious way, as though to show that
even in this dire pass the appreciation of humour still remained
with them. At times, when any of their number alluded to
the examination or detailed the questions which had been
propounded to Brown or Baker the day before, the mask of
unconcern would be dropped, and the whole assembly would
glare eagerly and silently at the speaker.' Some Job's com-
forter went about suggesting abstruse questions and hinting
that they represented a particular examiner's hobby. For
example:

'What do you know about cacodyl?'

'Cacodyl? It's some sort of antediluvian reptile, isn't it?'

'No. It's an organic explosive chemical compound. You're
sure to be asked about cacodyl.'

At which point the delighted questioner left his discomfited
victim.

Doyle passed his final examination 'with fair but not notable
distinction' in 1881, qualifying as Bachelor of Medicine in
August of that year, and taking his Doctor's degree in 1885.
He had intended to start his professional life as a ship's
surgeon, partly because he wanted to see something of the
world and partly to make enough money to set up in practice.
To this end he had applied for a job on a passenger ship; but
he had heard nothing for months and was seriously thinking
of joining the Army or the Navy or the Indian Service when
a telegram arrived offering him the post of medical officer at
£12 a month on the African Steam Navigation Company's
Mayumba. He sailed from Liverpool on October 22nd, 1881,
and spent the four most miserable months of his existence
going from place to place on the west coast of Africa. It was
a neat little steamer of 4000 tons, carrying a cargo of mixed
goods and a score or so of passengers. He started well by
saving the lives of everybody on board. The ship was running
before a fierce gale in a thick fog down the Irish Sea when,
through a rift in the fog, Doyle suddenly spotted a lighthouse
on the port side. Knowing that they were supposed to be
well down on the Irish coast, but not wishing to lay himself
open to ridicule as a landsman, he casually drew the mate's
attention to the lighthouse and asked, as if for information,
'Is that all right?' Apparently it was not all right, because
the mate nearly jumped out of his skin and for several moments
clamour reigned on the ship. They had been heading straight

for the rocks. The passengers included some nice white women and some nasty negro traders, who were patrons of the line and had to be humoured. These palm oil chiefs were wealthy, spending their money on drink and women, and Doyle noted that one of them 'had a choice selection of the *demi-monde* of Liverpool to see him off'.

The first part of the journey was stormy, everyone was seasick, and Doyle was kept busy; but life became endurable further south, and he was able to enjoy Madeira and the Canaries. They touched at Freetown, Sierra Leone, where white people used to die quickly in beautiful surroundings, at the capital of Liberia, and so on down that burning, surf-lined, flat, monotonous, and seemingly endless coast. Trade in those days was conducted in a rough-and-ready fashion: 'Once we moved on while a hundred native visitors were still on board. It was funny to see them dive off and make for their canoes. One of them had a tall hat, an umbrella, and a large coloured picture of the Saviour—all of which he had bought at the trading booths which the men rig up in the forecastle. These impedimenta did not prevent him from swimming to his boat. At another minor port, since we were pressed for time, we simply threw our consignment of barrel staves over-board, knowing that soon or late they would wash up on the beach, though how the real owner could make good his claim to them I do not know.' At Lagos the ship had to do without her doctor, for a mosquito got at him and he was down with fever, which came with its usual suddenness, sent him reeling to his bunk, and laid him out senseless. 'As I was myself doctor there was no one to look after me and I lay for several days fighting it out with Death in a very small ring and without a second.' While he was engaged in the struggle another passenger succumbed; but his constitution pulled him through and in a week he was convalescent. At Old Calabar he got into a canoe with another fellow and paddled up to Creektown through gloomy mangrove swamps. Here they were in native territory, and the King, hearing of their presence, ordered them to report instantly to him. They paddled back to their steamer faster than they went to Creektown. Having seen the niggers sporting in the waters, Doyle considered that a white man should be equally free of the ocean, and at Cape Coast Castle he plunged in and swam round the ship. While drying himself on deck after this excursion he observed the high fin of a shark, which had heard the splashing and come up to look for him. The sight made him feel rather cold.

One day, while standing on the poop in a raging thunderstorm, he decided that this first trip must be his last. Existence on board ship was too comfortable for a young ambitious man. One more voyage and he would probably want to settle into the easy enervating rut of ship's surgeon for life. If he desired success as a doctor, there was a hard struggle ahead of him, and whereas one wander-year might be useful two would be fatal. So he thought; and with his determination to stop travelling the seas he made up his mind to stop drinking spirits for the rest of the voyage. The deadliness of Africa no less than the luxury of the boat palled on him, and he wrote a verse in his diary:

> Oh Africa, where are thy charms
> That sages have seen in thy face?
> Better dwell in Old England on alms
> Than be rich in that terrible place.

The return journey, spent in collecting oil and ivory from the places where they had dropped beads and umbrellas on the outward voyage, was enlivened during its last week by the ship catching fire. For the first two or three days they did not take it seriously, but when the smoke turned into a blaze they did. All hands exerted themselves for over twelve hours, the iron side of the ship getting hotter every hour until at one point it was red-hot and arrangements were being made to leave in the boats, but by the evening the danger was over and the 'pillars of smoke were down to mere wisps'. They reached Liverpool on January 14th, 1882.

The atmosphere of the west coast of Africa, to say nothing of the atmosphere of the *Mayumba*, had been unfavourable to literary conversation, and Doyle did not feel that he had made any mental or spiritual advance during the trip; but the American consul at Monrovia, a negro, had discussed Motley with him and had told him that if he wished to travel in Africa he should go unarmed: 'You would not like it in England if a body of men came armed to the teeth and marched through your land. The Africans are quite as sensitive.' Also a young Frenchman, dying of fever, had given him Flammarion's *L'Atmosphere* as a professional fee. Apart from these two incidents Doyle was thrown back on his old companions for mental nourishment, and on one of them in particular.

Glancing over his library a quarter of a century later, he told us which it was: 'If I had to choose the one book out of all that line from which I have had most pleasure and most profit, I should point to yonder stained copy of Macaulay's Essays. It seems entwined into my whole life as I look backwards. It was my comrade in my student days, it has been with me on the sweltering Gold Coast, and it formed part of my humble kit when I went a-whaling in the Arctic. Honest Scotch harpooners have addled their brains over it, and you may still see the grease stains where the second engineer grappled with Frederick the Great.'

CHAPTER III

DOCTOR BUDD

AFTER finishing at the University Budd had disappeared from Edinburgh, and as he never wrote letters Doyle had lost touch with him for some months. But one spring day in 1881 a wire arrived from Bristol: 'Come at once. I have urgent need of you. Budd.' He then remembered that Budd's father had been a leading Bristol physician and presumed that his friend was carrying on the family business. He was working in Birmingham at the time, but set off at once for Bristol, feeling sure that Budd had something good to offer him. The first person he saw on the station platform was Budd, with his hat as usual on the back of his head, an unbuttoned waistcoat, and the unusual addition of a collar round his neck. He greeted Doyle with a roar, pulled him out of the carriage, seized his carpet bag, and hustled him along the streets, talking about everything except the reason for his telegram. From football he jumped to his latest invention, concerning which he got so excited that he surrendered the bag to Doyle in order to gesticulate freely and discoursed in this manner:

'My dear Doyle, why was armour abandoned, eh? What! I'll tell you why. It was because the weight of metal that would protect a man who was standing up was more than he could carry. But battles are not fought nowadays by men who are standing up. Your infantry are all lying on their stomachs, and it would take very little to protect them. And steel has improved, Doyle! Chilled steel! Bessemer! Bessemer! Very good. How much to cover a man? Fourteen inches by twelve, meeting at an angle so that the bullet will glance. A notch at one side for the rifle. There you have it, laddie—the Budd patent portable bullet-proof shield! Weight? Oh, the weight would be sixteen pounds. I worked it out. Each company carries its shields in go-carts, and they are served out on going into action. Give me twenty thousand good shots, and I'll go in at Calais and come out at Pekin. Think of it, my boy!—the moral effect. One side gets home every time and the other plasters its bullets up against steel plates. No troops would stand it. The nation that gets it first will pitchfork the rest of Europe over the edge. They're bound to have it—all of them. Let's reckon it out. There's about eight million of them on a war footing. Let us suppose that only half of them have it. I say only half, because I don't want to be too sanguine. That's four million, and I should take a royalty of four shillings on wholesale orders. What's that, Doyle? About three-quarters of a million sterling, eh? How's that, laddie, eh? what?'

This statement, which gave Doyle an idea he was later to develop, was delivered in a dramatic style, punctuated with pauses, now whispered, now bawled, and accompanied by thumps, shrugs, and peals of laughter.

They arrived at a large house, standing in its own grounds, and when the door was opened by a footman in red plush knee-breeches Doyle felt that he was on velvet. Mrs. Budd looked pale and tired, and their surroundings were impressively ancestral, yet they had an uproarious supper which reminded Doyle of the evenings above the grocer's shop. Not a syllable was uttered during the meal in explanation of the 'urgent need' that had brought him to Bristol. Afterwards they retired to a small sitting-room, where the men lighted their pipes, Mrs. Budd her cigarette, and for a while they smoked in silence. Suddenly Budd jumped to his feet, dashed at the door, flung it open, discovered no one's ear glued to the key-hole, shut it, and returned to his arm-chair. He had an insanely suspicious nature and was firmly convinced that people were conspiring against him and spying on him. His fears temporarily allayed, he confided in his visitor:

'Doyle, what I wanted to tell you is, that I am utterly, hopelessly, and irretrievably ruined.'

Doyle, who was lazily tilting his chair backwards, nearly fell off it.

'Sorry to disappoint you, my boy. That's not what you expected to hear, I can see.'

'Well,' stammered Doyle, 'it *is* rather a surprise, old chap. I thought from the . . . from the . . .'

'From the house, and the footman, and the furniture. Well, they've eaten me up among them . . . licked me clean, bones and gravy. I'm done for, my boy, unless . . . unless some friend were to lend me his name on a bit of stamped paper.'

'I can't do it, Budd. It's a wretched thing to have to refuse a friend; and if I had the money . . .'

'Wait till you're asked,' snapped Budd, with a nasty gleam in his eyes. 'Besides, as you have nothing and no prospects, what earthly use would *your* name on a paper be?'

'That's what I want to know,' murmured Doyle, feeling a little mortified all the same.

'Look here, laddie; d'you see that pile of letters on the left of the table?'

'Yes.'

'Those are duns. And d'you see those documents on the right? Well, those are County Court summonses. And now d'you see that?' He showed a ledger with three or four names on the first page. 'That's the practice!' He laughed until the veins swelled on his forehead, his wife sympathetically joining in. Recovering himself, he proceeded: 'It's this way, Doyle. You have probably heard—in fact I have told you myself— that my father had the finest practice in Bristol. As far as I could judge, he was a man of no capacity, but still there you are—he had it. Well, he's been dead seven years, and fifty nets dipping into his little fish-pond. However, when I passed I thought my best move was to come down to the old place and see whether I couldn't piece the thing together again. The name ought to be worth something, I thought. But it was no use doing the thing in a half-hearted way. Not a bit of use in that, Doyle. The kind of people who came to him were wealthy, and must see a fine house and a man in livery. What chance was there of gathering them into a bow-windowed forty-pound-a-year house with a grubby-faced maid at the door? What do you suppose I did? My boy, I took the governor's old house, that was unlet—the very house that he kept up at five thousand a year. Off I started in rare style, and sank my last cent in furniture. But it's no use, laddie. I can't hold on any longer. I got two accidents and an epileptic—twenty-two pounds, eight and sixpence—that's the lot!'

'What will you do, then?'

'That's what I wanted your advice about. That's why I wired for you. I always respected your opinion, my boy, and I thought that now was the time to have it.'

Though the appeal flattered him, it occurred to Doyle that it was rather late in the day to ask his advice.

'You really think it's no use holding on here?'

'You take warning from it, Doyle. You've got to start yet

Take my tip, and go where no one knows you. People will trust a stranger quick enough; but if they can remember you as a little chap who ran about in knickerbockers, and got spanked with a hair brush for stealing plums, they are not going to put their lives in your keeping. It's all very well to talk about friendships and family connections; but when a man has a pain in the stomach he doesn't care a toss about all that. I'd stick it up in gold letters in every medical classroom —have it carved across the gate of the University—that if a man wants friends he must go among strangers. It's all up here, Doyle; so there's no use in advising me to hold on.'

Having ascertained that Budd owed £700, that the rent of his house was £200, that he had already raised money on the furniture, and that his total assets came to less than £10, Doyle advised him to call a meeting of his creditors and make a clean breast of it. 'They can see for themselves that you are young and energetic—sure to succeed sooner or later. If they push you into a corner now, they can get nothing. Make that clear to them. But if you make a fresh start elsewhere and succeed, you may pay them all in full. I see no other possible way out of it.'

Apparently Budd was entirely of his opinion: 'I knew that you'd say that, and it's just what I thought myself. Well, then, that settles it, and I am much obliged to you for your advice, and that's all we'll say about the matter to-night. I've made my shot and missed. Next time I shall hit, and it won't be long either.'

In a minute or two he was drinking whisky and rattling away as if there were no such things as duns and summonses. Unfortunately, two glasses of whisky had its usual effect on him, and after his wife had left them together he brought the subject round to boxing and suggested a few rounds. Doyle, who ought to have known better, could never resist a challenge, and donned the gloves. They pushed back the table, put the lamp on a high bracket, and faced one another. At once Doyle realised his error. The malignant glare in the eyes of Budd said as plainly as words that Doyle's refusal to back his paper was still rankling in his mind. Doyle wished to do a little friendly sparring, but Budd rushed at him, hitting hard with both hands, knocked him off his legs, forced him up against the door, and leaving him no elbow-space began to pummel him severely. Somehow Doyle managed to evade a terrific right-hander that would have settled the contest, and broke away.

'Look here,' said he, 'there's not much boxing about this game.'

'Yes, I hit pretty hard, don't I?' returned Budd complacently.

'If you come boring into me like that, I'm bound to hit you out again. I want to play light if you'll let me.'

He had hardly said the words when Budd made another onslaught. Doyle side-stepped; but his opponent was round in an instant, flew at him again, knocked him off his balance, and gave him a crack on the ear and a blow on the body. Doyle tripped over a footstool, and before he could right himself received another on the ear which made his head sing.

'Say when you've had enough,' said Budd, preening himself.

Doyle had had quite enough and was now prepared to repay some of it. This time he was ready for his antagonist, breaking his tempestuous assault with a left-hander on the nose and then giving him a jab on the jaw which floored him.

'You swine!' shrieked Budd, his face convulsed with maniacal rage. 'Take those gloves off and put your hands up.'

'Go on, you silly ass!' replied Doyle good-humouredly. 'What is there to fight about?'

'By God, Doyle,' yelled Budd, flinging away his own gloves, 'if you don't take 'em off I'll go for you, whether they're on or off.'

'Have a glass of soda water,' Doyle suggested.

'You're afraid of me,' snarled Budd; 'that's what's the matter with you.'

Doyle took his gloves off, and as he did so Mrs. Budd walked in.

'George!' she cried, horrified when she saw the lower part of his face covered with blood, his nose having bled profusely; and then, turning to his opponent, 'What is the meaning of this, Mr. Doyle?' Though there was a look of loathing in her eyes, Doyle's impulse was to pick her up and kiss her.

'We've only been having a little spar,' he said. 'Your husband was complaining that he never got any exercise.'

'It's all right, dear,' said Budd, putting on his coat. 'Don't be a little stupid. Are the servants gone to bed? Well, you might bring some water in a basin from the kitchen. Sit down,

Doyle, and light your pipe again. I have a hundred things that I want to talk to you about.'

With his remarkable talent as a quick-change artist, Budd chatted away as if nothing had occurred to ruffle their friendship, and the evening closed in harmony.

Next morning, though their features showed the wear and tear of the previous night, Budd was at the top of his form. He had a hundred ideas for making their fortunes, several of which will be familiar to readers of Doyle's stories. The great thing, according to Budd, was to get one's name in the papers. Quite simple! Doyle was to drop senseless in the roadway outside his house; a crowd would gather; he would be carried in; and a footman would run to the newspaper offices with a paragraph about it. Should the crowd be inconsiderate enough to take him to the rival practitioner on the other side of the road, different methods would have to be tried. Doyle could have a fit at Budd's very door; indeed he could have several fits, in various disguises, each fit to produce fresh copy for the press. When fits ceased to have any news value, Doyle could actually drop dead at a convenient spot, Budd would restore him to life, and England would ring with his fame.

While Budd was outlining these schemes for the betterment of his position, and Doyle was exploding with laughter, the doctor across the way was receiving a succession of patients, and every now and then the flow of Budd's ideas was checked while he anathematised both rival and patients. Whenever he caught sight of a new arrival on the opposite doorstep, he sprang from his chair and strode about the room, cursing and raving and gnashing his teeth.

'There you are!' he would suddenly yell. 'See that man with a limp! Every morning he goes. Displaced semilunar cartilage, and a three months' job. The man's worth thirty-five shillings a week!' A few minutes later he would interrupt himself with a shriek: 'There! I'm hanged if the woman with the rheumatic arthritis isn't round in her bath-chair again. She's all seal-skin and lactic acid. It's simply sickening to see how they crowd to that man. And such a man! You haven't seen him. All the better for you. What the devil are you laughing at, Doyle?'

Doyle was limp from laughter when he left Bristol.

A few months later he was on his way to the west coast of Africa. When he returned he heard indirectly that Budd had called his creditors together, reduced some of them to tears with a detailed account of his struggle with adversity, obtained their willing consent to let their bills stand over *sine die*, received a unanimous vote of confidence, and very nearly persuaded them to send round the hat and start him off with a cash testimonial.

After he got back Doyle was wondering whether he dared risk the plunge into practice on his own account when, in the late spring of 1882, he received a wire from Budd: 'Started here in Plymouth last June. Colossal success. My example must revolutionise medical practice. Rapidly making fortune. Have invention which is worth millions. Unless our Admiralty take it up shall make Brazil the leading naval power. Come down by next train on receiving this. Have plenty for you to do.' Doyle had returned to Birmingham and did not feel sufficient confidence in Budd to do as he suggested. Instead he wrote to say that he was quite comfortable where he was and would not leave his present job unless he could feel sure of a permanency. After a silence of ten days Budd telegraphed again: 'Your letter to hand. Why not call me a liar at once? I tell you that I have seen thirty thousand patients in the last year. My actual takings have been over four thousand pounds. All patients come to me. Would not cross the street to see Queen Victoria. You can have all visiting, all surgery, all midwifery. Make what you like of it. Will guarantee three hundred pounds the first year.' After talking over the matter with the doctor for whom he was working, Doyle left for Plymouth.

Again Budd was on the platform to welcome him with a roar and a thump on the back.

'My dear chap,' he began at once, 'we'll clear this town out. I tell you, Doyle, we won't leave a doctor in it. It's all they can do now to get butter to their bread; and when we get to work together they'll have to eat it dry. Listen to me, my boy! There are a hundred and twenty thousand folk in this town, all shrieking for advice, and there isn't a doctor who knows a rhubarb pill from a calculus. Man, we only have to gather them in. I stand and take the money until my arm aches.'

'But how is it?' asked Doyle, bewildered. 'Are there so few other doctors?'

'Few!' shouted Budd. 'By Crums, the streets are blocked with them. You couldn't fall out of a window in this town

without killing a doctor. But of all the—well, there, you'll
see them for yourself. You walked to my house at Bristol. I
don't let my friends walk to my house at Plymouth—eh, what?'

At this point there was an obviously prearranged bit of
comedy. A luxurious carriage drawn by two fine-looking black
horses awaited them, and an obsequious coachman asked Budd
which of his houses he would like to be driven to. Noting
with satisfaction that Doyle had been suitably impressed,
Budd said that as dinner would be nearly ready they had better
'drive to the town residential'. In the carriage Doyle ejacu-
lated his amazement and was informed that, for the time being,
Budd had contented himself with a town house, a country
house, and a house of business.

'Consulting- and waiting-room?' Doyle supposed.

'You cannot rise to a situation,' said Budd. 'I never met
a man with such a stodgy imagination. I have written to you
about my practice, and I've wired to you about it, and here
you sit asking me if I work it in two rooms. I'll have to hire
the market square before I've finished, and then I won't have
space to wag my elbows. Can your imagination rise to a great
house with people waiting in every room, jammed in as tight
as they'll fit, and two layers of them squatting in the cellar?
Well, that's my house of business on an average day. The
folk come in from the county fifty miles off, and eat bread
and treacle on the doorstep, so as to be first in when the housekeeper comes down. The medical officer of health made an
official complaint of the overcrowding of my waiting-rooms.
They wait in the stables, and sit along the racks and under
the horses' bellies. I'll turn some of 'em on to you, my boy,
and then you'll know a little more about it.'

The carriage pulled up on the Hoe at a corner house which
looked like a spacious hotel. Doyle later discovered that it
had been a leading club, the rent of which had been too high
for the members. An imposing sweep of steps led up to the
door, above which five or six storeys were capped by pinnacles
and a flagstaff. The thirty odd bedrooms had not been
furnished, but the ground-floor rooms and the hall were on
a spectacular scale. After modestly announcing that this was
his 'little place', Budd took Doyle upstairs. 'You see,' said he,
as he knocked a few nails into the door of Doyle's bedroom,
which contained a small iron bed and a basin mounted on a
packing-case, 'there's no good my putting a forty-pound suite

into a bedroom, and then having to chuck it all out of the window in order to make room for a hundred-pound one. No sense in that, Doyle, eh, what? I'm going to furnish this house as no house has ever been furnished. By Crums, I'll bring the folk from a hundred miles round just to have leave to look at it. But I must do it room by room.'

Mrs. Budd gave her visitor a cordial welcome and they sat down to a dinner which fulfilled the expectations aroused by the furniture, carpet, and curtains of the dining-room. Budd was in ecstasies about the huge prices he had paid, dragged Doyle about the room while the soup was getting cold to inspect the chairs, hangings, etc., and even swung the waiting-maid round by the arm to ask if Doyle had ever seen a neater one. Half-way through the meal he dashed from the room and returned with a bag full of cash, which he emptied on the table-cloth. 'Our day's take,' he explained. It came to £31 8s. 0d. When Doyle remarked that his Bristol creditors would be glad to hear that he was doing so well, Budd's geniality vanished, his expression turned to one of fiendish ferocity, and his wife sent the maid out of the room.

'What rot you do talk!' he cried. 'Do you suppose I am going to cripple myself for years by letting those debts hang on to me?'

'I understood that you had promised,' said Doyle. 'Still, of course, it's no business of mine.'

'I should hope not. A tradesman stands to win or to lose. He allows a margin for bad debts. I would have paid it if I could. I couldn't, and so I wiped the slate clean. No one in his senses would dream of spending all that I make in Plymouth upon the tradesmen of Bristol.'

'Suppose they come down on you?'

'Well, we'll see about that when they do. Meanwhile I am paying ready money for every mortal thing that comes up the doorsteps. . . . There's nearly four hundred pounds under this one ceiling.'

There was a tap at the door and a boy in buttons entered. 'If you please, sir, Mr. Duncan wishes to see you.'

'Give my compliments to Mr. Duncan, and tell him he may go to the devil!'

'My dear George!' exclaimed his wife.

'Tell him I am at dinner; and if all the kings in Europe were waiting in the hall I wouldn't cross that door mat to see them.'

After a minute's absence the boy was back again.

'Please, sir, he won't go.'

'Won't go? What d'you mean, you brat? What are you boggling about?'

'It's his bill, sir,' said the trembling boy.

'His bill, eh?' The veins on Budd's forehead began to swell. 'Look here!' He placed his watch on the table. 'It's two minutes to eight. At eight I'm coming out, and if I find him there I'll strew the street with him. Tell him I'll shred him over the parish. He has two minutes to save his life in, and one of them is nearly gone.'

A few moments later they heard the bang of the front door, and Budd gave himself up to mirth, sending forth peal upon peal of laughter. 'I'll drive him mad,' he said at last, wiping away his tears. 'He's a nervous, chicken-livered kind of man, and when I look at him he turns the colour of putty. If I pass his shop I usually just drop in and stand and look at him. I never speak, but just look. It paralyses him.' Doyle learnt that the man was Budd's corn merchant, who had cheated him once or twice: hence the treatment. But Budd told his wife to send the man £20 on account the following day.

Dinner over, they went into a back room where Budd conducted his experiments. There were pistols, cartridges, a rook rifle, an electric battery, and a large magnet. Doyle asked what it was all for. Budd turned to his wife and repeated the question. 'Naval supremacy and the command of the seas,' she dutifully replied.

'That's it,' he crowed. 'Naval supremacy and command of the seas. It's all here, right under your nose. I tell you, Doyle, I could go to Switzerland to-morrow, and I could say to them, "Look here, you haven't got a seaboard and you haven't got a port; but just find me a ship and hoist your flag on it, and I'll give you every ocean under heaven." I'd sweep the seas until there wasn't a match-box floating on them. Or I could make them over to a limited company, and join the board after allotment. I hold the salt water in the cup of this hand, every drop of it. . . . Oh, you may grin! You'll grin a little wider when you see the dividends coming in. What's the value of that magnet?'

'A pound.'

'A million pounds. Not a penny under. And dirt cheap to the nation that buys it. I shall let it go at that, though I could make ten times as much if I held on. I shall take it up to the First Lord of the Admiralty in a week or two; and if he seems to be a civil deserving sort of person I shall do business with him. It's not every day, Doyle, that a man comes into his office with the Atlantic under one arm and the Pacific under the other. Eh, what?'

Doyle tried hard to hold himself in check, but abandoned the effort and laughed himself tired. After a scowl of fury Budd joined in.

'Of course, it seems absurd to you,' he shouted, stamping about the room and gesticulating wildly. 'Well, I dare say it would to me if any other fellow had worked it out. . . . Now I'll show you. What an unbelieving Jew you are, trying to look interested, and giggling at the back of your throat! In the first place, I have discovered a method—which I won't tell you—of increasing the attractive power of a magnet a hundredfold. Have you grasped that?'

'Yes.'

'Very good. You are also aware, I presume, that modern projectiles are either made of or tipped with steel. It may possibly have come to your ears that magnets attract steel. Permit me now to show you a small experiment.' He bent over his apparatus, and Doyle heard the snapping of electricity. 'This,' he continued, going across to a packing-case, 'is a saloon pistol, and will be exhibited in the museums of the next century as being the weapon with which the new era was inaugurated. Into the breech I place a Boxer cartridge, specially provided for experimental purposes with a steel bullet. I aim point-blank at the dab of red sealing-wax upon the wall, which is four inches above the magnet. I am an absolutely dead shot. I fire. You will now advance, and satisfy yourself that the bullet is flattened upon the end of the magnet, after which you will apologise to me for that grin.'

Doyle had to admit that it was so.

'I'll tell you what I'd do!' cried Budd. 'I'm prepared to put that magnet in my wife's bonnet, and to let you fire six shots straight at her face. How's that for a test? You wouldn't mind, dear?'

Though his wife did not seem to mind, Doyle did.

'Of course, you see that the whole thing is to scale,' Budd went on. 'My warship of the future carries at her prow and stern a magnet which shall be as much larger than that as the big shell will be larger than this tiny bullet. Or I might have a separate raft, possibly, to carry my apparatus. My ship goes into action. What happens then, Doyle? Eh, what! Every shot fired at her goes smack on to the magnet. There's a reservoir below into which they drop when the electric circuit is broken. After every action they are sold by auction for old metal, and the result divided as prize money among the crew. But think of it, man! I tell you it is an absolute impossibility for a shot to strike any ship which is provided with my apparatus. And then look at the cheapness. You don't want armour. You want nothing. Any ship that floats becomes invulnerable with one of these. The warship of the future will cost anything from seven pound ten. You're grinning again; but if you give me a magnet and a Brixham trawler with a seven-pounder gun I'll show sport to the finest battleship afloat.'

'Well, there must be some flaw about this,' said Doyle. 'If your magnet is so strong as all that, you would have your own broadside boomeranging back upon you.'

'Not a bit of it! There's a big difference between a shot flying away from you with all its muzzle velocity, and another one which is coming towards you and only needs a slight deflection to strike the magnet. Besides, by breaking the circuit I can take off the influence when I am firing my own broadside. Then I connect, and instantly become invulnerable.'

'And your nails and screws?'

'The warship of the future will be bolted together by wood.'

On a later occasion he told Doyle that he had failed to impress the authorities with the vital need of his invention. 'I'm very sorry for my country,' he lamented, 'but there is no more command of the seas for her. I'll have to let the thing go to the Germans. It's not my fault. They must not blame me when the smash comes. I put the thing before the Admiralty, and I could have made a board school understand it in half the time. Such letters, Doyle! Colney Hatch on blue paper. When the war comes, and I show those letters, somebody will be hanged. Questions about this—questions about that. At last they asked me what I proposed to fasten my magnet to. I answered to any solid impenetrable object, such as the head of an Admiralty official. Well, that broke the whole thing up. They wrote with their compliments, and they were returning my apparatus. I wrote with my compliments, and they might go to the devil. And so ends a great historical incident, Doyle—eh, what?'

When Doyle went to bed that first evening he realised that Budd had neither explained his success as a doctor nor broached the subject of their partnership; and when he was awakened the following morning by Budd, who charged into the room in his dressing-gown, vaulted over the rail at the bottom of the bed, and did a somersault which brought his heels on to Doyle's pillow, it was quite a different topic that his host had come to discuss.

'I tell you one of the first things I mean to do, Doyle. I mean to have a paper of my own. We'll start a weekly paper here, you and I, and we'll make them sit up all round. We'll have an organ of our own, just like every French politician. If anyone crosses us, we'll make them wish they had never been born. Eh, what, laddie? What d'you think? So clever, Doyle, that everybody's bound to read it, and so scathing that it will just fetch out blisters every time. Don't you think we could?'

'What politics?'

'Oh, curse the politics! Red pepper well rubbed in, that's my idea of a paper. Call it the *Scorpion*. Chaff the Mayor and the Council until they call a meeting and hang themselves. I'll do the snappy paragraphs, and you would do the fiction and the poetry. I thought about it during the night, and my wife has written to Murdoch's to get an estimate for the printing. We might get our first number out this day week.'

'My dear chap!' gasped Doyle.

'I want you to start a novel this morning. You won't get many patients at first, and you'll have lots of time.'

'But I've never written a novel in my life.'

'A properly balanced man can do anything he sets his hand to. He's got every possible quality inside himself, and all he wants is the will to develop it.'

'Could you write a novel yourself?'

'Of course I could. Such a novel, Doyle, that when they'd read the first chapter the folk would just sit groaning until the second came out. They'd wait in rows outside my door in the hope of hearing what was coming next. By Crums, I'll go and begin it now!'

Another somersault over the end of the bed, and he was gone.

Apart from Budd's extravagant claims and mannerisms, Doyle was much struck by the aphorisms which peppered his conversation, e.g. 'The greatest monument ever erected to Napoleon Bonaparte was the British National Debt', and 'The principal export of Great Britain to the United States is the United States'. Doyle wished he could jot them all down in a note-book, but his memory was fairly retentive.

After breakfast all three got into a carriage and drove to Budd's business address, a square whitewashed building with Dr. BUDD in enormous letters on a brass plate by the door, and the words 'May be Consulted Gratis from Ten to Four' underneath. The hall was crowded with people.

'How many here?' asked Budd.

'A hundred and forty, sir,' answered the page boy.

'All the waiting-rooms full?'

'Yes, sir.'

'Courtyard full?'

'Yes, sir.'

'Stable full?'

'Yes, sir.'

'Coach-house full?'

'There's still room in the coach-house, sir.'

'Ah, I'm sorry we haven't got a crowded day for you, Doyle. Of course, we can't command these things, and must take them as they come. Now then, now then, make a gangway, can't you?' he bawled at the patients. 'Come here and see the waiting-room. Pooh! what an atmosphere! Why on earth can't you open the windows for yourselves? I never saw such folk! There are thirty people in this room, Doyle, and not one with sense enough to open a window to save himself from suffocation.'

'I tried, sir, but there's a screw through the sash,' said one of the patients.

'Ah, my boy, you'll never get on in the world if you can't open a window without raising a sash,' said Budd, who promptly seized the man's umbrella and stuck it through two of the panes of glass. 'That's the way! Boy, see that the screw is taken out. Now then, Doyle, come along and we'll get to work.'

They climbed to the top floor, every room on the way being

filled with patients. Budd marched into a large chamber
which contained nothing but two wooden chairs and a table
with two books and a stethoscope on it.

'This,' he announced, 'is my consulting-room. It doesn't
look like four or five thousand a year, does it? Now, there is
an exactly similar one opposite which you can have for yourself. I'll send across any surgical cases which may turn up.
To-day, however, I think you had better stay with me, and
see how I work things.'

'I should very much like to,' said Doyle.

'There are one or two elementary rules to be observed in
the way of handling patients,' remarked Budd, sitting on the
table and swinging his legs. 'The most obvious is that you
must never let them see that you want them. It should be
pure condescension on your part seeing them at all; and the
more difficulties you throw in the way of it, the more they think
of it. Break your patients in early, and keep them well to heel.
Never make the fatal mistake of being polite to them. Many
foolish young men fall into this habit, and are ruined in
consequence. Now this is my form.' He rushed to the door
and bellowed downstairs: 'Stop your confounded jabbering
down there! I might as well be living above a poultry show!'
Dead silence ensued. 'There, you see! They will think ever
so much more of me for that.'

'But don't they get offended?'

'I'm afraid not. I have a name for this sort of thing now,
and they have come to expect it. But an offended patient—
I mean a thoroughly insulted one—is the finest advertisement
in the world. If it is a woman, she runs clacking about among
her friends until your name becomes a household word, and
they all pretend to sympathise with her, and agree among
themselves that you must be a remarkably discerning man. I
quarrelled with one man about the state of his gall duct, and
it ended by my throwing him down the stairs. What was the
result? He talked so much about it that the whole village
from which he came, sick and well, trooped to see me. The
little country practitioner who had been buttering them up
for a quarter of a century found that he might as well put up
his shutters. It's human nature, my boy, and you can't alter
it. Eh, what? You make yourself cheap and you become cheap.
You put a high price on yourself and they rate you at that
price. Suppose I set up in Harley Street to-morrow, and made

it all nice and easy, with hours from ten to three, do you think I should get a patient? I might starve first. How would I work it? I should let it be known that I only saw patients from midnight until two in the morning, and that bald-headed people must pay double. That would set people talking, their curiosity would be stimulated, and in four months the street would be blocked all night. Eh, what? Laddie, you'd go yourself. That's my principle here. I often come in of a morning and send them all about their business, tell them I'm going off to the country for a day. I turn away forty pounds, and it's worth four hundred as an advertisement!'

'But I understood from the plate that the consultations were gratis?'

'So they are, but they have to pay for the medicine. And if a patient wishes to come out of turn he has to pay half a guinea for the privilege. There are generally about twenty every day who would rather pay that than wait several hours. But mind you, Doyle, don't you make any mistake about this! All this would go for nothing if you had not something solid behind—I cure them. That's the point. I take cases that others have despaired of, and I cure them right off. All the rest is only to bring them here. But once here I keep them on my merits. It would all be a flash in the pan but for that. Now come along and see my wife's department.'

They went to the end of the passage, and found Mrs. Budd happily engaged in making pills.

'The best dispenser in the world,' said Budd, giving her an encouraging pat on the shoulder. 'You see how I do it, Doyle. I write on a label what the prescription is, and make a sign which shows how much is to be charged. The man comes along the passage and passes the label through the pigeon-hole. My wife makes it up, passes out the bottle, and takes the money. Now come on and clear some of these folk out of the house.'

Doyle then witnessed a series of scenes such as he could never have imagined or believed possible. Hour after hour the patients filed in and departed with their prescriptions. Budd's antics were incredible. He yelled, he raved, he cursed, he knocked his patients about, thumped them, prodded them, barged them against the wall, pulled them in, flung them out, and occasionally varied the proceedings by rushing from the room and bawling at the lot from the landing. Sometimes he

did not even allow them to utter a word, but with a loud
'Ssh!' ran at them, hit them on the chests, listened to their
hearts, wrote their labels, and shot them through the door.
He paralysed one old lady the moment she entered by scream-
ing, 'You've been drinking too much tea! You are suffering
from tea poisoning!' Before she could utter a syllable he seized
her black mantle, dragged her to the table, and shoved a copy
of Taylor's *Medical Jurisprudence* under her nose. 'Put your
hand on the book,' he thundered, 'and swear that for fourteen
days you will drink nothing but cocoa.' She lifted up her eyes,
swore the oath, and was instantly hustled off to the dispensary.
A portly male made a dignified entrance and was about to
explain his symptoms when Budd caught him by the armholes
of his waistcoat, thrust him backwards into the passage and
downstairs into the street, and staggered the passers-by by
bellowing after him, 'You eat too much, drink too much, and
sleep too much! Knock down a policeman, and come again
when they let you out.' Another female, who complained of
a 'sinking feeling', was advised to take her medicine, 'and if
that does no good, swallow the cork, for there is nothing better
when you are sinking'.

While Doyle was laughing himself silly throughout this
amazing exhibition he was conscious of the fact that Budd
showed considerable skill in diagnosis and not a little psycho-
logical insight, though his use of drugs was both heroic and
alarming, his idea being that doctors were too timid; they were
afraid of poisoning their patients; whereas he believed that the
whole art of medicine lay in judicious poisoning, and with him
it was a case of kill or cure. In many cases he relied on his
personal magnetism; his confidence gave his patients confidence; his vitality re-charged theirs. 'My dear,' he said to a
girl, swaying her about by the shoulders, his nose about three
inches from hers, 'you'll feel better to-morrow at a quarter
to ten, and at twenty past you'll be as well as ever you were
in your life. Now keep your eye on the clock and see if I'm
not right.' In the majority of such cases the trick worked.

At the close of that first day Budd was able to put £32 8s. 6d.
into his canvas bag, which, to Doyle's acute embarrassment,
he paraded through the streets, holding it at arm's length and
jingling it, his wife and Doyle on either side of him, like
acolytes supporting a priest.

'I always make a point of walking through the doctors'

quarter,' said Budd. 'We are passing through it now. They all come to their windows and gnash their teeth and dance until I am out of sight.'

Doyle thought such behaviour undignified and unfriendly, and said so, Mrs. Budd backing him up. Budd replied that his wife was annoyed because the other doctors' wives wouldn't call on her. 'Look at that, my dear,' he cried, shaking the bag; 'that's better than having a lot of brainless women drinking tea and cackling in your drawing-room. I've had a big card printed, Doyle, saying that we don't desire to increase the circle of our acquaintance. The maid has orders to show it to every suspicious person who calls.'

'Why should you not make money at your practice, and yet remain on good terms with your professional brethren?' Doyle wanted to know. 'You speak as if the two things were incompatible.'

'So they are. What's the good of beating about the bush, laddie? My methods are all unprofessional, and I break every law of medical etiquette as often as I can think of it. You know very well that the British Medical Association would hold up their hands in horror if it could see what you have seen to-day.'

'But why not conform to professional etiquette?'

'Because I know better. My boy, I'm a doctor's son, and I've seen too much of it. I was born inside the machine, and I've seen all the wires. All this etiquette is a dodge for keeping the business in the hands of the older men. It's to hold the young men back, and to stop the holes by which they might slip through to the front. I've heard my father say so a score of times. He had the largest practice in Bristol, and yet he was absolutely devoid of brains. He slipped into it through seniority and decorum. No pushing, but take your turn. Very well, laddie, when you're at the top of the line, but how about it when you've just taken your place at the tail? When I'm on the top rung I shall look down and say, "Now you youngsters, we are going to have very strict etiquette, and I beg that you will come up very quietly and not disarrange me from my comfortable position." At the same time, if they do what I tell them, I shall look upon them as a lot of infernal blockheads. Eh, Doyle, what?'

Doyle completely disagreed with him.

'Well, my boy, you may disagree as much as you like, but

if you are going to work with me you must throw etiquette to
the devil.'

'I can't do that.'

'Well, if you are too clean-handed for the job you can clear
out. We can't keep you here against your will.'

Doyle was silent, but the moment they got back he
went upstairs and began to pack his trunk, intending to
return to Birmingham that night. While he was doing so
Budd walked in and made abject apologies, which placated
Doyle.

After dinner the same evening a curious incident occurred.
They were shooting steel darts out of an airgun in the back
room when Budd suggested that Doyle should hold up a halfpenny between finger and thumb and let him knock it out.
No halfpenny being available, Budd produced a bronze medal
which Doyle held up. 'Plonk' went the gun, and down went
the medal.

'Plumb in the centre,' claimed Budd.

'On the contrary,' said Doyle, 'you never hit it at all.'

'Never hit it! I must have hit it!'

'I am confident you didn't.'

'Where's the dart, then?'

'Here,' said Doyle, holding up his bleeding forefinger with
the dart sticking out of it.

Budd collapsed and expressed his contrition so extravagantly
that Doyle had to laugh the incident off. The dart having
been extracted, and Budd having recovered, Doyle picked up
the medal and read the inscription: 'Presented to George Budd
for Gallantry in Saving Life, January 1879.'

'Hullo! you never told me about this,' he exclaimed.

'What, the medal?' rejoined Budd. 'Haven't you got one?
I thought everyone had. You prefer to be select, I suppose.
It was a little boy. You've no idea the trouble I had to get
him in.'

'Get him out, you mean.'

'My dear chap, you don't understand! Anyone could get
a child out. It's getting him in that's the bother. One
deserves a medal for it. Then there are the witnesses; four
shillings a day I had to pay them, and a quart of beer in the
evenings. You see you can't pick up a child and carry it to
the edge of a pier and throw it in. You'd have all sorts of
complications with the parents. You must be patient and

wait until you get a legitimate chance. I caught a quinsy walking up and down the pier before I saw my opportunity. He was rather a stolid fat boy, and he was sitting on the very edge, fishing. I got the sole of my foot on to the small of his back, and shot him an incredible distance. I had some little difficulty in getting him out, for his fishing-line got twice round my legs, but it all ended well, and the witnesses were as staunch as possible. The boy came up to thank me next day, and said that he was quite uninjured save for a bruise on the back. His parents always send me a brace of fowls every Christmas.'

Exit Budd, and they could hear his shouts of laughter as he ran upstairs for his tobacco. Doyle was gravely inspecting the medal, which had evidently been in constant use as a target, when Mrs. Budd warned him not to take her husband too seriously, as he got carried away by his flights of fancy; to prove which she showed Doyle a press cutting which described how Budd had saved a child's life in an ice accident, nearly losing his own in the process.

Doyle now settled down to his job, which was not a very fruitful one. Though a plate with his name in large letters appeared by the outside door, and he was given a room opposite Budd's, his methods were not exciting enough to attract customers. For the first three days he sat in his room doing nothing while his partner gambolled and scrimmaged with his patients on the other side of the landing or howled at them from the top of the stairs. On the fourth day an old soldier entered his room and displayed a cancerous nose, caused by the hot tobacco from a short clay pipe. Doyle sent him home, and two days later drove out in Budd's dog-cart to operate. It was his first operation, though the patient was fortunately unaware of the fact, and he was the more nervous of the two; but the result was successful, and the old soldier was proud of the aristocratic twist Doyle had given his nose. After that he had a trickle of cases, and though his patients were very poor his takings slowly increased: £1 17s. 6d. the first week, £2 the second, £2 5s. the third, and £2 18s. the fourth.

Meanwhile Budd was forging ahead with the newspaper, for which he was already writing articles, parodies, libellous paragraphs, doggerel poems, and a novel. Anything for publicity was his motto, and Doyle saw an almanac with a large local circulation containing such entries as this:

Sep. 15. Reform Bill passed, 1867.
Sep. 16. Birth of Julius Caesar.
Sep. 17. Extraordinary cure by Dr. Budd of a case of
          dropsy in Plymouth, 1881.
Sep. 18. Battle of Gravelotte, 1870.

Some months later Doyle cut an advertisement out of the
British Medical Journal, into which it had been copied from
the *Western Morning News*, and pasted it into his scrapbook:

'Dr. Budd's blood-tonic. This medicine is prepared from
a prescription designed by Dr. Budd of Plymouth. It possesses extraordinary power in renovating the blood and in
clearing it from impurities. It is the identical medicine
prescribed by him in the remarkable cure of dropsy effected
by him in September 1881, which was classed in the *Three
Towns Almanac* as one of the chief local events of the year.
A bottle containing twenty doses forwarded to any address
(carriage paid) on receipt of Post Office Order for three
shillings and sixpence, payable to Dr. George Budd,
1 Durnford Street, Plymouth.'

Budd's low opinion of the medical profession annoyed Doyle,
who felt that their motives should be primarily humanitarian.
'Why the devil should we do all the good?' objected Budd.
'A butcher would do good to the race, would he not, if he
served his chops out gratis through the window? He'd be a
real benefactor; but he goes on selling them at a shilling the
pound for all that. Take the case of a doctor who devotes
himself to sanitary science. He flushes out drains, and keeps
down infection. You call him a philanthropist! Well, I call
him a traitor. That's it, Doyle, a traitor and a renegade! Did
you ever hear of a congress of lawyers for simplifying the law
and discouraging litigation? What are the Medical Association
and the General Council and all these bodies for? Eh, laddie?
For encouraging the best interests of the profession. Do you
suppose they do that by making the population healthy? It's
about time we had a mutiny among the general practitioners.
If I had the use of half the funds which the Association has,
I should spend part of them in drain-blocking, and the rest in
the cultivation of disease germs, and the contamination of
drinking water.'

Not content with founding a paper and running a practice
that would have driven any other doctor into an asylum, Budd
got his partner to help him build a stable at his business address;
quite as much for his patients, thought Doyle, as for the horses.
Then, too, he was busy on a new invention, which he called
the 'Budd Spring-Shutter Screen', an ingenious method of
preventing a ship from foundering as a result of artillery fire
or running on the rocks, a shutter descending over every hole
made in her side. Even so his energy was not absorbed and
he decided to exercise himself on a frisky horse. He heard of
one belonging to an army officer, who had paid £150 for it
but wanted to get rid of it for £70 because it was dangerous.
This suited Budd, and the dealer brought it round. The
ensuing scene proved of value to Doyle, as it gave him some
hints for an incident in his romance *Sir Nigel*. Let him describe
the original episode exactly as it occurred:

'It was a beautiful animal, coal black, with a magnificent
neck and shoulders, but with a nasty backward tilt to its ears,
and an unpleasant way of looking at you. The horse dealer
said that our yard was too small to try the creature in; but
Budd clambered up upon its back and formally took possession
of it by lamming it between the ears with the bone handle of
his whip. Then ensued one of the most lively ten minutes
that I can remember. The beast justified his reputation; but
Budd, although he was no horseman, stuck to him like a limpet.
Backwards, forwards, sideways, on his fore feet, on his hind
feet, with his back curved, with his back sunk, bucking and
kicking, there was nothing the creature did not try. Budd was
sitting alternately on his mane and on the root of his tail—
never by any chance in the saddle—he had lost both stirrups,
and his knees were drawn up and his heels dug into the
creature's ribs, while his hands clawed at mane, saddle, or
ears, whichever he saw in front of him. He kept his whip,
however; and whenever the brute eased down, lammed him
once more with the bone handle. His idea, I suppose, was to
break its spirit, but he had taken a larger contract than he
could carry through. The animal bunched his four feet
together, ducked down his head, arched his back like a yawning
cat, and gave three convulsive springs into the air. At the
first Budd's knees were above the saddle flaps, at the second
his ankles were retaining a convulsive grip, at the third he
flew forward like a stone out of a sling, narrowly missed the

coping of the wall, broke with his head the iron bar which
held some wire-netting, and toppled back with a thud into
the yard. Up he bounded with the blood streaming down his
face, and running into our half-finished stables he seized a
hatchet, and with a bellow of rage rushed at the horse. I
caught him by the coat and put on a fourteen-stone drag,
while the horse dealer (who was as white as a cheese) ran off
with his horse into the street. Budd broke away from my
grip, and cursing incoherently, his face slobbered with blood
and his hatchet waving over his head, he rushed out of the
yard—the most diabolical-looking ruffian you can imagine.
However, luckily for the dealer, he had got a good start, and
Budd was persuaded to come back and wash his face. We
bound up his cut, and found him little the worse, except in
his temper. But for me he would most certainly have paid
seventy pounds for his insane outburst of rage against the
animal.'

Nearly every day Budd had a new plan for making money
on an unprecedented scale. Sometimes he would complain of
the wretched conditions of Plymouth where a fellow could
only scrape together a beggarly three or four thousand a year
out of the poorest classes. He wanted a continent to bustle
in; and once he announced that he would clear out and clear
up South America by concentrating on 'the eye'. There was,
he said, a fortune in eyes. A man grudged half a crown to
cure his chest or throat, but he would spend his last dollar
on his eye. There was money in ears, but the eye was a
gold mine.

'Look here, laddie!' said he. 'There's a great continent
from the equator to the icebergs, and not a man in it who
could correct an astigmatism. What do they know of modern
eye-surgery and refraction? Why, dammy, they don't know
much about it in the provinces of England yet, let alone Brazil.
Man, if you could only see it, there's a fringe of squinting
millionaires sitting ten deep round the whole continent with
their money in their hands waiting for an oculist. Eh, Doyle,
what? By Crums, I'll come back and I'll buy Plymouth, and
I'll give it away as a tip to the waiter.'

'You propose to settle in some large city, then?'

'City! What use would a city be to me? I'm there to
squeeze the continent. I work a town at a time. I send on
an agent to the next to say that I am coming. "Here's the

chance of a lifetime," says he; "no need to go back to Europe; here's Europe come to you. Squints, cataracts, iritis, refractions, what you like; here's the great Signor Budd, right up to date and ready for anything!" In they come of course, droves of them, and then I arrive and take the money. I work Bahia while my agent prepares Pernambuco. When Bahia is squeezed dry I move on to Pernambuco, and the agent ships to Monte Video. So we work our way round with a trail of spectacles behind us. It'll go like clockwork. Then I load up a steamer and come home, unless I elect to buy one of their little States and run it.'

'You will need to speak Spanish.'

'Tut, it does not take any Spanish to stick a knife into a man's eye. All I shall want to know is "Money down—no credit". That's Spanish enough for me.'

After Doyle had been five weeks at Plymouth his practice showed a decided upward tendency: he was beginning to make between £3 and £4 a week. Against this he did not seem to be on such friendly terms with the Budds. Sometimes he caught hostile glances from the wife; other times he noticed the husband glaring at him, and when he asked what was the matter received the reply, 'Oh, nothing!' Between times they both behaved quite amiably; yet he felt that something was wrong. He did not solve the problem until he had left them, but we may know the truth at once.

From the outset his mother had resented his association with Budd. She was very conscious of her ancestry. 'Not once, nor twice, but thrice did the Plantagenets intermarry with us,' wrote her son; 'the Dukes of Brittany courted our alliance, and the Percies of Northumberland intertwined themselves with our whole illustrious record. So in my boyhood she would expound the matter, with hearth-brush in one hand and a glove full of cinders in the other, while I would sit swinging my knickerbocker legs, swelling with pride until my waistcoat was as tight as a sausage skin, as I contemplated the gulf which separated me from all other little boys who swang their legs upon tables.' Doyle's mother was therefore pained when her boy linked his fortunes with a man whose behaviour and opinions, as reported to her by Arthur, showed so unmistakably that he had no Plantagenet blood in him, and her letters were very outspoken on the point. Arthur defended his partner to the best of his ability, but the more he defended

him the more violently did his mother attack him, and at last
there was almost a breach between mother and son. Unfortunately, the latter, being of an honest confiding nature, did
not burn her letters, which were extracted from his pockets
and read by the Budds. Even so it should have been clear
from the mother's letters that the son was taking their part;
but Budd was of a highly suspicious nature and instantly smelt
treason. Hence the glares and hostile glances which puzzled
their unsuspecting lodger.

One evening Budd's growing antagonism flared out in a
curious manner. They were playing billiards at a hotel, and
at the end of the game, wanting two to win, Doyle pocketed
the white. Instantly Budd screamed that it was bad form.
Doyle appealed to the marker, who supported him. Whereupon Budd began to abuse him violently, and when Doyle
said that it was 'a caddish thing to speak like that before the
marker' Budd lifted his cue as if to strike his opponent; but
thought better of it and marched out, after flinging his cue
on the ground and half a crown at the marker. In the street
his stream of abuse continued until Doyle checked him: 'That's
enough. I've already stood rather more than I can carry.'
For a moment or two it seemed as if there must be a fight
between them, which might have been good for business but
could not have cemented their partnership. Then Budd, with
one of his characteristic quick-changes, burst out laughing,
put his arm through Doyle's, and hurried him along the street,
saying, 'Devil of a temper you've got, Doyle! By Crums, it's
hardly safe to go out with you. I never know what you're
going to do next. Eh, what? You mustn't be peppery with
me, though; for I mean well towards you, as you'll see before
you get finished with me.'

At last matters were brought to a head. Budd was unusually
sulky one morning, and after finishing with his patients he came
stamping into Doyle's room with a savage look on his face.

'This practice is going to the devil,' said he.

'How's that?'

'It's going to little pieces, Doyle. I've been taking figures,
and I know what I'm talking about. A month ago I was seeing
six hundred a week. Then I dropped to five hundred and
eighty; then to five-seventy-five; and now to five-sixty. What
do you think of that?'

'To be honest, I don't think much of it. The summer is

coming on. You are losing all your coughs and colds and sore throats. Every practice must dwindle at this time of year.'

'That's all very well. You may put it down to that, but I think quite differently about it.'

'What do you put it down to, then?'

'To you.'

'How's that?'

'Well, you must allow that it's a very queer coincidence— if it is a coincidence—that from the day when your plate was put up my practice has taken a turn for the worse.'

'I should be very sorry to think it was cause and effect. How do you think that my presence could have hurt you?'

'I'll tell you frankly, old chap,' said Budd, with something between a smile and a sneer. 'You see, many of my patients are simple country folk, half imbecile for the most part, but then the half-crown of an imbecile is as good as any other half-crown. They come to my door and they see two names, and their silly jaws begin to drop, and they say to each other, "There's two of 'em here. It's Dr. Budd we want to see, but if we go in we'll be shown as likely as not to Dr. Doyle." So it ends in some cases in their not coming in at all. Then there are the women. Women don't care a toss whether you are a Solomon, or whether you are hot from an asylum. It's all personal with them. You fetch them, or you don't fetch them. I know how to work them, but they won't come if they think they're going to be turned over to anybody else. That's what I put the falling away down to.'

'Well,' said Doyle, 'that's easily set right.'

He walked downstairs, followed by Budd and his wife, got a hammer, and wrenched his name-plate from the side of the door.

'That won't interfere with you any more,' he remarked.

'What do you intend to do now?' asked Budd.

'Oh, I shall find plenty to do. Don't you worry about that.'

'But this is all rot,' said Budd, picking up the plate. 'Come along upstairs and let us see where we stand.'

Back they went, all feeling very awkward.

'It's this way,' said Doyle. 'I am very much obliged to you, and to you, Mrs. Budd, for all your kindness and good wishes, but I did not come here to spoil your practice; and, after what you have told me, it is quite impossible for me to work with you any more.'

'Well, my boy, I am inclined myself to think that we should
do better apart; and that's my wife's idea also, only she is too
polite to say so.'

'It's a time for plain speaking,' Doyle went on, 'and we
may as well thoroughly understand each other. If I have done
your practice any harm, I assure you that I am heartily sorry,
and I shall do all I can to repair it. I cannot say more.'

'What are you going to do, then?'

'I shall either go to sea or else start a practice on my own
account.'

'But you have no money.'

'Neither had you when you started.'

'Ah, that was different. Still, it may be that you are right.
You'll find it a stiff pull at first.'

'Oh, I am quite prepared for that.'

'Well, you know, Doyle, I feel that I am responsible to you
to some extent, since I persuaded you to leave another job.'

'It was a pity, but it can't be helped.'

'We must do what we can to make up. Now I tell you
what I am prepared to do. We were talking about it this
morning, and we agreed that if we allowed you a pound a
week until you got your legs under you, it would encourage
you to start for yourself, and you could pay it back as soon
as you were able.'

'It is very kind of you,' said Doyle. 'If you would let the
matter stand just now, I should like just to take a short walk
by myself, and to think it all over.'

Doyle went and sat on the Hoe, and brooded over a cigar.
He began by feeling depressed, but the flowers and the spring
air soon restored him, and he even experienced a sudden thrill
of happiness at the thought that his mother would be pleased,
that the strain of the last two weeks would be removed, and
that at last he would be on his own. 'As a drift of rooks
passed cawing over my head, I began cawing also in the over-
flow of my spirits.' On reaching their house he told Budd
that he had decided to accept his offer, and friendliness was
re-established over a bottle of champagne. They consulted
a map, and it was agreed that Doyle should try his luck at
Tavistock.

But his plans were upset the following morning. While he
was packing before breakfast Mrs. Budd knocked at his door.
'Would you mind coming down and seeing George?' she

begged. 'He has been very strange all night, and I am afraid
that he is ill.'

Doyle went down and found Budd sitting up in bed with
a pencil, a sheet of paper and a clinical thermometer before him.
'Deuced interesting thing,' said the patient. 'Come and
look at this temperature chart. I've been taking it every
quarter of an hour since I couldn't sleep, and it's up and
down till it looks like the mountains in the geography books.
We'll have some drugs in—eh, what, Doyle?—and, by Crums,
we'll revolutionise all their ideas about fevers. I'll write a
pamphlet from personal experiment that will make all their
books clean out of date, and they'll have to tear them up and
wrap sandwiches in them.'

Doyle noted that his temperature was above 102 and that
his pulse was not normal. 'Any symptoms?' he asked.

'Tongue like a nutmeg-grater,' said Budd, thrusting it out.
'Frontal headache, renal pains, no appetite, and a mouse
nibbling inside my left elbow. That's as far as we've got at
present.'

'I'll tell you what it is, Budd. You have got a touch of
rheumatic fever, and you will have to lie by for a bit.'

'Lie by be hanged! I've got a hundred people to see to-day.
My boy, I must be down there if I have the rattle in my
throat. I didn't build up a practice to have it ruined by a few
ounces of lactic acid.'

'George dear, you can easily build up another one,' cooed
his wife. 'You must do what Dr. Doyle tells you.'

'Well,' said Doyle, 'you'll want looking after, and your
practice will want looking after, and I am quite ready to do
both. But I won't take the responsibility unless you give me
your word that you will do what you are told.'

'If I am to have any doctoring it must come from you,
laddie; for if I was to turn my toes up in the public square,
there's not a man here who would do more than sign my
certificate. By Crums, they might get the salts and oxalic
acid mixed up if they came to treat me, for there's no love
lost between us. But I want to go down to the practice all
the same.'

'It's out of the question. You know the sequel of this
complaint. You'll have endocarditis, embolism, thrombosis,
metastatic abscesses—you know the danger as well as I do.'

'I take my complaints one at a time, thank you,' laughed

Budd. 'I wouldn't be so greedy as to have all those—eh, Doyle, what?—when many another poor devil hasn't got an ache to his back.' The bed rocked with his laughter. 'Do what you like, laddie—but I say, mind, if anything should happen, no tomfoolery over my grave. If you put so much as a stone there, by Crums, Doyle, I'll come back in the dead of the night and plant it on the pit of your stomach.'

For three weeks Doyle doctored Budd, and attempted to doctor Budd's patients. He could not prevent Budd from experimenting on himself, from covering reams of paper, from building models of his spring-shutter screen, and from firing off a pistol at his magnetic target; and he could not shriek at Budd's patients or knock them about or dance round them or prophesy miraculous cures or yell insults from the landing; but somehow Budd recovered, after which his business recovered.

At the close of those three weeks Doyle received another stinging letter from his mother. He had written to say he was leaving Budd, but by the next post he had written to say he was nursing him and keeping his practice going. This was altogether too much for the good woman, who replied after an interval that he was dragging his family honour in the dirt by continued association with a bankrupt swindler. The contents of this letter having been absorbed by the Budds without his knowledge, Doyle was naturally surprised when they suddenly became glacial, and rather upset when Budd, who was just up again, asked him how much he wanted for looking after the business.

'Oh, it was all in the day's work,' said Doyle.

'Thank you, I had rather have strict business,' answered Budd. 'You know where you are then, but a favour is a thing with no end to it. What d'you put it at?'

'I never thought about it in that light.'

'Well, think about it now. A locum would have cost me four guineas a week. Make it twenty. Well, I promised to allow you a pound a week, and you were to pay it back. I'll put twenty pounds to your credit account, and you'll have it every week as sure as Saturday.'

'Thank you,' said Doyle. 'If you are so anxious to make a business matter of it, you can arrange it so.'

Their manner made it clear that they wanted him to go, and on the day Budd resumed operations he set off for Tavistock. But as there seemed to be more doctors than patients in

Tavistock, he returned to Plymouth, where he had such a cold reception that he asked Budd what was wrong. Budd evaded the question with a forced laugh and a reference to his thin skin. This time Doyle determined to cut the painter, and as conditions at Portsmouth seemed analogous to those at Plymouth he boarded a steamer the following day with a brass plate, a hat-box, a trunk containing a stethoscope, a second pair of boots, two suits of clothes and some linen, a total capital of about £6 in his purse, and a piece of advice from Budd, who saw him off: 'You rely upon me, laddie. Get a good house in a central position, put up your plate and hold on by your toe-nails. Charge little or nothing until you get a connection, and none of your professional haw-dammy or you are a broken man. I'll see that you don't stop steaming for want of coal.'

Thus he left Plymouth, in complete ignorance of the real cause that had driven him forth, and wholly unconscious that Budd, in trying to ruin him as a doctor, had helped to make him as an author.

CHAPTER IV

DOCTOR DOYLE

H E arrived at Portsmouth on a July afternoon in 1882, feeling strangely elated. Naturally self-reliant, he enjoyed the prospect of having to depend solely upon his own energy and ability; and he gave expression to his exultation by cheering a regiment of soldiers about to embark for Malta. The first thing to be done was to find temporary lodgings. Leaving his luggage at the office, he took a tramcar into the town, the conductor advising him to get off at a 'shabby-genteel kind of thoroughfare' where there were innumerable apartments to be let. He rang the bell of the first establishment that took his fancy, where he was informed that a sitting-room could be had for 13s. a week. Never having hired a room before, he did not know whether this was a reasonable figure, and tried the experiment of raising his eyebrows in the hope of lowering the price. It was successful: the rent was reduced to 10s. 6d. Wondering whether a further reduction could be obtained by similar means, he again looked surprised, adding an ejaculation of amazement to be on the safe side; but this time the landlady's expression made it clear that the bidding was over, and he made the only kind of retreat that occurred to him.

'Your rooms are quite clean?'

'Quite clean, sir.'

'No vermin?'

'The officers of the garrison come sometimes.'

This might have been taken in two ways, but he decided to take it in the more respectable of the two, and having ordered tea he left to fetch his belongings.

As it was a lovely evening he went for a walk after tea to inspect his new surroundings. Thinking that his future practice would probably depend to a large extent on his personal appearance, and wishing to start well, he put on his frock-coat and top-hat and sallied forth with his metal-headed walking stick. He wandered along the common that lies between the houses and the beach and sat down for an hour near the band. But the sight of the families enjoying themselves made him feel lonely and 'music nearly always puts me into the minor key; so there came a time when I could stand it no longer, and I set off to find my way back to my lodgings'.

At the junction of several streets a crowd had gathered; and though the last thing in the world he wanted at that moment was to celebrate his arrival by engaging in a free fight, his curiosity got the better of him and he pushed his way to the front. A burly, red-faced, drunken man was kicking his wife, who, with a baby in her arms, was trying to entice him home before he had reached a condition in which he would have to be carried there. The crowd greeted each kick with a cry of 'Shame!' which had the effect of applause on the drunkard, who increased his efforts. Doyle's impulse was to go bald-headed at the brute and knock him out; but a sudden memory of what and where he was steadied him, and he tried conciliation. 'Come, come, my lad! Pull yourself together,' he said, placing his hand on the man's shoulder. His advice was taken with exceptional rapidity. The man pulled himself smartly together, and then let fly at Doyle, whose chin was up, catching him on the throat and making him swallow several times in quick succession. In an instant they were at it, the crowd dancing round them in an ecstasy of delight and yelling encouragement to the drunkard, who, being two inches shorter than Doyle and less presentably dressed, became the favourite. Doyle's top-hat was down to his ears, and he soon found himself locked in the arms of a man who had no respect for his frock-coat and kid gloves. It was an unpleasant situation for a newly arrived doctor to find himself in; and though he was a good enough boxer to take care of himself, his opponent was so tough that he made little impression on him. The suddenness of the attack had placed him at a disadvantage, and he was about to adopt a more formidable strategy when the matter was taken out of his hands. The crowd, swaying with excitement, gave them little space, and at last one of the onlookers, a rough jersey-clad sailor, was pushed between them. Doyle's opponent being too drunk and too furious to discriminate between a doctor and a sailor, he caught the latter a swinging smack on the ear. With a yell of fury and a stream of obscenity the sailor went for him; and Doyle retired. The sounds of strife were audible from the door of his lodging, and as he let himself in he felt greatly relieved that his first public appearance at Portsmouth would not be in the police court.

For a week Doyle worked, or rather walked, hard in search
of a 'desirable residence' to which he could attach his plate
and for which he would not have to pay rent in advance.
After obtaining a map of the town, he studied it closely and
planned a number of excursions which would take him through
every street in Portsmouth and Southsea. Immediately after
breakfast each morning he set out, walked till lunch, which
cost him threepence, and walked again till it was time for tea.
At the end of a week his map was marked with crosses at
all the empty houses and circles at all the doctors' residences,
and he had picked on a house in Southsea called Bush Villa
which was only £40 a year, plus another £10 for taxes, and
seemed ideal for his purpose, being close to the junction of
four roads, with a church on one side and a hotel on the other.
Having satisfied himself that he could find nothing better, he
called on the agent, who said that he must sign a year's
agreement and pay a quarter's rent in advance.

'In advance?' said Doyle, feeling very uncomfortable, but
putting on a manner of complete indifference.

'It is usual.'

'Or references?'

'Well, that depends, of course, upon the references.'

'Not that it matters much. Still, if it is the same to the firm,
I may as well pay by the quarter, as I shall do afterwards.'

'What names did you propose to give?'

Doyle casually gave the name of his uncle Henry Doyle,
a C.B., manager of the National Gallery in Dublin, and that
of Dr. Budd. The agent was duly impressed, and, restraining
an impulse to snatch the key from the man's hand, Doyle
went along to view his property. 'It was my own house—all
my very own! I shut the door again, the noise of the street
died down, and I had, in that empty, dust-strewn hall, such
a sense of soothing privacy as had never come to me before.
In all my life it was the first time that I had ever stood upon
boards which were not paid for by another.' He examined
the two rooms on the ground floor, his high spirits impelling
him to do a step dance in each, descended to the basement,
climbed to the first floor, and finally to the second, from the
windows of which he surveyed the grey backs of houses, some
green tree-tops, and patches of blue sky between drifting
clouds. A sudden sense of his own personality and of his
responsibility to something far greater than himself came upon

him, and he knelt down to pray. But though he tried to express his emotion in words he found that the old phrases had lost their meaning for him because the conventional idea of God as a magnified man who had to be asked, praised, and thanked, was no longer valid; and his prayer was so full of qualifying clauses that it seemed like a legal petition. Yet it comforted him and he felt the better for it as he went downstairs.

His first job was to obtain drugs and furniture. He ordered £12 worth of tinctures, infusions, pills, powders, ointments, and bottles at a wholesale house, giving Budd's name to ensure credit and prompt delivery; and he went down to an auction sale in Portsea that same evening where he collected two small tables, three chairs, a metal umbrella-stand, some curtains, a square of red drugget, a small iron bed, a fender, a toilet set, and three pictures, for just over £3. Next morning he moved in, suffering a spasm of shyness as he caught sight of his plate, which had been affixed to the railings by an ironmonger the previous evening. Then he set to work. With a broom that he had bought on the way, he swept out the hall and ground-floor rooms, and went upstairs to repeat the process, with the result that the lower rooms and hall were once more covered with dust and had to be swept again. Next came the problem of giving the house an appearance of being furnished: a little had to go a long way. The decorative key-note of the hall was a stern simplicity: an oakum mat, an umbrella-stand, and three pegs (6d.) on which his two hats reposed to give an impression of realism. Depressed by the large amount of bare floor still visible, he fixed a curtain about half-way down the hall, 'draping it back, so that it had a kind of Oriental look, and excited a vague idea of suites of apartments beyond. It was a fine effect, and I was exceedingly proud of it.' The most important feature, however, was the consulting-room, which was the only room in the house he could furnish at all and the only room he would be able to furnish for some time to come. The bit of red drugget occupied the centre of the floor, the effect heightened by brass-headed nails; but it looked like 'a postage stamp in the middle of an envelope'. The table stood on the carpet, and three medical books, a stethoscope, and dresser's case stood on the table. It took him about ten minutes to decide where the chairs should be placed to best advantage. One had to go behind the table, and at length he determined to place another on the right and the third in front of the table. The three pictures—'Spring', 'The Banjo Players' and 'Windsor Castle'—he nailed to three of the walls, and having placed the fender where fenders are usually placed, and his other table in the window, he darkened the room by fixing up the curtains and drawing them fairly closely together, 'which toned everything down, and made the dark corners look furnished'. The back room on the same floor was to be his kitchen-dining-room. Fortunately it contained a gas bracket, over which he suspended a kettle by driving a piece of wood into the wall. 'The attraction of the idea was that there was no immediate expense, and many things would have happened before I was called upon to pay the gas bill.' The furniture of this room consisted of his box, in which he could keep his food and on which he could sit and eat it. Even less thought and effort were given to his bedroom, as he only had a bed, a basin and a jug; but a packing-case which he found in the yard made a reasonably good wash-hand stand. The first few nights he slept in his overcoat on the iron bed, with Bristowe's *Principles of Medicine* wrapped in his second suit of clothes under his head; but later he received blankets, sheets, a pillow and so forth from his mother, and made a mattress out of the straw and sacking in which his medicine bottles arrived.

That first day he was content to sit in his house revelling in the sense of privacy and the joy of proprietorship. In the evening he went out and bought half a pound of tea, a pound of sugar, a tin of Swiss milk and a tin of American potted meat, after which his total wealth was reduced to something under £2; but he did not worry about the future because he had written to Budd the moment he had taken the house and expected to receive the first weekly sum promised by his late partner in a day or two. He could not, of course, afford a servant, so had to face the prospect of opening the door to his patients, polishing his plate, keeping the front of his house presentable, cleaning the windows and dusting the interior. The more public part of these duties must, he felt, be reserved for the night-time.

His first week's callers were unprofitable. The curate of the parish came to express a wish that he should attend divine service, was shocked to discover that he thought Jesus Christ 'a frail mortal like ourselves', and hurried away in a condition of speechless indignation. His next visitor looked more promising. When the bell rang he rushed into the hall and saw through the glass panel a respectably dressed bearded man, wearing a top-hat. Though he had thrilled at the thought of his first patient, he was nervous now that the moment had come and for an instant felt that he would not open the door; but he mastered the weakness and opened the door with an 'air of insouciance, as though I had happened to find myself in the hall, and did not care to trouble the maid to ascend the stairs'.

'Dr. Conan Doyle?'

'Pray step in.'

To hide his nervousness he affected an extravagant geniality. Entering the consulting-room the man took a seat and coughed huskily.

'Ah!' said Doyle, 'bronchial, I perceive. These summer colds are a little trying.'

'Yes, I've had it some time.'

'With a little care and treatment. . . .'

'It's not about that I've come.'

'No?' Doyle's heart sank.

'No, doctor. It's about a small sum that's due on the meter.'

Apparently the previous tenant had gone off owing the gas company 8s. 6d., but though the sum was small it was too large for the present tenant. After a certain amount of hum-ing and ha-ing, Doyle said he would look into the matter 'and so escaped for the moment, badly shaken but still solvent'. Before leaving the man volunteered a number of details concerning his bronchial trouble, but as he was in the hands of another doctor, Doyle did not even take an academic interest in the subject.

Such disappointments were slight compared with the blow that fell upon him a few mornings after his arrival. He received a letter from Budd which clarified a previous mystery but clouded his future. 'When the maid was arranging your room after your departure,' it ran, 'she cleared some pieces of torn paper from under the grate. Seeing my name upon them, she brought them, as in duty bound, to her mistress, who pasted them together and found that they formed a letter from your mother to you, in which I am referred to in the vilest terms, such as "a bankrupt swindler" and "the unscrupulous Budd". I can only say that we are astonished that you could have been a party to such a correspondence while you were a guest under our roof, and we refuse to have anything more to do with you in any shape or form.'

From motives of economy Doyle had given up smoking, but the situation called for a pipe, which he managed to fill by collecting the tobacco-dust from the linings of his pockets. Then he 'smoked the whole thing over'. Surely, he thought, the Budds must have realised that his mother's attack was in answer to his defence. 'Why should we write a duet each saying the same thing?' Besides, it was not his habit to tear up letters and scatter them in the grate; he usually let them accumulate until his pockets were bursting. At this point in his reflections he searched the jacket he had usually worn at Plymouth, and almost the first letter he opened was the one from which Budd had quoted. Obviously therefore the picture of the Budds piecing the letter together, though funny, was a fake. At last he began to understand Budd's explosions of temper and the hostility of Mrs. Budd: they had made a daily practice of going through his pockets and reading his correspondence. But in that case why had not Budd taxed him with treachery to his face? Presumably because he could not do so without confessing that he had played the spy. Having considered the matter from every angle, Doyle came to the conclusion that Budd had lured him on with promises in order to abandon him the moment he had committed himself, with the result that he would have to compound with his creditors and be what his mother had called Budd: a bankrupt swindler. Budd's villainy was inexplicable to Doyle and left its trace in his writings, which are peppered with blackguards whose behaviour has the same groundless and nightmare quality. 'It was as though in the guise and dress of a man I had caught a sudden glimpse of something subhuman—of something so outside my own range of thought that I was powerless against it.' Doyle replied briefly to Budd: 'I said that his letter had been a source of gratification to me, as it removed the only cause for disagreement between my mother and myself. She had always thought him a blackguard, and I had always defended him; but I was forced now to confess that she had been right from the beginning. I said enough to show him that I saw through his whole plot; and I wound up by assuring him that if he thought he had done me any harm he had made a great mistake; for I had every reason to believe that he had unintentionally forced me into the very opening which I had most desired myself.'

To finish with Budd. His business declined when the novelty of his methods wore off and the findings of one or two coroner's inquests suggested that his use of drugs was unconventional. His abnormally suspicious nature made his last years exciting. He was afflicted with the notion that someone was trying to poison him with copper, and he took the most extravagant precautions, sitting at meals with a complicated chemical apparatus and innumerable retorts and bottles at his side, and testing each dish before eating it. He died in the late eighties, leaving his wife very little money on which to maintain his memory.

Doyle now had to face life with not much more than a pound in his pocket and nothing in prospect wherewith to pay the rent. The first thing he did was to write a letter to the editor of *London Society*, in which a few of his short stories had already appeared ('feeble echoes of Bret Harte' he later described them), explaining the situation, sending a new story for their next Christmas number, and begging for payment in advance. The editor sent £10, which settled the first quarter's rent, and Doyle was grateful. But when, after Doyle's reputation was made, the editor published all his juvenilia in a volume under his own name, he was not so grateful.

Following the visit of the gas company's man, business flagged. For three days the bell did not ring. Doyle sat in his bedroom counting the passers-by who took notice of his plate. 'Once (on a Sunday morning) there were over a hundred in an hour, and often I could see from their glancing over their shoulders as they walked on, that they were thinking or talking of the new doctor. This used to cheer me up, and make me feel that something was going on.' He did his shopping between nine and ten at night, returning as a rule with a loaf of bread, some fried fish, or some saveloys. After dinner he quietly emerged from the house with a broom, and if anyone passed while he was busy he dropped the broom and gazed at the stars in a meditative manner. Later, when all respectable citizens were in bed, he brought out a rag, a tin of polishing paste and a chamois leather, and set to on his plate, which shone so brightly in the daytime that no one could help noticing it.

The first person to break the three-days' silence was the

man he had fought on the evening of his arrival. He did not recognise Doyle, and as he had called to see whether the doctor had any scissors to grind Doyle's interest in him was brief. The next person was his first *bona fide* patient: 'a little anaemic old maid, a chronic hypochondriac, I should judge, who had probably worked her way round every doctor in the town, and was anxious to sample this novelty. . . . She said that she would come again on Wednesday, but her eyes shifted as she said it. One and sixpence was as much as she could pay, but it was very welcome. I can live three days on one and sixpence.' Which was true, because when he jotted down his daily expenditure on food he found that it came to about sixpence a day. His daily ration of tea, sugar, and Swiss milk worked out at a penny; his loaf of bread was twopence three farthings; whilst his dinner cost twopence if he had two saveloys or two pieces of fried fish or a quarter of an eightpenny tin of Chicago beef, and twopence halfpenny if he had a third of a pound of bacon. He gave up butter, as well as tobacco, but the military doings in Egypt thrilled him and he could not resist the luxury of a halfpenny evening paper. One might suppose that such a diet would have toned down the vitality of so large a man, 'but I never felt more fit in my life. So full of energy am I that I start off sometimes at ten at night and walk hard until two or three in the morning. I dare not go out during the day, you see, for fear that I should miss a patient.'

A few weeks after his arrival his little brother Innes came from Edinburgh to keep him company. Out of school hours Innes was helpful, blacking the boots, carrying medicine, opening the door, shopping, scrubbing, and so on; and he was very companionable, accompanying his big brother on long walking expeditions and taking almost as much interest in the imperial associations of Portsmouth and the news from Egypt. From a letter written by the lad to their mother in August '82 it appears that business was looking up: 'We have made three bob this week. We have vaxenated a baby and got hold of a man with consumtion.' But sometimes it was the doctor who paid for the consultation. One morning a gipsy's van, covered with baskets and chairs, stopped outside the house, and the bell rang. Thinking that the owner wanted to sell him something, Doyle yelled from upstairs, 'Go away!' The bell rang again, and Innes repeated the order through the letter-box.

The gipsy swore volubly and said that he wanted the doctor to see his baby. Meanwhile, Doyle, not realising that the conversation was being held through the letter-box, kept bawling, 'Shut that door!' But the moment he heard that his professional services were required his manner changed from that of an outraged householder to that of a solicitous doctor and he descended to open the door. 'Pray step in, madam,' said he to the baby's mother. The entire family stepped in, and he discovered that the baby was in the early stages of measles. They were so poor that the visit ended in his giving the medicine for nothing and adding all his small change, fivepence, to the gift. 'A few more such patients,' he thought, 'and I am a broken man.'

There were occasions in those early days when the inmates of Bush Villa (which was later to be called Doyle House) had to live on a crust of bread. Rather than break into those ten pounds, which he had set aside for the quarter-day's rent, Doyle would have starved. Sometimes he could not even afford a stamp for a letter home, and the position of affairs in Egypt had to be gleaned from the posters. Three times he had to pawn his watch, and it occurred to him that instead of paying a poor rate he ought to be collecting it. During the first six months he lost a stone in weight. The few patients were so poor that they could seldom afford more than eighteen pence, and throughout that time he was called upon to do nothing but listen 'to the throb of the charwoman's heart and the rustle of the greengrocer's lungs'. Had he been a little less honest he might have done better, for his uncle sent him a letter of introduction to the Catholic bishop, and there was no Catholic doctor in the town; but as he could no longer believe in that creed, he resisted the temptation and destroyed the letter.

After a while some luck came his way. He happened to be passing a grocer's shop when the owner fell down in a fit of epilepsy. 'You may believe that I saw my chance, bustled in, treated the man, conciliated his wife, tickled the child, and gained over the whole household.' The fits were periodical, and Doyle arranged to buy his food at the shop, balancing his account against the grocer's. 'It was a ghoulish compact, by which a fit to him meant butter and bacon to me, while a spell of health for him sent me back to dry bread and saveloys.' At last the grocer died, and Doyle had to do without butter again. Then there were two small road accidents near his door, from which he derived little profit; but taking a leaf out of Budd's book he hurried off to the local newspaper, described the accident, and managed to get himself into the news: 'The driver, though much shaken, is pronounced by Dr. Conan Doyle, of Bush Villa, to have suffered no serious injury.' A more dangerous accident was more profitable. He was feeding in his back room when he heard a noise in the street, rushed to the door and met a crowd of folk carrying a lawyer who had fallen from his horse and been trampled on. 'They flooded into my house, thronged my hall, dirtied my consulting-room, and even pushed their way into my back room, which they found elegantly furnished with a portmanteau, a lump of bread, and a cold sausage. However, I had no thought for anyone but my patient, who was groaning most dreadfully. I saw that his ribs were right, tested his joints, ran my hand down his limbs, and concluded that there was no break or dislocation. He had strained himself in such a way, however, that it was very painful for him to sit or to walk. I sent for an open carriage, therefore, and conveyed him to his home, I sitting with my most professional air, and he standing straight up between my hands. The carriage went at a walk, and the crowd trailed behind, with all the folk looking out of the windows, so that a more glorious advertisement could not be conceived. It looked like the advance guard of a circus. Once at his house, however, professional etiquette demanded that I should hand the case over to the family attendant, which I did with as good a grace as possible—not without some lingering hope that the old-established practitioner might say, "You have taken such very good care of my patient, Dr. Doyle, that I should not dream of removing him from your hands." On the contrary, he snatched it away from me with avidity, and I retired with some credit, an excellent advertisement, and a guinea.'

Doyle had a strong feeling that a doctor who opened his own door forfeited the confidence of his patients, and one morning early in '83 he had a brain-wave. Business was improving; now and again he was able to indulge in a pipe; and the milkman was calling daily, 'which gives you a great sense of swagger when you have not been used to it'. He therefore paid a shilling for three insertions of the following advertisement in the evening paper: 'To Let. A basement floor, in exchange for services. Apply Bush Villa.' One insertion would have been enough: he was deluged with applicants. 'I should have been prepared at the outset to take anything in a petticoat; but as we saw the demand increase, our conditions went up and up: white aprons, proper dress for answering door, doing beds and boots, cooking—we became more and more exacting. So at last we made our selection. . . . She was a hard-faced, brusque-mannered person, whose appearance in a bachelor's household was not likely to cause a scandal. Her nose was in itself a certificate of virtue. She was to bring her furniture into the basement, and I was to give her and her sister one of the two upper rooms for a bedroom.' All went well at first, but coming down earlier than usual one morning Doyle saw a small bearded man who was just about to leave by the front door. An explanation of his presence being demanded, he said that he was married to the woman whom Doyle had engaged. 'Dreadful doubts of my housekeeper flashed across my mind, but I thought of her nose and was reassured. An examination revealed everything. She was a married woman. The lines were solemnly produced. Her husband was a seaman. She had passed as a miss, because she thought I was more likely to take a housekeeper without encumbrances. Her husband had come home unexpectedly from a long voyage, and had returned last night. And then— plot within plot—the other woman was not her sister, but a friend. . . . She thought I was more likely to take two sisters than two friends. So we all came to know who the other was.'

He allowed the seaman to remain, and allotted the other bedroom on the top floor to his wife's friend. It seemed to Doyle that, from absolute solitude, he was 'rapidly developing into the keeper of a casual ward'. In return for the lodging he made the seaman clean the place twice a week 'until the boards were like a quarterdeck'.

Finding a few shillings in his pocket at about this time, and having no immediate expenses to meet, Doyle purchased a four-and-a-half gallon cask of beer and placed it in the cellar, firmly determined that it should not be touched except on special occasions or when a guest had to be entertained. His male lodger went to sea again in three weeks, and the sound of quarrelling came up from the basement. Soon the unmarried woman tearfully explained that the other made life impossible, and announced her intention of leaving and of setting up a small shop. Doyle having expressed his regret, she suddenly said, 'Take a drink of your own beer,' and left hurriedly. Doyle dived into the cellar, found his beer-cask empty, and after an unpleasant scene with the seaman's wife gave her notice to leave on the spot. 'But we were demoralised by luxury. We could no longer manage without a helper— especially now in the winter-time, when fires had to be lit —the most heart-breaking task that a man can undertake.' So he went in search of the woman who had left the house after warning him about the beer. 'She was quite willing to come, and saw how she could get out of the rent; but the difficulty lay with her stock. This sounded formidable at first, but when I came to learn that the whole thing had cost eleven shillings, it did not appear insurmountable. In half an hour my watch was pawned, and the affair concluded. I returned with an excellent housekeeper, and with a larger basketful of inferior Swedish matches, bootlaces, cakes of black lead, and little figures made of sugar, than I should have thought it possible to get for the money.'

He decided to pay her a small, a very small, salary; and from that moment life at Bush Villa was more comfortable. She became an admirable housekeeper, and nursed his practice by pretending to every caller that he was in great demand. 'Dear me, now!' she would say; 'he's been hurried off again. If you'd been here half an hour ago he might have given you a minute.' Or, consulting an imaginary list, she would do her best to fit someone in: 'Let us see! He will be clear at seven minutes past eight this evening. Yes, he could just manage it then. He has no one at all from seven past to the quarter past.' If the patient, who arrived at the minute named, could have realised that he was the first to be seen that day, which had probably been spent by the doctor at cricket, he might not have been so punctual, nor valued so highly the advice he received.

Gradually the practice increased, not because of Doyle's ability as a doctor but because of his adaptability as a man. He at length came to the conclusion that it was no good waiting in for patients: one might sit on one's chair until it broke without making the least progress. So he determined to go out and fetch them in. That is, he began to take part in the social activities of the place. He joined a football club, a bowling club, a political club, a literary club, and several

cricket clubs. He mixed with as many men as possible in as
many walks of life as possible; and although he might have
missed a patient or two by attending a smoking concert, he
soon discovered that the loss was more than balanced by the
fact that he had passed a noisy evening with eighty potential
patients. But he was very careful to keep his own boisterous-
ness within limits; he did not forget why he was there; he was
friendly, genial, convivial, but he never drank a drop too
much, never lost the respect which he felt was his due as a
doctor, knowing well that, while the rest of the company
condoned drunkenness in one another, they would not over-
look it in the man to whom they might commit their lives.

In all these activities Doyle was, as always, very thorough.
Whatever he took up was carried through with every scrap of
energy and conviction he possessed. He played games for all
he was worth, and soon found himself on the club committees,
with requests to act as secretary or chairman. He lectured to
literary gatherings, and was accepted as an authority. He
debated at political meetings, and was soon in demand as a
speaker; though in his early days he was so nervous that the
bench he was sitting on, as well as everyone else who sat upon
it, shook with his emotion for a minute or two before he got
on his legs. Meanwhile he kept himself to the fore as a doctor
by writing to the newspapers in support of vivisection or
criticising the anti-vaccinationists. His popularity was partly
gained by his performances in the field of sport. He was a
very good all-round cricketer and became captain of the
Portsmouth Cricket Club. As a footballer he was described
as 'one of the safest Association backs in Hampshire'; while
his billiards and bowls were well above the average. He was
further helped by the catholicity of his interests, for he became
joint secretary of the Portsmouth Literary and Scientific
Society, to which he read papers on Gibbon and Carlyle, and
vice-president of the Liberal-Unionist Association. He seemed
indeed to take an interest in everything, from the battles in
Egypt, descriptions of which he pasted into a scrapbook, to
the mystery of Edwin Drood, of which he wrote his own
solution; from vaccination, which he thought should be made
compulsory, to verse, wherein he exercised himself by writing
a mock heroic poem on a football match between the ancient
gods and heroes.

Apart from the number of male patients he collected by

these means, it seems that his manner fascinated old ladies.
We have record of two fairly tough cases. One was Mrs. Mary
Harriet Abbott of Garden Terrace, Southsea, who at the age
of 101 suffered a fall and injured herself, but she was attended
by Dr. Conan Doyle, 'whose services', according to the local
paper, 'resulted in her complete recovery'. Six weeks after
her accident she sallied forth to enjoy a Turkish bath, after
which she returned home in a cutting east wind, which brought
on congestion of the lungs. This was too much for Doyle,
and even too much for Mrs. Abbott. The second old lady
was tall, haughty, dignified, and horse-faced. She lived in a
small house, and was attended by a small servant. Passers-by
used to admire her picturesque poise as she sat framed in her
window, looking like an aristocrat of the *ancien régime*. But
once every two months or so she indulged in a drinking bout,
which lasted about a week, and the admiration of the passers-by
changed to consternation as she skimmed plates at them
through the window, varying the sport by shouting, singing,
and chasing her servant about the house with derisive yells.
Doyle was called in during one of her field-days, soon discovered how to control her, and thenceforth was fetched whenever the plates began to soar through the window. Once she
spotted him coming in at the gate and was about to receive
him with crockery when she caught the look in his eye and
forbore. She had a collection of curios, jugs, statues, pictures,
and so forth, many of which she loaded him with on these
occasions, begging him to accept them as a mark of her
appreciation, and he used to 'stagger out of the house like one
of Napoleon's generals coming out of Italy'. But with the
return of sanity she always despatched a porter with a
polite note asking for their return. 'Once when she had been
particularly troublesome,' he wrote many years later, 'I retained a fine lava jug, in spite of her protests, and I have got
it yet.'

Doyle's practice never became large. He made £154 the
first year, £250 the second, and then by degrees his income
rose to £300, where it stayed: he never earned more as a
doctor in any one year while he was at Southsea from 1882
to 1890. When he filled in and sent off his first income tax
form, it was returned with the comment: 'Most unsatisfactory.'
He wrote 'I entirely agree' underneath and posted it back
again. Whereupon he was ordered to appear in person. An

inspection of his ledger stumped the officials, and they parted on cordial terms.

Though he made little money as a doctor, his practice brought him a wife. He was taken into consultation over a youth who suffered from cerebral meningitis. The boy's mother, a widow named Mrs. Hawkins, had come from Gloucestershire to settle in Southsea, and there was also a daughter, Louise, 'a very gentle and amiable girl'. As the lad required constant attention, and their lodgings were unsatisfactory, Mrs. Hawkins and her daughter called to ask Doyle whether he could recommend a doctor who would take him in as a patient. Doyle considered the matter carefully, and then rang for his housekeeper. 'Do you think we can furnish a bedroom by to-night, so as to take in a gentleman who is ill?' he asked. The housekeeper was equal to the occasion. 'Easily, sir, if the patients will only let me alone. But with that bell going thirty times an hour, it's hard to say what you're going to do.' The room was furnished by the evening, and the boy moved in. Doyle was now assured of one regular patient, and felt rather ashamed of the gratitude expressed by Mrs. Hawkins and her daughter. But the boy only lived for a few days, and Doyle was caused a good deal of anxiety because the death had occurred in his house; in fact he would have been very awkwardly placed if he had not asked the doctor who had taken him into consultation over the case to see the patient the day before he died. Also a funeral from a doctor's house is not the sort of advertisement for which he craves. However, the affair ended happily, because a friendship commenced between himself and the family of Hawkins, and very soon he was engaged to Louise.

In 1885 his brother Innes left him to enter a public school in Yorkshire, and in the same year he married. His income at the time was about £270, but as his wife had a hundred or so of her own they were able to enjoy 'the decencies, if not the luxuries, of life'.

CHAPTER V

WHILE WAITING

ODD stories, some of them very odd, had been written by Doyle between 1878 and 1883, and a few had been accepted by the editors of magazines that appealed to boys and elderly boys. Three or four guineas was the average payment for one of these, and they never yielded more than £15 a year. In 1883 he got into what he called good company, and experienced his first thrill of recognition when James Payn accepted his tale 'Habakuk Jephson's Statement' for the *Cornhill*, paying him twenty-nine guineas for it. The contributions were anonymous, but Doyle was too elated over the appearance of his work in a magazine that had been founded and edited by Thackeray to keep the news to himself, and he experienced a thrill of another sort when a friend ran after him in the street, waving a London evening paper and shouting, 'Have you seen what they say about your *Cornhill* story?'

'No, no. What is it?'

'Here it is! Here it is!'

Trembling with excitement, swelling with pride, but making a desperate attempt to appear modest, Doyle peeped over his friend's shoulder and began to read, 'This month's *Cornhill* opens with a story which will make Thackeray turn in his grave. . . .' When relating the incident long afterwards Doyle added, 'There were several witnesses about, and the Portsmouth bench are severe upon assaults, so my friend escaped unscathed.' He was comforted when another critic said that his yarn might have been written by R. L. Stevenson.

After that he sent all his stories to James Payn, who was compelled to return five out of six. Unfortunately Payn's writing was almost wholly illegible, and between the reception of his letter and the return of the MS. Doyle suffered agonies of uncertainty as to whether his work had found favour or not. Two more of his tales appeared in the *Cornhill*, and *Blackwood's* took another. But he was still utterly unknown, and feeling it was necessary that his name should appear on the back of a volume he wrote a novel which he entitled *The Narrative of John Smith*. Unfortunately it was lost in the post on its first journey to a publisher; and although Doyle was to confess in after years that 'my shock at its disappearance would be as nothing to my horror if it were suddenly to appear again —in print', his biographer feels differently about it. The title alone assures us of its autobiographical nature, and as the author said that it was 'of a personal-social-political complexion', and that it steered 'perilously near to the libellous', we cannot share his later thankfulness that the countless blue forms sent him by the Post Office were filled up in vain.

The shock of its loss did not paralyse him, and in 1884 he commenced another novel: *The Firm of Girdlestone*. In this, the first of his novels to survive, though it was not published until he had made his name with stories of a very different brand, his peculiar merits and faults as a writer are at once apparent. All the 'action' episodes are first-rate, and we are given a good specimen of the humorous observation that was later to make his best short stories so entertaining: 'Their faces wearing that pained and anxious expression which the British countenance naturally assumes when dancing, giving the impression that the legs have suddenly burst forth in a festive mood, and have dragged the rest of the body into it very much against its will.' On the other hand the book is padded out with descriptions of a dozen things that have nothing to do with the story. There is a lot of information about Edinburgh University; there are descriptions of a rectorial election, of a 'rugger' match between England and Scotland, and of a first professional examination; with the result that the reader may sometimes wonder whether he is reading a guide-book for undergrads or a 'thriller'. Doyle had obviously been wallowing in Dickens, for he apostrophises one of his characters thus: 'Perhaps, Thomas Gilroy, that ill-spared half-crown of yours may bring in better interest than the five-and-twenty pounds of your employer.' And he dismisses his characters at the end of the novel in this style: 'I see them going on down the vista of the future, gathering wisdom and happiness as they go. . . . I see Kate and her husband, chastened by their many troubles, and making the road to the grave pleasant to the good old couple who are so proud of their son. . . .' Finally, we are made aware of the essential simplicity of the author, whose hero has only told one lie in his life and that a noble one, and whose villains, portrayed as shrewd business men, place themselves open-eyed at the mercy of blackmailing blackguards without taking any precautions: they even employ one of these rascals, who has already tried to ruin them, to murder a girl whose money they will get at her death. Their creator had a trusting nature.

The patchwork effect of the book is partly due to the conditions in which it was written. Doyle's practice between '84 and '86, though poor, was busy, and there were constant interruptions. In the middle of a chapter this sort of thing would occur:

Enter his housekeeper.

'Mrs. Thurston's little boy wants to see you, doctor.'

'Show him in,' says Doyle, trying to fix in his memory the scene he has been planning.

'Well, my boy?'

'Please, doctor, mother wants to know if she is to add water to that medicine?'

'Certainly, certainly.'

It pays doctors to be decisive. The boy goes, and Doyle continues his novel. The boy returns hurriedly.

'Please, doctor, when I got back mother had taken the medicine without the water.'

'Tut, tut! It really does not matter in the least.'

The boy looks suspiciously at the doctor as he leaves the room, and Doyle adds a paragraph to his chapter. Suddenly the husband arrives.

'There seems to have been some misunderstanding about that medicine,' he says frigidly.

'Not at all: it really didn't matter.'

'Then why did you tell the boy that it should be taken with water?'

Doyle tries to explain but fails to convince the husband, who shakes his head gloomily and says, 'She feels very queer. We should all be easier in our minds if you came and looked at her.'

So Doyle has to abandon his heroine at a crucial moment in her fortunes and concern himself with pills and pulses.

No publisher would consider *Girdlestone*, and its regular reappearance at Bush Villa depressed the author but did not surprise him.

Meanwhile he never stopped reading because he thought it 'a great mistake to start putting out cargo when you have hardly stowed any on board'. He was much attracted by the plots of Gaboriau's tales and he absorbed a deal of detective fiction. Poe's Dupin had always been a favourite of his, and it occurred to him that he could humanise some such character by modelling it on Dr. Bell, whose deductive faculty had so much impressed him at Edinburgh University. We shall learn more of this in the next chapter. Sufficient here to say that Sherlock Holmes made his first appearance in *A Study in Scarlet*, which Doyle wrote in 1886. Realising its merit he was deeply disappointed when this story began to repeat the monotonous journeys to and from the publishers which *Girdlestone* had made. At last the firm of Ward, Lock & Co. offered £25 for the copyright, if the author did not 'object to its being held over till next year'. The author objected not only to the delay but to the offer, and wrote to ask for a percentage on sales. The firm replied on November 2nd, 1886:

'DEAR SIR,

'In reply to your letter of yesterday's date we regret to say that we shall be unable to allow you to retain a percentage on the sale of your work as it might give rise to some confusion. The tale may have to be inserted together with some other in one of our annuals, therefore we must adhere to our original offer of £25 for the complete copyright.
'We are, dear Sir,
'Yours truly,
'WARD, LOCK & CO.'

Doyle never made a penny more than £25 out of *A Study in Scarlet*, which first appeared in 'Beeton's Xmas Annual' in 1887. While waiting for it to be published, he decided to spread himself on a historical theme, or, as he put it, 'feeling large thoughts rise within me, I now determined to test my powers to the full'. The toughness, not the teachings, of the Puritans had always appealed to him, and with Macaulay as his main inspiration he did about a year's reading and five months' writing before producing *Micah Clarke*, which was finished early in '88. By that time his Holmes book was out, but the favourable notice it had received did not help *Micah Clarke*, which went the usual round of publishers and returned in the usual way. Blackwood's informed him that 'many of your characters, for instance, strike us as belonging more to the 19th than to the 17th century', but the reason why no magazine would touch it was given by the Globe Newspaper

Syndicate, to which he had sent it with the suggestion that it might appeal to the readers of one of their papers, *The People*. The manager's department replied on August 31st, 1888, to Dr. A. Corran Boyle, Bush Villa, Southsea:

'DEAR SIR,

'The gentleman who reads our Tales for us has carefully perused your *Micah Clarke*, and, whilst fully admitting that it is written well, and has much interest of a kind, is not from the nature of its subject or its style suitable for the serial publication in a popular newspaper like *The People*.

'I may just mention that one great failure in it is the fact that it has next to no attraction for female readers who form undoubtedly a large percentage of our subscribers. Again it is hardly sensational enough.

'I thank you for the offer, and am sorry that we cannot make use of the MS.

'How and where shall we send it?

'Yours faithfully,

' . . .'

After reading this letter, which he pasted into his scrapbook, 'Dr. Corran Boyle' understood why the style and theme of his book would not appeal to the readers of *The People*, to say nothing of *The Globe*. But the constant refusals worried him. 'I remember smoking over my dog-eared manuscript when it returned for a whiff of country air after one of its descents upon town, and wondering what I should do if some sporting, reckless kind of publisher were suddenly to stride in and make me a bid of forty shillings or so for the lot.' As a last hope he sent it to Longmans, and by a stroke of good luck it fell into the hands of Andrew Lang, who advised the firm to publish it. Of the period before it came out in February '89 Doyle was able to say that 'during ten years of hard work, I averaged less than £50 a year from my pen'. But success was now on the way. *A Study in Scarlet* had been generously pirated and handsomely reviewed in the United States, and when the firm of Lippincott sent over a representative to commission a few books by British authors James Payn wrote to Doyle: 'I recommended you to Lippincott the other day, I hope with success. I am ill so excuse brevity.' Doyle was invited to dinner, took a day off, and found that his fellow guests were also Irish: a Member of Parliament named Gill, and Oscar Wilde. 'It was a golden evening for me,' he recorded. 'Wilde to my surprise had read *Micah Clarke* and was enthusiastic about it, so that I did not feel a complete outsider. His conversation left an indelible impression upon my mind. He towered above us all, and yet had the art of seeming to be interested in all that we could say.' As a result of that dinner Wilde wrote *The Picture of Dorian Gray* for Lippincott's and Doyle *The Sign of Four*, in which Sherlock Holmes made his second appearance.

The welcome given to *Micah Clarke* by the critics had stimulated Doyle, and he spent close on two years over his next historical romance, *The White Company*, having read well over a hundred volumes on the period, French and English, before starting to work. He considered the reign of Edward III 'the greatest epoch in English history', giving the whimsical reason that 'both the French and the Scottish kings were prisoners in London'. Such a view, curious in a writer, is natural in a soldier, and it explains why Doyle, a born man of action, was always at his best in describing action, and why he was so gravely concerned with accuracy in the historic background to his romances. He believed Charles Reade's *The Cloister and the Hearth* to be the greatest novel in the English language, mainly because the author takes the reader by the hand and leads him through the Middle Ages, 'and not a conventional study-built Middle Age, but a period quivering with life, full of folk who are as human and real as a bus-load in Oxford Street. He takes him through Holland, he shows him the painters, the dykes, the life. He leads him down the long line of the Rhine, the spinal marrow of mediaeval Europe. He shows him the dawn of printing, the beginnings of freedom, the life of the great mercantile cities of South Germany, the state of Italy, the artist-life of Rome, the monastic institutions on the eve of the Reformation. . . .'

As we know, Conan Doyle was immensely impressed by the encyclopaedic mind of Macaulay, and here again we note his love of information for its own sake. True, he paid a tribute to the imaginative quality in Reade's book, but one feels that for him *The Cloister and the Hearth* was primarily a great encyclopaedia of the Middle Ages, a super-Baedeker. That is the chief fault of his own romances. He steeped himself in his subject but could not imaginatively transmute it; and in

his serious novels he was being either painfully historical or
joyfully romantic, and he failed to fuse the two main elements.
'I am fairly tied to the chariot-wheels of history now,' says
Micah Clarke, which indeed was Doyle's trouble whenever he
set out to reproduce a period. To the end of his life it never
occurred to him that the accumulation of detail, however
accurate or picturesque, does not vivify an age but nullifies
it. Here, for example, is a passage from his last industrious
attempt to recapture the past in *Sir Nigel*:

> 'The great influx of foreign knights who had come in
> their splendour from all parts of Christendom to take part
> in the opening of the Round Tower of Windsor six years
> before, and to try their luck and their skill at the tourna-
> ment connected with it, had deeply modified the English
> fashions of dress. The old tunic, over-tunic, and cyclas
> were too sad and simple for the new fashions, so now
> strange and brilliant cote-hardies, pourpoints, courtepies,
> paltocks, hanselines, and many other wondrous garments,
> parti-coloured, or diapered, with looped, embroidered or
> escalloped edges, flamed and glittered round the king. He
> himself, in black velvet and gold, formed a dark right centre
> to the finery around him.'

He picked up this trick from Sir Walter Scott, in whose
historical productions the scenery and properties are sometimes as important as the story and characters. The passage
reads like a series of stage-directions: it is the work of a pageant-
producer, not a poet. But whenever Doyle forgot the notes
he had taken from the books he had read on the period with
which he was dealing, and let himself rip, no one but Dumas
could write more stirring scenes of action. Then the martial
man seized the pen, and the book came to life; only to die
again when the soldier in him, who had such a profound respect
for the scholar, recalled his period and handed back the pen
to the fellow who had so laboriously studied it.

Doyle had a high opinion of his historical novels. Towards
the close of his life he declared that, taken together, *The
White Company* and *Sir Nigel* 'did thoroughly achieve my
purpose, that they made an accurate picture of that great age,
and that as a single piece of work they form the most complete,
satisfying and ambitious thing that I have ever done'. As a

onsequence he under-estimated the stories he wrote with ase. Nowadays we can see that the facile saga of Sherlock Holmes is far more valuable even as a 'period piece' than the diligent epic of Edward the Third. The work that comes spontaneously from a man, the work he considers beneath his best, is often the work that survives, the classic example being the Gilbert and Sullivan operas.

When he wrote the last words of *The White Company*, Doyle felt 'a wave of exultation, and with a cry of "That's done it!" I hurled my inky pen across the room, where it left a black smudge upon the duck's-egg wall-paper. I knew in my heart that the book would live and that it would illuminate our national traditions.' It certainly became popular and established his reputation as a 'serious' writer, largely because of its appeal to an age that longed to escape from the stuffiness of commerce into the invigorating atmosphere of chivalry, an age that had forgotten the reality of war and so idealised it. Doyle was the mouthpiece of his age, expressing its vague aspirations more completely and whole-heartedly than any other writer of his time. He was 'the average man' made articulate. Lacon Watson, in his *Lectures to Living Authors*, says that Doyle achieved his position by sheer hard work, that he was the novelist of the average male Briton, and that his opinions harmonised with those of the majority. We need seek no further for the explanation of his success.

The age was not only bursting for bloodshed but thirsting for mystery—yearning for anything that would temporarily release it from the stifling air of merchandise and respectability—and while Doyle was waiting for his patients between 1885 and 1890 he wrote a number of short stories in addition to his long romances. Most of these eventually appeared in *The Captain of the Polestar*, but two of them reveal another side of his nature, which represented a similar urge in the ordinary man.

Like all spiritually undeveloped folk, Doyle was greatly attracted to such subjects as telepathy, theosophy, hypnotism, and anything else that went beyond the borderland of normal experience; and during his Southsea days he passed through various esoteric phases, starting with telepathy and hypnotism, continuing with occultism and Buddhism, and ending up with table-turning and spiritualism. Of the last we shall hear more later on; but his telepathic and theosophic phase resulted in

two stories, neither of which appeared in book form until th
middle 'nineties. The first he called *The Parasite*. It is
powerful little yarn, with perhaps more than a tinge of auto
biography in it, about a doctor who does not believe that th
spirit is something apart from the body and is converted by
lame and unattractive female mesmerist, who falls passionatel
in love with him and forces him to behave in a manner h
regards as infamous and criminal while under the spell of he
power. One day, when he is with her, she faints: he promptl
regains control of himself in her presence, and when she come
round tells her exactly what he thinks of her. As it is extremel
uncomplimentary her passion turns to hate, and recoverin
her strength she uses her telepathic power to make him tal
nonsense at his lectures. To anyone who has listened t
professorial lectures the effect of this is extraordinary: he
suspended from his chair by the authorities of the university
Having shown what she can do with him, she asks whether h
wishes to retract the words he addressed to her while out o
her power. He refuses, and she determines to ruin hi
socially. Under the trance into which she sends him he trie
to break into a bank. Finally she compels him to take a bottl
of vitriol to the house of the girl to whom he is engaged i
order to disfigure her. While waiting for the girl in her roo
he emerges from the trance, realises what has happened, an
rushes round to the mesmerist with the intention of killin
her. On arrival he is told that she died at 3.30—the precis
moment at which he had come to himself in his fiancée's roo
with the bottle of vitriol ready for action.

Doyle then moved on to Buddhism, and showed what i
devotees could do in *The Mystery of Cloomber*. The scientis
says he, should 'look to the East, from which all great move
ments come', where the savants 'are many thousand yea
ahead of him in all the essentials of knowledge'; and he co
cludes that 'the occult philosophy has been the work of th
very cream of humanity'. After reading the novel som
readers would prefer a philosophy that comes from the ve
beer of humanity. Briefly, an English officer, in the course
his duty in the East, kills a Buddhist holy man. From th
moment he is doomed, and spends the rest of his life fleei
and hiding from the other holy men who are on his track a
who at intervals convey to him by signals that he cannot esca
his fate. At last they come for him in a boat which

conveniently wrecked on the lonely bit of Scottish coast where he has fortified himself in a large house, the implication being that Buddhist holy men can create a storm at sea as easy as winking. He makes no resistance, follows them obediently, and comes to a sticky end in a bog. The chronicler is not in a position to inform us whether the soldier's last regrets were that he had failed to make a clean sweep of holy men while serving in the East.

Doyle was always hankering after a life of action, and though he could not join the army in Egypt he managed to get in touch with the army at home when there was a call for doctors to do the work of those in the Medical Service who were serving on the Nile. Most of the civilian doctors who volunteered made certain stipulations, and when Doyle appeared before the Board of Selection he was bawled at by the President: 'And you, sir! What are you prepared to do?' 'Anything,' said Doyle, and promptly got the job.

What with cricket, literature, his practice, his marriage, and the birth of a daughter, life was flowing along pleasantly enough in 1890, and at a later date he wrote: 'As I have never had personal ambitions, since the simple things of life have always been the most pleasant to me, it is possible that I should have remained in Southsea permanently but for this new episode in my life.' The new episode resulted from an announcement by a German doctor named Koch that he would demonstrate his discovery of a cure for consumption. For no apparent reason, since he took little interest in such matters and was sceptical about cures for anything, Doyle felt 'a great urge' and 'an irresistible impulse' to visit Berlin and witness the demonstration. The probability is that, without knowing it, he wanted to get away from Southsea, an unconscious ambition being responsible for the urge and the impulse. No doubt domesticity was extremely pleasant, but as a rule men of action enjoy the prospect of it more than the experience. He acted immediately on the impulse and arrived in Berlin with letters of introduction to the British Ambassador and the correspondent of *The Times*, collected *en route* from W. T. Stead, who asked him to do a character-study of Koch for *The Review of Reviews*. The Ambassador would not help him; the *Times* correspondent was unable to help him; Koch refused to see him; Bergmann the demonstrator was rude to him; and if it had not been for a good-natured American, who made full notes of the lecture and allowed him to study them the following morning along with the cases that were exhibited, his journey to Berlin would have been wasted. He came to the conclusion that 'the whole thing was experimental and premature', wrote a letter to the *Daily Telegraph* saying so, and was justified by the event.

In the train to Berlin he had passed most of the night talking with a Harley Street skin specialist named Malcolm Morris, who told him that he was wasting his time in the provinces, and, finding that he was interested in eye work, advised him to set up in London as an eye specialist after six months' study in Vienna. 'Thus,' said Morris, 'you will have a nice clean life with plenty of leisure for your literature.' Doyle returned to Southsea 'a changed man', Morris's suggestion buzzing in his head. Mrs. Doyle favoured the move, and after arranging for their little daughter to stay with her grandmother they began to pack up. 'There were no difficulties about disposing of the practice, for it was so small and so purely personal that it could not be sold to another and simply had to dissolve.' On December 12th, 1890, Doyle was given a Farewell Dinner at the Grosvenor Hotel by the members of the Portsmouth Literary and Scientific Society, and a few days later he bade farewell to Bush Villa, recalling the thrill with which he had entered it eight and a half years before, and thrilling once more with a sense of freedom and adventure as he left it for fresh bricks and mortar new.

They reached Vienna on Monday night, January 5th, 1891. It was bitterly cold, with a blizzard, and Doyle felt that his career as an eye specialist was starting inauspiciously, a feeling that deepened when he attended the lectures, which he could have followed more easily if he had previously familiarised himself with the German names for all the technical terms. He began to keep a diary in January '91 and continued to do so for about twenty years; but as the entries were unusually laconic, and in later years were almost exclusively concerned with cash receipts and cricket results, we can learn little from them, though we shall find the diary for 1891, his *annus mirabilis*, illuminating. The entry for January 6th, the day after his arrival at Vienna, runs: 'Began "Raffles Haw",' after which there is no entry until January 23rd, when we read 'Finished "Raffles Haw".' Turning over a few empty pages we then come across, under February 3rd, 'Raffles Haw £150.'

It was like Doyle to sit down and begin a story the moment
he reached Vienna in order to pay the expenses of the trip.
The story he wrote is the feeblest he ever wrote. *The Doings
of Raffles Haw* is about a chemist who, having discovered how
to transmute other metals to gold, becomes a billionaire. But
he has a moral mission; he wishes to do good; so he helps the
needy. The net result is that he turns hard-working men
into loafers, breeds universal discontent, makes an enthusiastic
artist a lazy good-for-nothing, breaks a love-match, sends a
man mad, and generally speaking corrupts the community.
At the conclusion of the parable one suspects that Doyle chose
the theme in order to display his knowledge of chemistry.

In his autobiography Doyle says that he and his wife spent
four very pleasant months at Vienna, enjoying some gay
society and excellent skating; but his diary tells a different
story. From it we learn that he stayed no more than two
months at Vienna, instead of the six he had been advised to
put in there; so we may conclude that the lectures were almost
wholly unintelligible, and that after eight weeks of skating
and gay life his conscience pricked him. Here are the tell-tale
entries:

March 9th.	Started for Semmering.
March 10th.	For Venice.
March 16th.	For Milan.
March 19th.	Reached Paris.
March 24th.	Reached London.

The White Company was running serially in the *Cornhill*
when he arrived in London, which gave him confidence, but
he still believed that medicine meant money; and after taking
rooms in Montagu Place for his family and himself, he looked
round for a spot in the Harley Street neighbourhood where
he could put up a plate and earn a living as an oculist. At
length he found what he wanted at the top of Wimpole Street.
For the sum of £120 a year he obtained the sole use of a front-
room and part use of a waiting-room at No. 2 Devonshire
Place, noting in his diary under Monday, April 6th: 'Got
Consulting Room in Order.' But only three days before, on
Friday the 3rd, he had made an entry which opened a strange
epoch in the history of fiction:
'Sent "A Scandal in Bohemia" to A. P. Watt.'

CHAPTER VI

SHERLOCK HOLMES

THE writer whose fictional characters were better known to the average Englishman than any others outside the plays of Shakespeare had lived for a time in Devonshire Terrace; and it was fitting that the first tales in which Sherlock Holmes achieved world-notoriety should have come from much the same address, for Holmes was to surpass in fame even the best known of Dickens's characters. G. K. Chesterton once remarked that if Dickens had written the Holmes stories he would have made every character as vivid as Holmes. We may reply that if Dickens had done so he would have ruined the stories, which depend for their effect on the radiance of the central character and the relative glimmer of the satellites. True, Watson's glimmer amounts to genius, but it adds to the splendour of Holmes, and Dickens would have made a fearful mess of Watson.

At the present time there are only three other creations in English literature to compare with Holmes in the mind and mouth of the man in the street. Any coal-heaver, docker, charwoman, or publican would recognise what was meant on hearing someone described as 'a reg'lar Romeo' or 'a blasted Shylock' or 'a blinkin' Robinson Crusoe' or 'a bleedin' Sherlock Holmes'. Other characters, such as Quixote, Bill Sikes, Mrs. Grundy, Micawber, Hamlet, Mrs. Gamp, Scrooge, the Artful Dodger, and so on, are known to the literate and the semi-literate; but those four are known to over ninety per cent. of the population, to millions who have never read a line of the works in which they appear; the reason being that each of them is a symbolical figure, representing a permanent passion in human nature. Romeo stands for love, Shylock for avarice, Crusoe for adventure, and Holmes for sport. Few readers think of Holmes as a sportsman, but that is how he figures in the popular imagination: he is a tracker, a hunter-down, a combination of bloodhound, pointer, and bulldog, who runs people to earth as the foxhound does the fox; in fact a sleuth. He is the modern Galahad, no longer in quest of the Holy Grail, but hot on the scent of the bloody trail, a figure from

olklore with the lineaments of real life. The curious thing
bout him is that, while not a four-square creation like all the
reatest characters in literature, it is impossible not to believe
n his existence. Wholly lacking the mystery and suggestive-
ess of a great portrait, he is as vivid as a snapshot. One knows
ow he would look and what he would say in certain given
ircumstances; indeed we all ape his look and say his words,
iven the circumstances. More than any character in fiction
e stimulates the sense of association. For those of us who
id not live in it, the London of the eighties and nineties of
ast century is simply the London of Holmes, and we cannot
ass down Baker Street without thinking of him and trying to
ocate his lodgings. Of whom but Holmes has a literature
prung up solely concerned with the question of where he
ived? One topographer, Mr. Ernest Short, has gone into the
natter with a zeal worthy of no better cause and has shown
y diagrams and description that the present number 109 was
robably the residence of Sherlock Holmes, whose Christian
ame has been given to a mews at the rear of the opposite
ouses.[1]

Doyle himself was singularly unobservant: he gave the
odgings a bow-window; and the distinguishing feature of
Baker Street is that there is not a bow-window from one end
f it to the other. Doyle made dozens of such slips. In going
hrough the stories recently I jotted down a few of them:
1) In 'The Yellow Face' we are told that even when Holmes
rred the truth was still discovered, as in the affair of the
econd stain. But in the story of 'The Second Stain' it is
Iolmes who discovers the truth. (2) Colonel Sebastian Moran
s, we presume, executed for murder in 1894; but Holmes says
e is still living in 1902. (3) Holmes disappears on May 4th,
891, and returns on March 31st, 1894; yet the adventure of
Wisteria Lodge' occurs in March 1892, when Holmes must
ave been travelling incognito in Tibet and was thought to
e dead by Dr. Watson and the rest of the world. The fact
s that it never dawned on Doyle that he was creating an
mmortal character; he was far more careful when relating the
istory of Nigel Loring, compared with whose exploits he

---

[1] Further, Holmes is the only fictional character who has been honoured by a bio-
raphy, his Life having been written by Mr. Vincent Starrett; and several societies,
uch as the Baker Street Irregulars and the Speckled Band Club, have been established
o his glory in America.

described those of Holmes as 'a lower stratum of literary achievement'. Many years later he wrote in his diary that he had been re-reading the plays of Shakespeare and had been much struck by his many blunders. We pay the same tribute to Doyle whenever we re-read the adventures of Holmes. No one cares a rap for the improbabilities and contradictions in a character that gives so much delight. Like Hamlet, Sherlock Holmes is what every man desires to be; like Don Quixote, he is a knight-errant who rescues the unfortunate and fights single-handed against the powers of darkness; and like Quixote he has a Sancho Panza in the person of Dr Watson.

There were living models for both Holmes and Watson. Doyle always declared that Dr. Joseph Bell, surgeon at the Edinburgh Infirmary, was the model for Sherlock Holmes, but Bell once confessed that Doyle owed 'much less than he thinks to me'. What happened, obviously, was that Bell stimulated Doyle's fancy, which, once released, far surpassed the original. Bell, a thin, wiry, dark man, had sharp, piercing grey eyes, an eagle nose, and a high, strident voice. Sitting back in his chair, with fingers together, he would quickly note the peculiarities of the cases that were ushered into his room by Doyle, whom he had appointed as his out-patient clerk, and would treat his circle of students and dressers to this sort of thing: 'Gentlemen, I am not quite sure whether this man is a cork-cutter or a slater. I observe a slight *callus*, or hardening, on one side of his forefinger, and a little thickening of the outside of his thumb, and that is a sure sign he is either one or the other.' Another case was simple: 'I see you're suffering from drink. You even carry a flask in the inside breast pocket of your coat.' A third patient listened open-mouthed as Bell, after saying 'A cobbler, I see,' turned to his students and pointed out that the inside of the knee of the man's trousers was worn; that was where the man had rested the lapstone, a peculiarity only found in cobblers. One example of Bell's diagnosis impressed Doyle so much that he never forgot it:

'Well, my man, you've served in the army.'
'Aye, sir.'
'Not long discharged?'
'No, sir.'
'A Highland regiment?'

'Aye, sir.'

'A non-com. officer?'

'Aye, sir.'

'Stationed at Barbados?'

'Aye, sir.'

'You see, gentlemen,' explained Bell to his students, 'the man was a respectful man but did not remove his hat. They do not in the army, but he would have learned civilian ways had he been long discharged. He has an air of authority and he is obviously Scottish. As to Barbados, his complaint is elephantiasis, which is West Indian and not British.'

Bell described his own methods in Holmesian style: 'The precise and intelligent recognition and appreciation of minor differences is the real essential factor in all successful medical diagnosis. . . . Eyes and ears which can see and hear, memory to record at once and to recall at pleasure the impressions of the senses, and an imagination capable of weaving a theory or piecing together a broken chain or unravelling a tangled clue, such are the implements of his trade to a successful diagnostician.'

But Holmes has been fathered on several fictional characters as well, and it is probable that his precise method first appeared in Voltaire's *Zadig*. A man who has lost a camel asks Zadig whether he has seen it. 'You mean a camel with one eye and defective teeth, I suppose?' returns Zadig. 'No, I have not seen it, but it has strayed towards the west.' Then if he has not seen it, how on earth does he know of its physical omissions, to say nothing of its direction? Elementary, my dear Watson. 'I knew it had but one eye because it cropped the grass on one side of the road only. I knew it had lost some of its teeth because the grass was not bitten off. I knew it had strayed towards the west because of its footprints.' D'Artagnan's reconstruction of the duel in *Louise de la Vallière* is also done in the Holmesian manner, and there are those who trace the greatest of all detectives to Dickens and Wilkie Collins. 'As I was brought up on Dickens's Inspector Bucket, Wilkie Collins's Sergeant Cuff, and Poe's Dupin, I thought nothing of Sherlock Holmes,' Bernard Shaw informed me; 'but the Brigadier Gerard stories were first rate.' Doyle himself admitted his obligation to Poe on several occasions, but others have compared Holmes unfavourably with Dupin and made statements which cannot be substantiated: for example, Miss Dorothy

Sayers, who asserts that Doyle's stories miss 'the analytical purity' of Poe. She talks of 'Poe's stern example of laying all the clues before the reader'. Yet Poe's detective, Dupin, springs a vital clue on his friend at the conclusion of his analysis of a crime when all the facts have been laid bare. 'I disentangled this little tuft from the rigidly clutched fingers of Madame L'Espanaye,' says he. We should at least have seen him disentangle it. And later, when his friend is amazed at his deduction that the owner of the ape is a sailor, Dupin produces a small piece of ribbon which has 'evidently been used in tying the hair in one of those long queues of which sailors are so fond'. This he has picked up on the scene of the crime. But his friend, and the reader, should have seen him pick it up. So much for Poe's 'stern example'; and if, as Miss Sayers assures us, Doyle's stories lack the analytical purity of Poe, so do Poe's stories.

Doyle, however, would have been the first to admit that he took a few hints from Poe's detective. Dupin, like Holmes, is a phenomenal pipe-smoker; is subject to 'moody reverie', sometimes refuses to talk of a case while pondering on it, breaks in on his friend's train of thought and continues his reflection for him, showing the various stages of his reverie; traps a man who can clear up the crime by an advertisement in the paper; arranges a tumult in the street, and while the attention of his companion is diverted removes one letter and substitutes another; and, like Holmes, has a low opinion of his official colleague, who is 'too cunning to be profound'.

But all this is beside the point, which is that Doyle was the first writer to give vitality and personality to a detective, and will probably be the last writer to produce short stories that are as thrilling and entertaining as the chief characters are vivid. Dupin is still-born, a mere talking-machine; the longest story in which he appears, *Marie Roget*, is boring; and none of Poe's characters come to life. In fact Doyle's successors have been influenced by Poe far more than Doyle ever was. The scientific approach to a problem, the mass of details, the tedious reconstructions of events, the padding and trade-tools of modern detective fiction are blessedly absent in the Holmes saga, because Doyle did not in this case confuse entertainment with instruction; and while he spoilt his historical romances by making the history more important than the romance, he never made the same mistake with his detective fiction, where the fiction is always more important than the detection. It almost seems as if he wrote history with the pen of Holmes, who preferred a scientific treatise to an exciting story; but he chronicled Holmes with the pen of Watson, who preferred an exciting story to a scientific treatise.⌋

⌈So please grip this fact with your cerebral tentacle,
The doll and its maker are never identical,

wrote Doyle to a critic who had suggested that Holmes's views on Poe's Dupin were those of his creator.⌋ We must be careful not to make the same error by assuming that Dr. Watson was Dr. Doyle. Nevertheless there was enough of Doyle in Watson to make it unnecessary for us to look further for a model. He frequently and unconsciously pictured himself in the character. 'Your fatal habit of looking at everything from the point of view of a story instead of as a scientific exercise has ruined what might have been an instructive and even classical series of demonstrations,' says Holmes to Watson, and it emphasises what we have just been saying. Doyle was a born story-teller, and whenever he sacrifices action for accuracy his hold on the reader's attention weakens. Again Doyle was thinking of himself when he makes Holmes tell Watson: 'You will realise that among your many talents dissimulation finds no place.' Yet again: 'My dear Watson, you were born to be a man of action. Your instinct is always to do something energetic.' And when, in the adventure of 'The Abbey Grange', Holmes decides to let the murderer off, he clinches our Watson-Doyle identification: 'Watson, you are a British jury, and I never met a man who was more eminently fitted to represent one,' which gives us Doyle's nature in a sentence.

The notion of writing a series of short stories round the character of Holmes came to Doyle when he read the monthly magazines that were then beginning to cater for the train-travelling public. 'Considering these various journals with their disconnected stories, it had struck me that a single character running through a series, if it only engaged the attention of the reader, would bind that reader to that particular magazine. On the other hand, it had long seemed to me that the ordinary serial might be an impediment rather than a help to a magazine, since, sooner or later, one missed one number

and afterwards it had lost all interest. Clearly the ideal com-
promise was a character which carried through, and yet instal-
ments which were each complete in themselves, so that the
purchaser was always sure that he could relish the whole
contents of the magazine. I believe that I was the first to
realise this and *The Strand Magazine* the first to put it into
practice.' His agent, A. P. Watt, sent 'A Scandal in Bohemia'
to the editor of *The Strand*, Greenhough Smith, who liked it
and encouraged Doyle to go ahead with the series. As he was
uninterrupted by the arrival of a single patient throughout
the whole of his time as an eye specialist, he spent his days
writing, from ten in the morning till four in the afternoon.
'My rooms in Devonshire Place,' said he, 'consisted of a
waiting-room and a consulting-room, where I waited in the
consulting-room and no one waited in the waiting-room.'

We may see how quickly he worked by glancing at his diary.
On Friday, April 10th, a week after sending off 'A Scandal in
Bohemia', he noted: 'Finished "A Case of Identity".' On
Monday the 20th he 'Sent off "The Red-Headed League".'
On the 27th he 'Sent off "The Boscombe Valley Mystery".'
After that he wrote 'The Adventure of the Five Orange Pips'
but it was not despatched until Monday the 18th May because
he was prostrated by a severe attack of influenza on the 4th,
when, on his morning walk to Devonshire Place, he was
attacked by 'icy shivers'. Returning to his lodgings he
collapsed. For a week he was in grave danger and for another
week was as feeble as a baby; but in the later stages of the
illness his mind became clear and he perceived that it was
silly to finance himself as an oculist, whom no one wanted to
consult, out of his earnings as a writer, whom everyone wanted
to read. 'I determined with a wild rush of joy to cut the
painter and to trust for ever to my power of writing. I remember in my delight taking the handkerchief which lay upon the
coverlet in my enfeebled hand, and tossing it up to the ceiling
in my exultation. I should at last be my own master. No
longer would I have to conform to professional dress or try
to please anyone else. I would be free to live how I liked and
where I liked. It was one of the great moments of exultation
of my life. The date was in August 1891.' He gives the
month as August in his autobiography, but the diary tells us
May, and the diary is right. As in the case of his sojourn in
Vienna, his memory exaggerated the period of his probation.

which largely explains the relief he felt when at length he decided to drop doctoring and take up writing as a profession. It was not a particularly risky step, for we learn from the April entries of his diary that he received £57 8s. 9d. for a short story called 'Lot No. 249', that he got £40 for the American serial rights of *Raffles Haw*, and that he was paid £30 12s. for the English serial rights and £50 for the American serial rights of 'A Scandal in Bohemia'. In the years ahead he was to earn about ten times as much for a single Holmes story as he received for the first; but the average payment for each of the first six *Adventures* to appear in *The Strand* was just over £30, rising to £45 for the last six.

Recovering from his attack of influenza, he began to move about with the aid of a stick and to interview house-agents. After spending two or three weeks in search of a suburban home, he at last chose No. 12 Tennyson Road, South Nor-wood, where he and his family settled in on June 25th. Almost simultaneously 'A Scandal in Bohemia' appeared in the July number of *The Strand*, and Doyle quickly became a figure of note in the literary world. The two long stories, *A Study in Scarlet* and *The Sign of Four*, had not popularised Holmes, but the short stories in *The Strand* made his name a household word. A name which now seems to us so inevit-able was not an inspiration but the result of patient con-sideration. Doyle took a slip of paper and abandoned him-self to the task of fitting Christian names to surnames. At first the sound of 'Sherringford Holmes' pleased him; then he dallied with 'Sherrington Hope'; finally, at the bottom of the slip, appeared 'Sherlock Holmes'. He worked on each 'adventure' with as much care as he had given to the leading character's name, first of all thinking out the prob-lem and its solution, then sketching the main outline, then writing the story. Among his papers I discovered a *scenario* for an uncompleted tale which gives us a rough idea of the early stages of his work before he filled it out and pulled it together though it is quite likely that he had bought the plot from someone else:

Plot for Sherlock Holmes Story.

A girl calls on Sherlock Holmes in great distress. A murder has been committed in her village—her uncle has been found shot in his bedroom, apparently through the open window. Her lover has been arrested. He is suspected on several grounds.

(1) He has had a violent quarrel with the old man, who has threatened to alter his will, which is in the girl's favour, if she ever speaks to her lover again.

(2) A revolver has been found in his house, with his initials scratched on the butt, and one chamber discharged. The bullet found in the dead man's body fits this revolver.

(3) He possesses a light ladder, the only one in the village, and there are the marks of the foot of such a ladder on the soil below the bedroom window, while similar soil (fresh) has been found on the feet of the ladder.

His only reply is that he never possessed a revolver, and that it has been discovered in a drawer of the hatstand in his hall, where it would be easy for anyone to place it. As for the mould on the ladder (which he has not used for a month) he has no explanation whatever.

Notwithstanding these damning proofs, however, the girl persists in believing her lover to be perfectly innocent, while she suspects another man, who has also been making love to her, though she has no evidence whatever against him, except that she feels by instinct that he is a villain who would stick at nothing.

Sherlock and Watson go down to the village and inspect the spot, together with the detective in charge of the case. The marks of the ladder attract Holmes's special attention. He ponders—looks about him—inquires if there is any place where anything bulky could be concealed. There is—a disused well, which has not been searched because apparently nothing is missing. Sherlock, however, insists on the well being explored. A village boy consents to be lowered into it, with a candle. Before he goes down Holmes whispers something in his ear—he appears surprised. The boy is lowered and, on his signal, pulled up again. He brings to the surface *a pair of stilts*!

'Good Lord!' cries the detective, 'who on earth could have expected this?'—'I did,' replies Holmes.—'But why?' —'Because the marks on the garden soil were made by two perpendicular poles—the feet of a ladder, which is on the slope, would have made depressions slanting towards the wall.'

(N.B. The soil was a strip beside a gravel path on which the stilts left no impression.)

This discovery lessened the weight of the evidence of the ladder, though the other evidence remained.

The next step was to trace the user of the stilts, if possible. But he had been too wary, and after two days nothing had been discovered. At the inquest the young man was found guilty of murder. But Holmes is convinced of his innocence. In these circumstances, and as a last hope, he resolves on a sensational stratagem.

He goes up to London, and, returning on the evening of the day when the old man is buried, he and Watson and the detective go to the cottage of the man whom the girl suspects, taking with them a man whom Holmes has brought from London, who has a disguise which makes him the living image of the murdered man, wizened body, grey shrivelled face, skull-cap, and all. They have also with them the pair of stilts. On reaching the cottage, the disguised man mounts the stilts and stalks up the path towards the man's open bedroom window, at the same time crying out his name in a ghastly sepulchral voice. The man, who is already half mad with guilty terrors, rushes to the window and beholds in the moonlight the terrific spectacle of his victim stalking towards him. He reels back with a scream as the apparition, advancing to the window, calls in the same unearthly voice —'As you came for me, I have come for you!' When the party rush upstairs into his room he darts to them, clinging to them, gasping, and, pointing to the window, where the dead man's face is glaring in, shrieks out, 'Save me! My God! He has come for me as I came for him.'

Collapsing after this dramatic scene, he makes a full confession. He has marked the revolver, and concealed it where it was found—he has also smeared the ladder-foot with soil from the old man's garden. His object was to put his rival out of the way, in the hope of gaining possession of the girl and her money.

Presumably Doyle scrapped this because he felt on reflection that the episode of the stilts was rather tall.

As we have seen, he seldom took more than a week to write a story. While living in South Norwood, where the last seven of the *Adventures* and all the *Memoirs* were written, he worked from breakfast to lunch and from five to eight in the evening, averaging three thousand words a day, and many of his ideas came to him in the afternoons when walking or cricketing or tricycling or playing tennis. In August 1892 he told an interviewer that he was fearful of spoiling a character of which he was particularly fond, but that he had enough material to carry him through another series (the *Memoirs*), the opening story of which was in his view so unsolvable that he had bet his wife a shilling she would not guess the explanation. It was a safe bet: 'Silver Blaze' is one of his most brilliant bits of work. His fondness for Holmes did not survive the *Memoirs*. After killing his detective in the December (1893) number of *The Strand*, the method having been suggested by a visit with his wife to the Reichenbach Falls in Switzerland, he wrote to a friend: 'I couldn't revive him if I would, at least not for years, for I have had such an overdose of him that I feel towards him as I do towards *pâté de foie gras*, of which I once ate too much, so that the name of it gives me a sickly feeling to this day.' But he was to have no peace until he resurrected Sherlock. Readers implored him, editors cajoled him, agents worried him, publishers tried to bribe him, some people even threatened him. For a long time he turned a deaf ear to both curses and prayers, but at last his rate of expenditure decided the issue, and when a friend told him the legend of a ghostly Dartmoor hound he completely transformed it into an early adventure of Sherlock Holmes, which, as *The Hound of the Baskervilles*, appeared in *The Strand* from August 1901 to April 1902. This merely whetted the appetite of the public, and Doyle brought Holmes back to life in October 1903, when 'The Empty House' commenced a new series in *The Strand*.

But his readers could not have a surfeit of Sherlock and went on asking for more; which made Doyle hate Holmes, whose notoriety interfered with a proper appreciation of what he considered his best work, and gave him a lot of trouble into the bargain. His dislike of Holmes took the curious form of praising Watson. Monsignor R. A. Knox writes to me: 'Long ago, when we were boys, my brothers and I questioned him about an inconsistency in one of the Holmes stories, and he wrote back quite kindly to say it was an error. Later, about 1912 or 1913, when I published an article on "The Mind and Art of Sherlock Holmes", a skit which gave impetus to that Holmesology which has since become rather tiresome, Sir Arthur wrote to me admitting that there were plenty of

inconsistencies, but claiming that at least he had made Watson
a consistent character all through.' He received hundreds of
letters from all parts of the world, some addressed to Holmes
begging him to solve problems, some addressed to Watson
offering him substantial sums if he could prevail with his
friend to undertake cases, some addressed to Doyle himself
requesting his assistance in unravelling mysteries. Occasionally
he was attracted by the problem put before him and helped
to clear it up, for which purpose he had to lock himself in a
room and imagine he was Sherlock Holmes. Now and then
he was successful, though it would be difficult to imagine a
man less like the Holmes of print or picture. Incidentally the
Holmes of the well-known pictures was not the Holmes as
Doyle had pictured him. Sidney Paget, who did the first
illustrations for *The Strand*, took his younger brother as a
model, with the result we know; but Doyle had originally seen
Holmes with a thin, razor-like face, 'a great hawks-bill of a
nose, and two small eyes, set close together on either side of
it'. However, Paget's Holmes remains that of the popular
fancy, reinforced by the detective's impersonators on the stage
and screen.

Doyle was to be dogged by Holmes for the rest of his life,
and three additions were made to the series after *The Return*:
another long story called *The Valley of Fear*, the first and
best of the 'gangster' yarns which achieved such an extraordinary vogue in the heyday of Edgar Wallace, and further
collections of short stories in *His Last Bow* and *The Case-Book*.
Doyle knew that the ideal detective story is short; and in his
four long ones he is careful not to overdo Holmes, but to
maintain the interest by telling a story within the story.
Although the continued demand for Holmes annoyed him so
much that he came to undervalue the work that had made
him world-famous, he always took great pains over every
addition to the saga, and some of the best stories were written
after the resurrection in 1903. 'I was determined,' said he,
now that I had no longer the excuse of absolute pecuniary
pressure, never again to write anything which was not as good
as I could possibly make it, and therefore I would not write
a Holmes story without a worthy plot and without a problem
which interested my own mind, for that is the first requisite
before you can interest anyone else. If I have been able to
sustain this character for a long time, and if the public find,

as they will find, that the last story is as good as the first, it is entirely due to the fact that I never, or hardly ever, forced a story.'* His claim is substantiated by my discovery among his papers of a complete unpublished Holmes story entitled 'The Man Who Was Wanted', which is certainly not up to scratch, though the opening is worth quoting because it carries the authentic trade-mark.

In the summer of 1895 Dr. Watson sends his wife to Switzerland for a holiday, his practice, which has 'grown much', keeping him in town. Let Doyle continue:

'One of my best patients was in a very critical state at the time, and it was not until August was gone that he passed the crisis and began to recover. Feeling then that I could leave my practice with a good conscience in the hands of a locum tenens, I began to wonder where and how I should best find the rest and change I needed.

'Almost at once the idea came to my mind that I would hunt up my old friend Sherlock Holmes, whom I had seen nothing of for several months. If he had no important enquiry in hand I would do my uttermost to persuade him to join me.

'Within half an hour of coming to this resolution I was standing in the doorway of the familiar old room in Baker St.

'Holmes was stretched upon the couch with his back towards me, the familiar dressing-gown and old briar pipe as much in evidence as of yore.

' "Come in, Watson," he cried cheerily, without glancing round. "Come in and tell me what good wind blows you here."

' "What an ear you have, Holmes," I said. "I don't think that I could have recognised your tread so easily."

' "Nor I yours," said he. "If you hadn't come up my badly lighted staircase taking the steps two at a time with all the familiarity of an old fellow-lodger. Even then I might not have been sure who it was, but when you stumbled over the new mat outside the door, which has been there for nearly three months, you needed no further announcement."

'Holmes pulled out two or three of the cushions from the pile he was lying on and threw them across into the arm-chair.

... Hesketh Pearson would not have retained this passage in later editions.

' "Sit down, Watson, and make yourself comfortable—you'll find cigarettes in a box behind the clock."

'As I proceeded to comply Holmes glanced whimsically across at me.

' "I'm afraid I shall have to disappoint you, my boy," he said. "I had a wire only half an hour ago which will prevent me from joining in any little trip you may have been about to propose."

' "Really, Holmes," I said, "don't you think this is going a little *too* far. I begin to fear you are a fraud and pretend to discover things by observation when all the time you really do it by pure out-and-out clairvoyance!"

'Holmes chuckled. "Knowing you as I do, it's absurdly simple," said he. "Your surgery hours are from 5 to 7, yet at 6 o'clock you walk smiling into my rooms. Therefore you must have a locum in. You are looking well though tired, so the obvious reason is that you are having, or about to have, a holiday. The clinical thermometer, peeping out of your pocket, proclaims that you have been on your rounds to-day; hence it's pretty evident that your real holiday begins to-morrow. When, under these circumstances, you come hurrying into my rooms—which, by the way, Watson, you haven't visited for nearly three months—with a new Bradshaw and a time-table of excursion bookings bulging out of your coat pocket, then it's more than probable you have come with the idea of suggesting some joint expedition.'

' "It's all perfectly true," I said, and explained to him, in a few words, my plans. "I'm more disappointed than I can tell you," I concluded, "that you are not able to fall in with my little scheme." '

Needless to say, Holmes has a case on hand and Watson is delighted to accompany him. They leave St. Pancras station at 1.30 a.m. for Sheffield in a first-class carriage, and another Holmesian trait is recorded:

'It was one of Holmes' characteristics that he could command sleep at will. Unfortunately he could resist it at will also, and often and often have I had to remonstrate with him on the harm he must be doing himself when deeply engrossed in one of his strange or baffling problems he would go for several consecutive days and nights without one wink of sleep. He put the shades over the lamps, leant

back in his corner, and in less than two minutes his regular
breathing told me he was fast asleep. Not being blessed
with the same gift myself, I lay back in my corner for some
time nodding to the rhythmical throb of the express as it
hurled itself forward through the darkness. Now and again
as we shot through some brilliantly illuminated station or
past a line of flaming furnaces, I caught for an instant a
glimpse of Holmes' figure coiled up snugly in the far corner
with his head sunk upon his breast.'

The problem and its solution show that Doyle was right to
shelve the story, though the fact that he did not destroy it
suggests either that he hoped to make the rest of it worthy
of the opening or that he wished to make use of the opening
in a worthier episode.* When people complained that the later
tales were not on a level with the earlier ones, he usually
protested. To John Gore, who made the accusation while the
concluding series were coming out in *The Strand*, he wrote:

'I read with interest, and without offence, your remarks
about the Holmes stories. I could not be offended for I have
never taken them seriously myself. But still even in the
humblest things there are degrees, and I wonder whether the
smaller impression which they produce upon you may not be
due to the fact that we become blasé and stale ourselves as we
grow older. My own youthful favourites no longer appeal.

'I test the Holmes stories by their effect on fresh young
minds and I find that they stand that test well. I believe in
my own critical capacity, for it is very detached, and if I were
to choose the six best Holmes stories I should certainly include
"The Illustrious Client" which is one of the last series, and
also "The Lion's Mane" which is the next to appear. "The
Noble Bachelor" which you quote would be about the bottom
of the list.

'I have always said that I would utterly abolish him the
moment he got below his level, but up to now, save for your
note (which may perhaps prove symptomatic) I have seen no
sign that he has lost his grip.'

The sixtieth and final adventure of Sherlock Holmes
'Shoscombe Old Place', appeared in *The Strand* for April 1927
when Doyle made his last bow as the creator of two characters
who have probably given more pleasure to millions of people
all over the world than any others in fiction and as the author

of the best of all fairy-tales for grown-ups. 'And so, reader,
Farewell to Sherlock Holmes,' he wrote. 'I thank you for your
constancy and can but hope that some return has been made
in the shape of that distraction from the worries of life and
stimulating change of thought which can only be found in the
fairy kingdom of romance.'

CHAPTER VII

FRIENDS AND FAME

VISITORS at No. 12 Tennyson Road, South Norwood, were surprised to find their host about as unlike his famous creation as it was possible for a man to be. Walking up a well-kept drive, they saw a red brick house with a projecting balcony over the entrance. From the grounds they could enjoy an unimpaired view of a broad stretch of fertile open country backed by the Surrey hills. They were shown into a comfortable room with a view of the lawn, whereon, as likely as not, they would see a gentleman practising shots with a golf club. He was dressed in a suit of 'rough heather mixture' and looked like a Life Guardsman. Noting that he was treating the turf with some familiarity, and that a number of golf balls lay about awaiting his attention, they would assume that he was a near relation, or at least a close friend of the family. It was a large walled garden and the Life Guardsman seemed quite at home in it. A servant approached him, spoke a few words, and he, dropping his club, made for the house. It took the visitors some time to realise that the soldierly man who now entered the room and gave them such a friendly greeting was the creator of Sherlock Holmes. The shock of disillusionment was followed by a sense of relief, it being instantaneously obvious that the healthy, hefty fellow before them was quite incapable of inferring anything about them from anything else about them.

He soon made friends, because he was so homely, so unassuming, so eager, so ingenuous, and indeed so friendly. The general impression he made was summed up in the statement that there was 'no nonsense about him'. This simply meant, in those days, that he had nothing of the artist about him, for it was an effeminate affectation among late-nineteenth and early-twentieth-century writers (an affectation against which Oscar Wilde was in healthy revolt) that the sword, the platform, and the cricket bat were manlier than the pen, and that a story-teller was a mere scribbler who felt abashed in the presence of a man of action, reverent in the presence of a politician, and humble in the presence of a sportsman. Anthony

Hope, whose *Prisoner of Zenda* scored a bull's eye in the 'nineties, expressed his envy of Doyle, 'who wrote good books, yet looked as if he had never heard of such a thing in his life'.

One of his first friends in the literary world was Jerome K. Jerome, whose *Three Men in a Boat* convulsed his contemporaries and to whose paper *The Idler* Doyle contributed stories. In his autobiography Doyle described Jerome as 'hot-headed and intolerant in political matters'. When Jerome read this he was amazed. 'It is precisely what I should have said myself concerning Doyle,' he retorted. They went for a holiday to Norway in those early years of friendship, and Doyle started to learn Norwegian on the boat, picking it up so quickly that he began to air his knowledge on all sorts of occasions. Then one day, according to Jerome, 'he lost his head'. They had gone up to a rest-house among the mountains in stoljas—one-person carriages drawn by small sturdy ponies. While they were at lunch a young officer entered and addressed them in Norwegian. Doyle rose, bowed, and answered him. The officer was charmed. Doyle became eloquent. And after a while the officer left. Asked what they had talked about, Doyle replied carelessly, 'Oh, just about the weather, and the state of the roads, and how some relation of his had hurt his leg. Of course I didn't understand *all* of it.' He changed the conversation. Lunch over the stoljas were brought out, but Doyle's pony was missing. Enquiries were made and Doyle was informed that he had lent it to the young officer, whose own pony had gone lame. The waiter had overheard the conversation and assured Doyle that he had said, 'Certainly, with pleasure,' and 'Don't mention it', several times in Norwegian. Fortunately a member of their party decided to put in a day or two at the rest-house and lent his stolja to Doyle, who talked less Norwegian for the remainder of the trip.

A fellow-contributor to *The Idler* was Eden Phillpotts, who, in a letter to me (November 1941) remembered Doyle as 'a typical Englishman and a most kindly man who loved sport and literature in about equal proportions. I never met him again after he went over, lock, stock, and barrel, to the spiritualists, and my memory of him embraces no shadow of the interests he afterwards developed. I only recollect a rare, big-hearted, friendly man who loved cricket and billiards. . . .' Two other contemporaries gave me their impressions of Doyle in the 'nineties. 'He struck me as a strong, direct sort of man,' wrote W. W. Jacobs; while Sir Bernard Partridge touched a different note: 'He always seemed to me a quiet, gentle, lovable character, with little of his real self showing on the surface.' Through those four pairs of eyes we are able to see Doyle in the first flush of his fame: a simple, reserved, proud, friendly, outspoken, warm-hearted, hot-headed, big boy of a man.

Perhaps the author he liked best among his contemporaries was James Barrie, whom he met in connection with *The Idler* and whose cricket team he joined. Doyle brought an element of gravity into the game which was not in harmony with the festive spirit in which Barrie's eleven played. 'Doyle was a serious cricketer and had no use for rotting,' I was told by A. E. W. Mason, who joined the team later on. But as, between 'quips and cranks and wanton wiles', it was necessary to put up some sort of a fight, Doyle was invaluable to his side, which he frequently saved from ignominious defeat by making more runs and taking more wickets than all the rest put together.

The transition from cricket to comic opera seemed natural, and Barrie asked Doyle to finish a libretto which he had been commissioned to write for D'Oyly Carte, who was frantically combing the world of wit for someone who could behave better than W. S. Gilbert and write as well. As time went on he discovered that everyone behaved better but that no one could write as well. Nothing could have been more courteous than the manners of Barrie and Doyle, nothing less witty than their libretto. Barrie sketched out the plot and wrote Act I. Then he handed it to Doyle, who toned up some of the lyrics in Act I and polished off Act II. The odd result, which was called *Jane Annie*, appeared at the Savoy in the spring of '93. Bernard Shaw's criticism in *The World* explains why it disappeared in the spring of the same year: 'It would ill become me, as a brother of the literary craft, to pretend to congratulate them seriously upon the most unblushing outburst of tomfoolery that two responsible citizens could conceivably indulge in publicly. . . . The high privilege of joking in public should never be granted except to people who know thoroughly what they are joking about—that is, to exceptionally serious and laborious people. Now in *Jane Annie* the authors do not impress me as having taken their work seriously or laboured honestly over it. I make no allowances for their performances in ordinary fiction; anybody can write a novel. A play—especially a music-play—is a different matter —different, too, in the sense of being weightier, not lighter.' After that Barrie and Doyle confined their collaboration to cricket.

On two later occasions Doyle was asked to finish the works of other men. R. L. Stevenson wrote to say that he had been retailing several Sherlock Holmes stories to his Samoan servants, and Doyle was delighted by the approbation of a writer he admired so much. After Stevenson's death his executors asked Doyle to finish *St. Ives*, of which R. L. S. had written about three-quarters. Doyle 'did not feel equal to the task'. Some years later Grant Allen made a dying request: would Doyle write the last two numbers of his novel *Hilda Wade*, then being serialised in *The Strand*? Under the circumstances he could not refuse and did the job, whether successfully or not I have taken no steps to find out.

The literary connection which made him especially proud in the South Norwood days was with George Meredith. Nowadays people wonder how it was that Meredith became the idol of his fellow-scribes during the last twenty years of his life. There are two reasons. First, his works were often difficult to read and frequently impossible to understand, which argued (1) that he was a great stylist and (2) that he was a profound thinker. Second, the general public never read him; and there being no likelihood of his competing with the current best-sellers, his contemporaries were on a safe wicket in cracking him up. Moreover, it is always a dignified thing for a profession to have a Grand Old Man, someone to look up to, an acknowledged monarch; and as Thomas Hardy was not respectable enough in the 'nineties, and Meredith was socially and politically 'safe', he was the obvious choice. Hardy's turn came later, when he was too old to be dangerous.

Having decided, after the death of Carlyle, that Meredith was the leading figure in contemporary literature, Conan Doyle wrote articles on his work and in November '92 lectured on him to the Upper Norwood Literary and Scientific Society. Naturally he was invited to see the master at Box Hill. The meeting began, and almost ended, at the garden gate. Pointing to the hill behind his house, Meredith said, 'I have just been up to the top for a walk.' Doyle, having read in the papers that Meredith's health had been poorly, said in surprise, 'You must be in good trim to do it.' Meredith replied angrily, 'That would be a proper compliment to pay to an octo- genarian.' Doyle was nettled. 'I understood that I was talking to an invalid,' said he. Meredith swallowed his wrath, and Doyle absorbed a bottle of Burgundy over lunch while listening to his host's conversation. Afterwards they climbed the steep and narrow path to the summer-house where Meredith worked. Doyle, who went first, heard Meredith slip and fall on the path behind him; but he had learnt his lesson, did not look round, and went on as if unconscious of the other's accident. 'He was a fiercely proud old man, and my instincts told me that his humiliation in being helped up would be far greater than any relief I could give him.' Safe at the summer-house Meredith read an unfinished novel, which Doyle liked so much that Meredith said he would complete it; so the world probably owes *The Amazing Marriage* to Doyle's tact in not hauling the author to his feet.

Meanwhile, between cricket matches and literary adventures, Doyle was working very hard and doing pretty well. His diary, which has no interest for us after his first year as a professional author, shows his upward progress during 1891. Here are a few extracts:

> June 1. 'Contracted with Good Words to write "Good Cheer" (42,000) at £150. MS to be ready by Sept. 1st.'

This story, which he called *Beyond the City*, and despatched on July 8, was of a domestic nature, and the combination of Good Words with 'Good Cheer' had a cramping effect on his style.

> July 7. 'Bought 250 shares in "Newnes Ltd."'
> Aug. 15. 'Started for Holland.'
> Aug. 26. 'Arrived from Holland.'

He went with a cricket team and played several games, finishing the tour at The Hague, where they were matched against United Holland and where Doyle saved his side by taking the last four wickets for as many runs. Transported by his per- formance, the stalwarts of the English team hoisted him on to their shoulders and carried him from the field; but his sixteen stones were too much for them, and their Dutch opponents were not displeased when he fell to the ground with a crash that left him breathless. In other respects he continued to rise:

> Oct. 5. 'Signed Agreement with Cassell's they to pay 20 per cent. Royalty on published price, accounts made up June 30, December 30. 100 down on passing of proofs.'
> Oct. 26. 'White Company Came Out. Received £250.'
> Nov. 13. 'Received £125 from Balestier for American Rights of "The White Company".'
> Nov. 16. 'Paid £260 for 200 more shares in Titbits, being 26/– per share.'
> Dec. 3. 'Paid £19 10s. for 15 more shares in Tit Bits at 26/–.'

He made about £1500 from his pen in 1891, which was not bad as a start-off, and he was careful to note that he had written 210,000 words during the year, of which he estimated 30,000 for the first hundred and fifty pages of a new historical novel, *The Refugees*, which deals with the French Huguenots, whom he admired as much as the English Puritans. His earlier romances had been influenced by Scott, but this one was influenced by Dumas, and, except for two or three of Stanley Weyman's, *The Refugees* is the best novel in English of the Dumas school. Of course Doyle's book suffers from his unshakable conviction that in order to recreate a period one has to introduce a number of prominent people who lived in it, and so the romance halts while all the leading figures of the time parade before us; but whenever he is not busy unrolling his panorama of history, and providing us with a Court Guide for the reign of Louis XIV, the tale goes at a rattling pace, and the action-episodes are as thrilling as anything of the kind in Dumas. Part II, which takes us to Canada, owes something to the historian, Francis Parkman, whom Doyle, impressed by his industry, considered America's 'greatest serious writer'.

He wrote two more works while at South Norwood: *The Stark Munro Letters*, which is largely autobiographical and deals with his Plymouth and Portsmouth experiences; and *The Great Shadow*, wherein his boyish admiration for Napoleon first bubbled over into a book. He seems to have written it for the sole purpose of describing the battle of Waterloo, which he does with all the gusto of one who savours slaughter from a comfortable distance. He tells, for example, how a ball 'knocked five men into a bloody mash, and I saw it lying on the ground afterwards like a crimson football. Another went through the adjutant's horse with a plop like a stone in the mud, broke its back and left it lying like a burst gooseberry.' Always anxious to see fighting at close quarters, Doyle applied for the job of war correspondent to the Central News and got it. There was a chance in the early 'nineties of a scrap with France in Egypt, but nothing came of it, and Doyle had to content himself with heroism on paper. He turned one of his short war stories, 'A Straggler of '15', into a one-act play, which Henry Irving bought outright for £100 in 1892. A few years later it was rechristened *A Story of Waterloo* and produced at the Lyceum, when Irving, as Corporal Brewster, made a deep impression on all the critics except Bernard Shaw, who said that 'he depicts with convincing art the state of an old man's joints'. It became a stock piece with Irving, and although he had purchased the copyright he paid the author a guinea for every performance. Doyle himself thought that Irving's son, H. B., was better in the part of Brewster. If so, Shaw's criticism of the original was justified, for I remember H. B.'s acting in the playlet as a grotesque caricature of old age. Before Henry Irving accepted it Doyle sent the MS. to George Moore and asked whether he had any suggestions to make. 'I do not know if your play would act—that is to say if a few alterations would fit it for the stage,' Moore told the unpractised playwright, 'but I do know that it made me cry like a child. I think it is the most pathetic thing I ever read in my life.' Doyle had 'laughed and sobbed' while writing it, and audience after audience laughed and sobbed when witnessing it, so everybody was pleased.

His increasing success enabled Doyle to help his family. His mother left Edinburgh and settled down at East Grinstead. One of his sisters had died at Lisbon before he could make life easier for her, but the other two, Lottie and Connie, had a second home with him whenever they cared to make use of it and were no longer forced to do uncongenial work. His brother Innes also benefited from his prosperity. Connie lived with them at Tennison Road, where Doyle's son Kingsley was born, and a regular visitor was E. W. Hornung, who eventually married Connie and emphasised the family relationship by converting Holmes into 'Raffles' and Watson into 'Bunny'.

In claiming that Hornung had 'a finer wit' than Dr. Johnson, Doyle made the mistake of preserving two specimens. When shown a newspaper cutting in which someone stated that he had run 100 yards in less than ten seconds, Hornung said, 'It's a sprinter's error.' When asked why he refused to play golf, Hornung declared that it was 'unsportsmanlike to hit a sitting ball'. Neither of those remarks, though neat enough, qualifies for the class of wit we associate with Johnson. In fact Doyle, while praising the doctor heartily, did not speak of him with much intelligence. He wondered how Johnson on his visit to Paris could have failed to foresee the French Revolution. 'We read that an amiable Monsieur Sansterre showed him over his brewery and supplied him with statistics as to his output of beer,' wrote Doyle. 'It was the same foul-mouthed Sansterre who struck up the drums to drown Louis' voice at the scaffold. The association shows how near the unconscious sage was to the edge of that precipice and how little his learning availed him in discerning it.' It is not always easy, even for a lexicographer, to infer a foul-mouthed murderer from an amiable merchant, or blood from beer. Doyle must have confused Dr. Johnson with Sherlock Holmes.

As we know, the holiday that Doyle and his wife took in Switzerland suggested a satisfying method of killing Sherlock Holmes; but it also very nearly killed Mrs. Doyle. A few weeks after their return she developed a cough and was seized with pain in her side. Doyle sent for 'the nearest good physician' and was alarmed to hear that her lungs were seriously affected. A specialist confirmed that she had 'galloping consumption', and declared that she had only a few months to live. 'I then set all my energy to work to save the situation. The home was abandoned, the newly bought furniture was sold, and we made for Davos in the High Alps where there seemed the best chance of killing this accursed microbe which was rapidly eating out her vitals. And we succeeded . . . we postponed the fatal issue from 1893 to 1906.' His sister Lottie went with them, and as Mrs. Doyle seldom suffered from pain, and was cheerful and contented by nature, the family were able to enjoy the scenery.

By the time Sherlock Holmes disappeared at the falls of Reichenbach Doyle's fame was becoming international. He had already done a certain amount of lecturing in England and Scotland, and had rather enjoyed it. In '94 he was asked

to give a series of talks and readings in America, and as there
was already a marked improvement in the condition of his
wife he set forth in October of that year, promising to be
back for Christmas and taking as a companion his brother
Innes who was about to become a subaltern in the army. His
visit was successful and he could have returned with a small
fortune if he had continued to the end of the season. As usual
people were taken aback by his appearance. 'A thrill of disappointment ran through the hall as he stepped on to the
platform.' But after recovering from the blow the audience
warmed to him. Though he read his works without the least
attempt to bring out their dramatic qualities, there was something about himself, a calmness, a solidity, an air of self-
possession, that his listeners found attractive. Naturally they
wanted to meet him and were greatly disappointed when his
impresario, Major Pond, had to break the news that he had
made a bee-line for the stage-door at the conclusion of the
reading. On one occasion Pond promised a group of prominent
New York ladies that they should be introduced to the lecturer,
and begged Doyle, who was just about to appear on the stage,
to remain behind for the purpose. 'Oh, Major, I cannot, I
cannot,' was the agitated reply. 'What do they want of me?
Let me get away. I haven't the courage to look anybody in
the face.' But whenever he was cornered he braced himself
to the ordeal and made a good impression.

Pond noticed that he was a hot-blooded man, who seldom
wore an overcoat even in the coldest weather and removed
his waistcoat when lecturing in the afternoon, buttoning up
his 'Prince Albert coat' instead. He liked everything in the
States, except the heat of the hotel lobbies, of the public halls
and the railway cars, and seemed to like everyone he met.
Not a single American custom or institution drew an unfavourable comment from him, and wherever he went he
expressed his hope for a permanent Anglo-American friendship
and his belief that civilisation depended upon the union of
the two countries. He surprised the members of the Lotos
Club, who entertained him to dinner, by saying that the
Americans, who visited the Old World in order to capture
the spirit of romance and thought their own life prosaic, were
hedged in with romance on every side. 'I feel keenly the
romance of Europe,' said he. 'I love the memories of the
shattered castle and the crumbling abbey, of the steel-clad

knight and the archer; but to me the romance of the redskin
and the trapper is more vivid, as being more recent. It is so
piquant also to stay in a comfortable inn, where you can have
your hair dressed by a barber, at the same place where a century
ago you might have been left with no hair to dress.' An
enthusiast for European romance could have rejoined that
the real charm of being manicured in some Old World city
lay in the reflection that only two centuries before one might
have been fitted with thumbscrews on the same spot. Doyle
would probably have agreed, for he went on to say that in
the rush of cable cars and the ringing of telephone bells he
seemed to catch the echoes of the woodsman's axe and of the
scout's rifle. Such an appreciative visitor was naturally
popular, and we learn without surprise that he was 'tendered
more honours from clubs and societies' than any other Englishman; and six years later Major Pond declared that he would
give Doyle 'more money to-day than any Englishman I know
of if he would return for a hundred nights'.

In 1894 a less appreciative Briton was residing in the United
States and expressing opinions which implied that his conception of Utopia did not include an Anglo-American alliance.
Doyle wrote to remonstrate, and received an invitation to
visit Mr. and Mrs. Rudyard Kipling at Vermont, where he
spent two days. 'The poet read me "McAndrew's Hymn",
which he had just done, and surprised me by his dramatic
power which enabled him to sustain the Glasgow accent
throughout, so that the angular Scottish greaser simply walked
the room. I had brought up my golf clubs and gave him
lessons in a field while the New England rustics watched us
from afar, wondering what on earth we were at, for golf was
unknown in America at that time. We parted good friends,
and the visit was an oasis in my rather dreary pilgrimage as
a lecturer.'

Altogether Doyle gave forty readings, visiting all the big
cities, from Boston to Washington, from New York to Chicago.
In spite of his social and professional engagements he found
time to play golf in all weathers and indulge his fancy in
literary pilgrimages: to the grave of Oliver Wendell Holmes,
to places associated with Poe, to the Parkman country. He
made about £1000 over and above the expenses of his brother
and himself, and having been impressed by the energy and
enthusiasm of Sam McClure he decided to invest that sum in

the magazine which McClure was trying to keep afloat. He therefore called at the office and planked down the cash, saying, 'McClure, I believe in you and in the future of your magazine.' McClure was down to his last cent and had spent a part of that morning on his knees offering up prayers for succour, so Doyle's arrival seemed like the direct answer of Providence. In exchange for the cash McClure gave 1000 shares in a rocky concern at face value, which caused Doyle to wonder, as the years went by and he received no benefit from the transaction, why Providence had been so one-sided in her favours. But eventually she justified her mysterious ways, for twenty years later Doyle was able to dispose of his shares 'at a reasonable advance'.

The Aldine Club gave him a farewell dinner on December 6th, when he entertained the members with numerous stories. The next day he sailed, so thoroughly exhausted by his labours that he spent most of the time between New York and Liverpool in his bunk.

Among the readings from his own works that he had given at Daly's Theatre, New York, was an unpublished tale entitled 'The Medal of Brigadier Gerard'.

CHAPTER VIII

THE BRIGADIER

AT Davos the lives of Doyle and his family were 'bounded by the snow and fir which girt us in', and his time was taken up by work and sport. An English translation of *The Memoirs of Baron de Marbot* had been issued in 1892, and this had stimulated him to re-read the French version, which he described as 'the first of all soldier books in the world'. Having been inspired to write the adventures of a soldier of the Empire, with Marbot as his model, he devoured every book on the Napoleonic wars that he could borrow or buy in order to get his details historically accurate. The first story, which he had read to his American audiences, appeared in *The Strand* for December 1894, and from April to September '95 *The Exploits of Brigadier Gerard* thrilled the readers of that magazine, the last of them being published in the December number.

Let us see to what extent the creator of Brigadier Gerard was indebted to the 'Memoirs' of Marbot.

First of all we notice that Marbot does not think much of the brains of his superiors, whose valour he indulgently praises —sometimes. His own intelligence is implied throughout, while his valour is stated in more exact terms: 'I may, I think, say without boasting that nature has allotted to me a fair share of courage; I will even add that there was a time when I enjoyed being in danger, as my thirteen wounds and some distinguished services prove, I think, sufficiently.' He explains why official recognition of his bravery is so tardy: 'Nowadays, when promotions and decorations are bestowed so lavishly, some reward would certainly be given to an officer who had braved danger as I had done in reaching the 14th regiment; but under the Empire a devoted act of that kind was thought so natural that I did not receive the cross, nor did it ever occur to me to ask for it.' However, the time comes when Napoleon can no longer ignore his deserts: 'Augereau spoke of the devoted manner in which I had carried orders to that regiment through the swarming Cossacks, and entered into full details of the dangers which I had run in accomplishing that mission, and of the really miraculous manner in which I had escaped death after being stripped and left naked on the snow. The Emperor replied: "Marbot's conduct was admirable, and I have given him the Cross for it." ' He is never backward in giving examples of his courage, which certainly deserve his notice. At one engagement, though wounded and only able to use an arm, he insists on taking part in a cavalry action 'in order to put still more dash into my regiment, and to show that, so long as I could sit on my horse, I felt bound in honour to command it in the hour of danger'. At Jena, after the battle, he hears cries from a house, rushes in, and sees 'two charming young ladies of eighteen to twenty years old, in night-dresses, struggling with four or five Hessian soldiers. . . . The men were far gone in liquor; but though they did not understand a word of French, and I very little German, the sight of me and my threats produced an effect on them, and being used to the stick from their officers they took without a word the kicks and blows which, in my indignation, I administered to them freely as I drove them down the stairs. Perhaps I was imprudent, for in the middle of the night, in a town where utter disorder prevailed, being all alone with these men, I ran the risk of being killed by them; but they ran away, and I placed a guard from the marshal's escort in one of the lower rooms. Then I returned to the young ladies' rooms; they had hurriedly put on some clothes, and I received from them warm expressions of gratitude.' In Russia, following an action, Napoleon sends promotions and decorations to the 23rd Chasseurs commanded by Marbot: 'I assembled all the captains, and, guiding myself by their advice, I drew up my list and went to present it to Marshal Oudinot, begging him to let me announce it on the spot to the regiment. "What? here among the cannon-balls?" "Yes, marshal, among the cannon-balls; it would be more chivalrous."'

Marbot is, he assures us, 'both beloved and valued' by his regiment. 'On seeing me resume my place at their head in spite of my wound, officers and men received me with a general cheer, which, as showing the esteem and regard which the good fellows had conceived for me, touched me deeply.'

He has a very exalted sense of honour. During the Spanish campaign, when the roads and mountains are infested with bandits, he cannot be deterred from his duty: 'I remarked to the excellent man that my honour required me to brave all dangers in order to get to my general.' Single-handed he

Dr. Doyle in the chair (1894)

Three aspects of Doyle: an artist's impression of him in Egypt in 1896; at Bloemfontein during the Boer War; and on the occasion of his marriage to Miss Jean Leckie

Brigadier Gerard salutes his emperor, from *The Strand* of 1895

A studio portrait of Conan Doyle's second wife, taken shortly before her marriage

Above left Dr. George Budd   *Above right* George Meredith
Below left J. M. Barrie   *Below right* Jerome K. Jerome

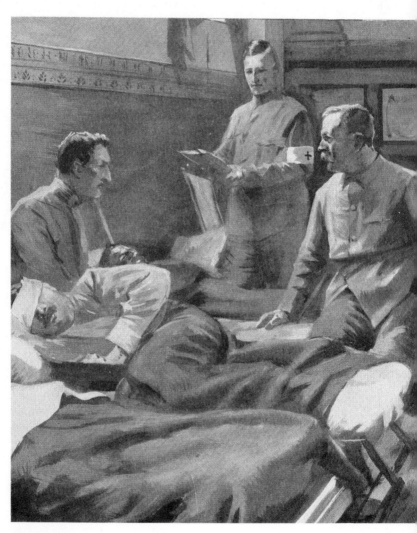

Conan Doyle tending patients in the Langman hospital during the
Boer War

Arthur Conan Doyle at home

Conan Doyle visited America in 1922 and 1923; here he is shown with
Lady Doyle, Mary Pickford and Douglas Fairbanks

saves a Frenchman from being flogged for trying to escape from the Prussians, as a result of which Napoleon warns both Prussians and Russians that if any of his soldiers are flogged he will shoot all their officers who fall into his hands. After the battle of Leipzig a gang of Prussians commence a massacre of the unarmed French who are on the run. Marbot sees this and orders his regiment to exterminate the Prussians. 'I dreaded lest I might actually find pleasure in killing some of the scoundrels with my own hand. So I sheathed my sword, and left the task of exterminating the assassins to my troopers.'

Some of his Spanish experiences, especially his single-handed fight with and escape from five Spanish carabineers, are as thrilling as anything Doyle could devise; while his crossing of the torrential Danube by night in order to capture an enemy who can give valuable information to Napoleon would have made Dumas lift his eyebrows. Occasionally Doyle takes an incident from Marbot and changes it for the purpose of his story. At Jena, for example, Marbot summons a Saxon hussar to surrender at the sabre's point. The hussar hands over his weapon but Marbot is 'generous enough to give it back to him', and although by the laws of war his horse belongs to Marbot, his captor does not deprive him of it. He thanks Marbot warmly and follows him. 'But as soon as we were 500 paces from the French chasseurs, the confounded Saxon officer, who was on my left, drew his sabre, laid open my horse's shoulder, and was on the point of striking me had I not thrown myself upon him, although I had not my sabre in my hand. But as our bodies were in contact he had not room to bring his blade to bear on me, seeing which he caught me by the epaulette—for I was in full uniform that day—and pulled hard enough to make me lose my balance. My saddle turned round, and there I was with one leg in the air and my head downwards, while the Saxon, going off at full gallop, returned to what remained of the enemy's army. I was furious both at the position in which I found myself and at the ingratitude with which the stranger repaid my kind treatment of him. So, as soon as the Saxon army was captured, I went to look for my hussar officer and give him a good lesson, but he had disappeared.' Readers of Gerard's adventures will recognise this incident, with the setting altered and the characters transposed, in the story called 'How the Brigadier Held the King'.

Thus it is clear that Doyle owed something to Marbot, just as Shakespeare owed something to Plutarch. Yet Doyle rises as much above Marbot in the realm of fancy as Shakespeare rises above Plutarch in the realm of the imagination. There are touches on almost every page of the Gerard stories that make the Brigadier stand out with a comic vividness unequalled by his model, who, to do him justice, did not see himself as a comic character. Meeting an officer whose troop of horsemen are a little out of hand, Gerard says, 'I gave them a glance which stiffened them in their saddles.' The officer asks him as a personal favour to undertake an adventure. Gerard replies that duty compels him to refuse. The officer then admits that there is an element of personal danger in the adventure. 'It was a crafty thing for him to say,' remarks Gerard. 'Of course I sprang from Rataplan's back and ordered the groom to lead him back into the stables.' When in a ticklish corner, with death staring him in the face, he confesses, 'I shed tears as I thought of the general consternation which my premature end would give rise to.' A lady presses him to tell her the story of his exploits. 'Never have I had so delightful a conversation,' says he. He rides through Rheims with a companion, whose behaviour draws this comment: 'In his insane conceit he ogled the girls as they waved their handkerchiefs to me from the windows.' Gerard indulges in a love-affair, remarking: 'You will wonder why it should be, if this maiden was so beautiful, that I should be left without a rival. There was a very good reason, my friends, for I so arranged it that my rivals were in the hospital.' In a particularly tight corner he prays for help, 'but I am a little out of practice at such things, and the only words I could remember were the prayer for fine weather which we used at the school on the evening before holidays'. Marshal Berthier tempts him to betray the Emperor, and he makes an impassioned reply: 'I was so moved by my own words and by the fine position which I had taken up, that my voice broke, and I could hardly refrain from tears.' The emotion of others moves him too: 'When he saw me his little pink eyes filled with tears, and, indeed, I could not but shed a few myself at the sight of his joy.' Massena wishes to send him on a dangerous mission, and the scene between them opens thus:

'He was nervous and ill at ease, but my bearing seemed to reassure him. It is good to be in contact with brave men.

‘ "Colonel Étienne Gerard," said he, "I have always heard that you are a very gallant and enterprising officer."

'It was not for me to confirm such a report, and yet it would be folly to deny it, so I clinked my spurs together and saluted.

‘ "You are also an excellent rider."

'I admitted it.

‘ "And the best swordsman in the six brigades of light cavalry."

'Massena was famous for the accuracy of his information.'

Every scene is superbly executed, every character is brilliantly etched, and every episode is heightened by a humour that ranges from satire to burlesque, the contrast between the boastfulness of the protagonist and the humiliating situations in which he sometimes finds himself providing much of the fun. The Brigadier is by turns shrewd and obtuse; his stupidity is matched by his intrepidity; his brain is slow but his impulses are brilliant; he is both Quixote and Panza, a sort of Watsonish Holmes, and, with d'Artagnan, the liveliest hero in romantic fiction. The odd thing is that the absurdity of the leading character never lessens the excitement of the narrative: the humour gives reality to the romance. Doyle never wrote anything else as good as these tales, which welled so spontaneously out of him that their gaiety and enthusiasm infect the reader. They have a zest and a naturalism that lift them right above his more sober historical romances. As with the Holmes saga, our chronicler was not weighed down by the seriousness of his mission.

The English reader will accept a Frenchman as a hero so long as he is ridiculous, and Gerard instantly became popular. No one can resist a man who is both likeable and laughable, and Doyle showed a masterly cunning in creating a figure who aroused the reader's admiration, won his affection, and flattered his self-esteem. There was a demand for more 'exploits', and the first of the *Adventures of Gerard* came out in *The Strand* for August 1902, the remainder appearing monthly from November of that year to May 1903.

Doyle did not place these stories among his highest flights of fiction, no doubt because, like those of Holmes, they were the natural product of his fancy. He wrote them with relative ease, and travail was his watchword.

CHAPTER IX

THE MAN OF ACTION

THE family spent the summer of '94 at Maloja, but they were back for the winter at Davos, where in the early months of '95 Doyle introduced a form of sport which in after years became the chief pastime of Switzerland, though there is no evidence that the people who made fortunes out of it acknowledged his pioneer work with cash, or even thanks. Having read Nansen's account of how he had crossed Greenland on skis, Doyle became interested in the subject and felt that Switzerland would provide a good ski-ing ground. Two tradesmen in Davos named Branger caught his enthusiasm, and they sent to Norway for skis. Beginners are always popular, and their early efforts provided the inhabitants with a good deal of light entertainment. But at the end of a month they emerged from the comic phase of their development and went up the Jacobshorn, the flags in Davos dipping in their honour when they got to the top. The return journey, though varied by 'an occasional cropper', was exhilarating, and they decided to cross the high pass between their valley and Arosa, which could only be reached from Davos in winter by a very tedious and circuitous railway journey. They had no rope, and, knowing nothing, they had to use their wits. The experience was not pleasant and occasionally frightening. 'We came to an absolute precipice,' wrote Doyle, 'up which no doubt the path zigzags in summer. It was not of course perpendicular, but it seemed little removed from it, and it had just slope enough to hold the snow. It looked impassable, but the Brangers had picked up a lot in some way of their own. They took off their skis, fastened them together with a thong, and on this toboggan they sat, pushing themselves over the edge, and going down amid a tremendous spray of flying snow. When they reached safety, they beckoned to me to follow. I had done as they did, and was sitting on my ski preparatory to launching myself when a fearsome thing happened, for my ski shot from under me, flew down the slope, and vanished in huge bounds among the snow-mounds beyond. It was a nasty moment, and the poor Brangers stood looking up at me some hundreds of feet below me in a dismal state of mind. However, there was no possible choice as to what to do, so I did it. I let myself go over the edge, and came squattering down, with legs and arms extended to check the momentum. A minute later I was rolling covered with snow at the feet of my guides, and my skis were found some hundreds of yards away, so no harm was done after all.' In signing the hotel register at Arosa, one of the Brangers wrote 'Sportesmann' after Doyle's name.

Having laid out a golf course Doyle left Davos in the early summer of '95 and took his family to Caux, where he finished the first Gerard series and began *Rodney Stone*. He had always been fond of boxing, had revelled in the history of the prize-ring, and in *Rodney Stone* his enthusiasm and knowledge are apparent. The book did a lot to popularise boxing, which was so little esteemed in the 'nineties that no one but the creator of Sherlock Holmes could have persuaded *The Strand* to serialise a novel on that theme. As usual the action-episodes are first-rate; and as usual the historical personages are not an integral part of the story. Nothing could be better than the description of the fights or of the race from Brighton to London; but Doyle wanted to reconstruct an age, and so Nelson, the Prince Regent, Sheridan, Fox, Beau Brummell, 'Junius', Cochrane, Collingwood, Lady Hamilton and others, pop in and out of the pages for the sole purpose of creating a 'period piece'. The author takes us round London, shows us the sights, carries us to Watier's, remarks on the habits and the manners of the time, and provides us with a sort of *Who's Who* in the sporting and social world of the Regency.

He repeated the process in another novel written a little later, *Uncle Bernac*, which is a good 'thriller' spoilt by the same defect. In the Gerard yarns Napoleon, Wellington and the rest are introduced for a purpose proper to the events in which they take part: they influence the life of the hero and forward the story. But in *Uncle Bernac* the tale is held up while Doyle presents us with the results of his reading. The two chapters in which Napoleon is portrayed are, the author is careful to remind us, 'the quintessence of a score of books'. Everyone of note, even the American Robert Fulton who is trying to interest Napoleon in steam navigation, turns up and bumps into the hero, and while the background is being filled in the foreground fades out.

In the autumn of '95, while on a short visit to England, Doyle heard from Grant Allen that the soil and air of Hindhead in Surrey had cured him of consumption. Doyle did not hesitate for a moment: he went down to Hindhead, bought a piece of land, engaged an old Southsea friend named Ball as architect, chose a builder, dashed back to Caux, and started off with his wife and sister to Egypt, where they decided to winter before settling down in their Surrey home. They stayed at the Mena Hotel, close to the Pyramids, about seven miles from Cairo. Mrs. Doyle was already much better, and they hoped that a few months in Egypt would complete the cure. One of the first things they heard on arrival was that the Sherlock Holmes stories had been translated into Arabic and issued to the local police as a text-book.

Doyle climbed the Great Pyramid once, for the satisfaction of being able to say that he had, and thereafter observed with interest the crowds of people enduring the discomforts of the ascent so that they might make a similar boast. He played golf on the primitive links of the Mena Hotel, and found that the graves of the early Egyptian monarchs made very effective bunkers. He practised riding, and on one occasion the horse ran away with him, pitched him over its head and kicked him in the eye, an accident which nearly resulted in the loss of it and left him with a slightly drooping eyelid for life. He mixed in the diplomatic and military society of Cairo, and tried to converse with such natives as he came across. 'Some men have the gift of pantomime and some have not. I know by experience that I have not,' he once admitted. 'On the occasion of the eclipse of the moon I endeavoured to explain the cause of it to an Arab. I pointed to the moon and to the earth. Then I pointed to a horse and his shadow. Presently the Arab rose and began to examine the horse's hind legs, and I found that I had convinced him that the animal was ill. I have given up gestures since then.'

Early in '96 he took the family up the Nile on one of Cook's boats as far as Wady Halfa, visiting so many temples on the way that he lost count of them. In those days camel-raids to the banks of the river used to be made by wild tribesmen from the south; and finding himself one day with 'a drove of helpless tourists' and an escort of four negro soldiers on the rock of Abousir, Doyle conjured up a fearsome picture of what would happen if a troop of Moslem fanatics were suddenly to appear.

'It was the strong impression which I there received which gave me the idea of taking a group of people of different types and working out what the effect of so horrible an experience would be upon each.' The result was *The Tragedy of the Korosko*, in which he tells a story as well as ever and portrays the various characters with a clarity and subtlety unmatched in his other novels. The Colonel in particular is lifelike, which shows that Doyle had closely observed the English officers in the clubs and messes around Cairo. Lacon Watson once said that the merit of Doyle's humour 'lies in a quick sense of the incongruous, and a simple, straightforward manner of exposing it'. There is no better example of this in all his work than the Colonel's speech to the interpreter when the Emir who has captured them threatens to torture the women unless they become Moslems. Hoping for the arrival of a rescue party, the Colonel makes his suggestion in order to gain time: 'I think I see a way out. See here, dragoman! You tell that grey-bearded old devil that we know nothing about his cursed tinpot religion. Put it smooth when you translate it. Tell him that he cannot expect us to adopt it until we know what particular brand of rot it is that he wants us to believe. Tell him that if he will instruct us, we are perfectly willing to listen to his teaching, and you can add that any creed which turns out such beauties as him, and that other bounder with the black beard, must claim the attention of everyone.'

When they returned from their trip up the river Doyle accompanied an Egyptian Army officer on a visit to the old Coptic monastery by the Salt Lakes some fifty miles from Cairo. Most of the journey was done in a gilded and fantastically decorated coach which Doyle thought had come out of a circus but which proved to be the coach that had been specially constructed for Napoleon III in the belief that he was going to open the Suez Canal. In this extraordinary chariot they lumbered across the Libyan desert, the officer running a large part of the journey in order to keep fit. Darkness came on and a storm of rain came down and the driver lost his way. Doyle found it by spotting Charles's Wain through a gap in the clouds and guessing they were south of the track. Then they walked ahead of the coach with lanterns, so as not to lose the track, and came to a tent, where a German surveyor pointed the way and said that the Monastery was nearby. Off they went, and after losing the track again, and wandering about for an hour or more, they saw a light ahead, hailed it with joy, and found themselves back with the German surveyor. They spent the night in a wooden hut and next morning reached the Monastery, where their arrival evoked no interest. Doyle found the place depressing; no one seemed to have anything to do; and several of the monks looked debauched; but a livelier atmosphere prevailed when the Abbot said he was feeling ill, because Doyle, instead of taking this as a delicate hint that the holy man was feeling inhospitable, promptly banged him about in a thoroughly professional manner and ordered him to take the medicine which would shortly arrive from Cairo. Leaving the Abbot to think things over, they returned to headquarters, where they heard that war had been declared in their absence and that the army was advancing on Dongola.

'It is impossible to be near great historical events and not to desire to take part in them, or at the least to observe them,' wrote Doyle, who instantly cabled to *The Westminster Gazette* asking for the appointment of 'honorary correspondent *pro tem*', and getting it by return. A glimpse of some tommies poking their heads through the window of a troop-train leaving for the front prompted him to write a passage which reflected his own emotion: 'Look at those eight bullet heads, close-cropped and red-eared, with flushed bruiser faces and gap-toothed mouths, howling in chorus. They are not beautiful, certainly, and it would be hard to deny that they are brutal, but what a sense of vigorous high-blooded animalism they leave behind them.'

Hurriedly collecting his kit, he started up the river with several junior officers, getting as far as Assouan, where they were stranded for a week. Doyle, with his eager emotional nature, was surprised by the casual bearing of his companions, who might have been enjoying a Cook's Tour instead of taking part in a campaign. 'Only once did I see them really excited. I had returned to the hotel which was the general headquarters, and as I entered the hall I saw a crowd of them all clustering round the notice-board to read a telegram which had just been suspended. They were on the toes of their spurred boots, with their necks outstretched and every sign of quivering and eager interest. "Ah," thought I, "at last we have got through the hide of these impenetrable men. I suppose the Khalifa is coming down, horse, foot, and artillery, and that we are on the eve of battle." I pushed my way in, and thrust my head among all the bobbing sun-helmets. It was the account of the Oxford and Cambridge Boat-race.'

At Assouan Doyle joined up with the other war correspondents, and they decided to trek south on their own, though they were advised to travel with a force of Egyptian cavalry for safety. Mounted on camels they set out for Korosko with a small army of servants, doing their longest marches before and just after dawn. 'I am still haunted by that purple velvet sky,' wrote Doyle nearly thirty years later, 'by those enormous and innumerable stars, by the half-moon which moved slowly above us, while our camels with their noiseless tread seemed to bear us without effort through a wonderful dream world.' The dream world turned to reality when his camel spotted some green stuff on the track and went on its knees to eat it, for Doyle did a rapid slide down its neck, head first, and felt rather surprised on reaching the earth. Tarantulas, lizards and snakes were also not part of the dream world; and once the sight of a fierce Nubian warrior, streaking past their camp in the dawn, was sufficiently alarming to inspire Doyle with a short story, 'The Three Correspondents'. From Korosko they went by water to Wady Halfa, where Kitchener asked him to dinner and told him that nothing exciting would happen for months. All the same he cameltrekked to Sarras, the last British post, and thought it 'wonderful to look south and to see the distant peaks said to be in Dongola, with nothing but savagery and murder lying between'. Presenting his camel to the army, he returned by a cargo boat, eating tinned apricots and reading Rousseau's *Confessions* all the way, and getting so heartily sick of both that he never wished to see a tinned apricot or to glance at Rousseau for the rest of his life. Already, at the end of April, the heat was too much for his wife, so they left Egypt at once; and on May 1st Doyle was a guest at the Royal Academy Banquet, noting on his wrists 'the ragged little ulcers where the poisonous jiggers which had burrowed into my skin while I lay upon the banks of the Nile were hatching out their eggs under the august roof of Burlington House'.

The 'considerable mansion' he had planned at Hindhead was too considerable to be ready for them, so they took a furnished house in Haslemere for a year, then went to a boarding-house called Moorlands in order to be near the new residence, into which they moved in June '97. He called it 'Undershaw' because 'it stood under a hanging grove of trees'. Apart from his wife's health, life was very pleasant for him: he wrote assiduously and rode vigorously. The Central News asked him to act as their special correspondent in the event of a European war, and he took riding-lessons in a Knights-bridge school. 'There will be a European war one of these days,' said he, 'and when there is I want to be in it, if only as a correspondent.' Meanwhile, failing larger game, there was a lot of fun to be got out of fox-hunting.

Having completed *Uncle Bernac*, *Korosko*, and several short stories of a rather gruesome nature, he decided to reveal another side of himself. It is more than likely that his wife was responsible for the subject-matter and the handling of his next book: her nerves may have been jarred by the neck-twisting episode in *Bernac*. 'I wish you'd write something that will make people realise what a treasure you are at home,' one can fancy her saying to him. 'Your stirring romances and sometimes rather horrifying scenes give your readers such a wrong impression of you.' Accordingly he produced *A Duet*, which contains some memories of the days when they were engaged, a knowledge of cooking and women's clothes which is surprising, and much information about certain historical figures which is not surprising. In the character of the hero Doyle quite consciously described himself, for he loved to picture himself as a sort of battleground in which the forces of good and evil perpetually strove: 'Strength, virility, emo-tional force, power of deep feeling—these are traits which have to be paid for. There was sometimes just a touch of the savage, or at least there were indications of the possibility of a touch of the savage, in Frank Crosse. His intense love of the open air and of physical exercise was a sign of it. He left upon women the impression, not altogether unwelcome, that there were unexplored recesses of his nature to which the most intimate of them had never penetrated. In those dark corners of the spirit either a saint or a sinner might be lurking, and there was a pleasurable excitement in peering into them, and wondering which it was. No woman ever found him dull. Perhaps it would have been better for him if they had, for his impulsive nature had never been long content with a chilly

friendship.' Like all relatively simple men, Doyle believed his
nature to be inextricably complex.[1]

As he had written something altogether unlike his usual
work, he thought it the best thing he had done, and evinced
some anxiety as to the advance orders from shops and libraries.
His publisher, Grant Richards, sent him bulletins, from which
he learnt that Simpkins did not 'take kindly' to the book, that
Mudies had only ordered 780 copies before publication, that
Smiths, who had sold 3000 of *Rodney Stone*, were contenting
themselves with 1300; and although it was pleasant to hear
that 'a young lady of rather special intelligence . . . did not
know when she had put down a book with greater reluctance',
it was not so comforting to be informed that the bookseller
who had shown her the work would not order a large number
because 'special intelligence' had added that it was 'too pure
and good to attract the multitude'. When it came out Doyle
showed more sensitiveness to criticism than was usual with
him; though in this case he had a real cause for grievance, because a Nonconformist named Robertson Nicoll criticised him
adversely, either anonymously or pseudonymously, in half a
dozen publications. From the Reform Club the indignant
author fired off a letter to the *Daily Chronicle*, in which he
complained that 'what to the uninitiated might seem to be a
general burst of praise or blame may really when analysed
prove to be the work of a single individual'. To put an end
to such a 'pernicious system', he said that 'a combination of

---

[1] The saint *v.* sinner theme occurs again in a poem he wrote about himself called
'The Inner Room', wherein he pictures Conan Doyles of all sorts, heroic and villainous,
anxious to assume control of his soul:

> There are others who are sitting,
>   Grim as doom,
> In the dim ill-boding shadow
>   Of my room.
> Darkling figures, stern or quaint,
> Now a savage, now a saint,
> Showing fitfully and faint
>   Through the gloom.
>
> And those shadows are so dense,
>   There may be
> Many—very many—more
>   Than I see.
> They are sitting day and night
> Soldier, rogue, and anchorite;
> And they wrangle and they fight
>   Over me.

authors who are opposed to wire-pulling and pluralism' should
see to it that their works were not advertised in the peccant
journals, 'and literary papers are dependent upon advertising'.
The drawback to his scheme was that the authors who
found favour with Robertson Nicoll could not be induced to
support it; and the pernicious system still is, or was until
Hitler interfered with the paper supply, in good running
order.

Whether *A Duet* was the cause or the effect we cannot say,
but Doyle was passing through a phase of pacifism round about
this period. The Tsar of Russia had recently invited the
powers to a Peace Conference at The Hague, and meetings
were being held all over Europe in support of his proposal to
limit armaments and to establish an international tribunal.
Doyle was all in favour of the Conference, took the chair at
a Hindhead meeting towards the end of January '99 and spoke
enthusiastically about the Tsar's move. To his amazement
a neighbour on Hindhead who had come to support him then
delivered himself as follows: 'All the statesmen of Europe, the
very men who are now ordering torpedo boats, are also
expressing approval of the Tsar's Rescript. Every one knows
that if the French submarine boats are a success, this country
will at once order them, Germany will order them, and the
Tsar himself will not have the power to prevent Russia from
ordering them. No good will be done by repeating the plati-
tudes which we put on our Christmas cards every year. We
must face the situation by making a sharp distinction between
two sets of proposals now before the world. One of these is
that war should be made less terrible than it is at present.
But I cannot too strongly insist that it is not armaments or
ironclads that fight, but men, and that if we do away with all
the weapons of war and reduce men to the aboriginal weapons
of their fists, teeth, and claws, they will fight just as horribly.'
By this time the pacifists were getting a bit jumpy, but as the
speaker went on to say that he supported the second proposal,
viz. the establishment of an international tribunal to which
public opinion would force nations to bring their quarrels
before resorting to the arbitrament of arms, the audience
calmed down. The speaker was Bernard Shaw, who used sometimes to visit Doyle when they both lived on Hindhead. 'We
were on pleasant terms,' Shaw told me, 'and I converted him
from Christmas-card Pacifism to rampant Jingoism—overdid it

in fact.' But this is questionable. Doyle felt as the average man feels. He was a Christmas-card pacifist at Christmas-time, becoming bellicose the moment the bugles rang out.

Before the end of the year he had forgotten all about the Tsar in his desire to fight Kruger, who declared war on Great Britain in October. Being a nation of Christmas-card pacifists, Great Britain was as usual unprepared, and in December suffered a series of reverses. But being bellicose when aroused, the country settled down to the job of beating the Boers. At a cricketers' smoking concert early in the war Doyle said: 'If ever England gets into a hole, you may depend on it that her sporting men will pull her out of it.' That indeed was the least they could do since they had helped to get her into it, the nation's preoccupation with sport keeping its mind off the muddle and corruption of politics. Like his fellow-Briton Doyle had a sportsman's attitude to war. 'One subject which always aroused his enthusiastic interest,' Francis Gribble informed me, 'was any movement to promote any sort of *entente* with "our friend, the enemy", whoever the enemy might be. His account of his experiences in the Boer War was full of praise for the sportsmanlike qualities of his opponents, and his dominating thought seemed to be: "What a splendid *entente* we shall be able to have when we're tired of fighting." I once said that when proposing his health at a public dinner over which he had presided; and he came up afterwards and thanked me, telling me that that was just what he liked people to say and think about him.'

After the 'black week' of December '99 Doyle tried to enlist in the Middlesex Yeomanry, but before his application was considered a friend of his, John Langman, who was sending a hospital unit to South Africa, asked him to go with it both as a doctor and as a general but unofficial supervisor. He agreed, and spent a week choosing the personnel. The War Office insisted that they should have a military chief, an Irishman named Major Drury, who caused a lot of trouble later on; but as he was amusing, and said that his sole object in life was to leave the service and marry a rich widow with a cough, Doyle tolerated him. The unit consisted of fifty men and fifty beds; and Langman footed the entire bill, Doyle alone receiving nothing for his services, but contributing his butler to the enterprise and paying his salary.

While waiting to embark Doyle experimented with a rifle,

anxious to devise a method whereby men who were concealed behind rocks could be killed with dropping bullets. After nearly murdering someone near Frensham Pond, he abandoned the experiments. Naturally he wrote to the War Office about his method, but nothing short of dynamite can move the War Office; and he wrote to *The Times* to complain of the War Office, but he might have saved himself the trouble; and then, having sent his wife to Naples for her health, and having been inspected by the Duke of Cambridge, who nearly died of apoplexy because the hospital tunic buttons carried no distinguishing mark, he sailed for South Africa on February 28th, 1900.

It was characteristic of Doyle that one of the first things he did on landing at Cape Town was to visit the Boer prisoners and distribute among them some money which had been given him in London 'for charitable purposes'. The news from the front was good. Lord Roberts had reached Bloemfontein, Cronje had been rounded up, Kimberley relieved, and the railway journey across the veldt was more exhilarating than dangerous. As he saw the camp-fires, and heard the answers yelled by the troops in the train to the questions shouted by the troops along the line, Doyle was enraptured by the atmosphere of war. 'When the millennium comes the world will gain much, but it will lose its greatest thrill," he reflected. In the early morning of April 2nd he reached Bloemfontein and was soon enveloped by an atmosphere that was still warlike but less uplifting. An appalling outbreak of enteric among the troops was caused by the simple fact that Lord Roberts had failed to take the waterworks (only 20 miles off) when he occupied the capital, an oversight of which the Boers took advantage by cutting the supply. Apparently he felt that the troops required rest after their exertions; so they drank water from the old wells of Bloemfontein and rested there, some 5000 of them for ever.

The Langman unit camped on the cricket-field, using the pavilion as chief ward, and for a month they 'lived in the midst of death—and death in its vilest, filthiest form. Our accommodation was for fifty patients, but 120 were precipitated upon us, and the floor was littered between the beds with sick and often dying men. Our linen and utensils were never calculated for such a number, and as the nature of the disease causes constant pollution of the most dangerous character and with the vilest effluvia, one can imagine how dreadful was the situation. The worst surgical ward after a battle would be a clean place compared to that pavilion. At one end was a stage with the scene set for "H.M.S. Pinafore". This was turned into latrines for those who could stagger so far. The rest did the best they could, and we did the best we could in turn. But a Verestschagin would have found a subject in that awful ward, with the rows of emaciated men, and the silly childish stage looking down upon it all. . . . Four weeks may seem a short time in comfort, but it is a very long one under conditions such as those, amid horrible sights and sounds and smells, while a haze of flies spreads over everything, covering your food and trying to force themselves into your mouth—every one of them a focus of disease. It was bad enough when we had a full staff, but soon the men began to wilt under the strain. They were nearly all from the Lancashire cotton mills, little, ill-nourished fellows but with a great spirit. Of the fifteen twelve contracted the disease and added to the labours of the survivors. Three died. . . . Our hospital was no worse off than the others, and as there were many of them the general condition of the town was very bad. Coffins were out of the question, and the men were lowered in their brown blankets into shallow graves at the average rate of sixty a day. A sickening smell came from the stricken town. Once when I had ridden out to get an hour or two of change, and was at least six miles from the town, the wind changed and the smell was all around me. You could smell Bloemfontein long before you could see it.'

Doyle cured one case by breaking a medical law and giving a square meal to a patient who was obviously dying and kept begging for food. 'Do you consider that this man is sure to die?' he asked the surgeon, Charles Gibbs. 'He is certainly as bad as he can be,' said Gibbs. 'Well then, I propose to give him a solid meal,' said Doyle. The other was shocked and shook his head: 'It is a great responsibility you take.' 'What's the odds, if he has to die anyhow?' returned Doyle. 'Well, it's just the difference whether you kill him or the disease does,' he was told. 'I'll take the chance,' said Doyle. He did so, the man recovered, and 'science' lost another victim.

At last the army continued the march to Pretoria, the water-works were taken with no resistance, and the conditions at the hospital improved so much that Doyle rode off to see a little fighting, being away with the army from the 1st to the 7th of May. We need not accompany him, though we may note that he was present at the capture of Brandfort, that he remained under fire during a two-hours artillery duel, and that he witnessed the looting of a farm, when the death of a pig shook him: 'A fat white pig all smothered in blood runs past. A soldier meets it, his bayonet at the charge. He lunges and lunges again, and the pig screams horribly. I had rather see a man killed.' He left the army to pursue its way and returned to duty, camping cheerfully on the veldt and writing a private memorandum: 'I felt happy because I had always wanted a baptism of fire and now I had had a fairly good one. As far as I could judge my own sensations I felt no nervousness at all—or at least far less than I should have expected—but my mind kept turning on other things all the time. For example I was so annoyed at the loss of my haversack that I really for some time forgot about the shells altogether as I bustled about looking for it. I think I was under fire about two hours. At the same time I could not have been as perfectly motionless as the Gunners—it was a wonderful exhibition of nerve.'

When he got back he found that Major Drury and the staff were at loggerheads, and he had to nip a mutiny in the bud. Then he fell ill himself, an illness that was aggravated by the buckling of two ribs in one of the football matches he had organised to keep the men's minds off enteric. With the capture of Pretoria he considered that his work was done, and as he had two jobs of his own on hand, a history of the war to write and a political election to fight, he determined to leave for England. Before going he visited Pretoria, interviewed Lord Roberts, obtained a number of first-hand accounts of the campaign for his book, and went down a gold mine at Johannesburg, receiving 'the usual tips as to which mines were going to boom—on all of which I acted, and all of which proved to be wrong'. After a visit to Sir Alfred Milner, he sailed for England on July 11th. The boat was packed with peers of the realm, whose presence did not prevent Doyle from telling a foreign officer that he was a liar for saying that the British had habitually used Dum-Dum bullets. The officer wrote an apology, and Doyle abated his fury.

Her stay in Naples had benefited Mrs. Doyle, and they were

able to settle down once more on Hindhead, where Doyle set to work on his History of the Boer War, an eminently fair record of the business, and probably the best. But what gave him greater satisfaction than the completion of the History was a pamphlet he wrote in nine days entitled *The Cause and Conduct of the War in South Africa*, which was inspired by the hostility to England then being expressed all over Europe. For once in a way France and Germany were in complete agreement, and the other countries joined the chorus of abuse. A firm belief in the iniquity of England and the barbarity of British soldiers cemented countries otherwise at variance. Not having had an opportunity then of showing what she could do when let loose, Germany was especially bitter; but nearly all the continental countries were anti-English, some of them violently so.

Early in 1902 Doyle set to work to check this feeling by expounding his country's case and exposing the current lies about the brutalities of her soldiers. He made an appeal in *The Times* for funds, got a publishing firm to assist the enterprise, obtained private subscriptions, made arrangements for translations, and produced a pamphlet which was sold for sixpence in Great Britain and distributed free throughout Europe. The sale in England and America brought in about £2500, and as the subscriptions came to much the same sum there was more than enough to cover the continental editions, the balance being used for various worthy purposes.

Doyle's pamphlet had a steadying effect on European opinion, and his reward followed quickly, for in 1902 he was created a knight and appointed Deputy-Lieutenant of Surrey.

CHAPTER X

TITANIC

LIKE so many people before and after him, Doyle thought that he ought to do something about the human race—or, as he put it, 'one likes to feel that one has some small practical influence upon the affairs of one's time'—and it never occurred to him, after he had done something about it, that he might have done better if he had left ill alone. His first attempt to improve his fellow-beings was made at his home town, when he stood for Parliament as a Liberal-Unionist candidate for Central Edinburgh in the 'khaki' election of 1900. He was given the chance of several 'safe' constituencies, but being a fighter he rejected them, preferring to attack one of the chief radical strongholds in the country. His main object was to fortify the Government in its job of beating the Boers, and when his committee drafted his election address he asked them who was going to honour the promises they had made in it. 'Why, you, of course,' they replied. 'Then I think it would be better if I made them,' said Doyle, who threw their draft into the waste-paper basket and wrote his own address. He entered with ardour into the campaign, but he was too honest for a politician and alienated the large Irish vote by pleading for a Catholic University in Dublin, which annoyed the Protestant northerners, and by withholding his support for Home Rule, which antagonised the Catholic southerners. 'This united Ireland, North and South, for the first time in history,' he declared. Still he was doing pretty well until an evangelical parson named Jacob Primmer covered the constituency with posters which stated that Doyle was a Roman Catholic, having been educated by the Jesuits, and that he was hostile to the Scottish Kirk and Covenant, because 'once a Jesuit always a Jesuit', and so on and so forth. This decided the issue. There was no time to reply, the election being next day, and Doyle lost the seat by a few hundred votes.

He made one more attempt to enter Parliament, as Tariff Reform candidate for The Border Burghs in 1905. He had not a chance of winning; for although it was obvious that the woollen industry of Hawick, Galashiels, and Selkirk had been badly hit by German competition, the doctrine of Free Trade was almost a religion in Scotland, and Doyle was subjected to such a barrage of questions and facetiae that his temper was severely strained. However, he held himself in check until the last moment, when, as luck would have it, one of his supporters got what was meant for his hecklers. He was standing on the platform waiting for the London train when a young enthusiast, brimming with kindly thoughts and burning with zeal, seized his hand and crushed it in a grip that was meant to be heartening. 'It opened the sluice,' Doyle confessed, 'and out came a torrent of whaler language which I had hoped that I had long ago forgotten. The blast seemed to blow him bodily across the platform, and formed a strange farewell to my supporters.'

He was asked to stand for Parliament on several later occasions, but declined, and for the rest of his life tried to influence the affairs of his time in a more direct way. For example: he founded the Undershaw Rifle Club, model and pioneer of the miniature rifle-ranges that sprang up all over the country, their value becoming apparent in the 1914–18 war; he advocated the Channel Tunnel (or tunnels), the lack of which was severely felt in the same war; he became President of the Crowborough and District Boy Scouts Association; for ten years he was President of the Divorce Law Reform Union; he worked for two years with E. D. Morel on the Congo Association, speaking of the atrocities up and down the country and producing a book, *The Crime of the Congo*, which had such an effect on public opinion that the Belgian government was forced to make life easier for the natives; in fact he could always be depended upon to fight for the underdog, and at a much later period in his life we find him taking up the cause of the chambermaids at the Metropole Hotel, Brighton, whose salaries were being reduced. 'The duty which we owe to the weak overrides all other duties and is superior to all circumstances,' wrote Doyle in *Micah Clarke*. He certainly recognised this duty more clearly than any man of his time. Many people will fight for humanity and become martyrs for abstract causes; but Doyle had the far rarer virtue of fighting for individual human beings, and courting ridicule for his eccentricity. Two instances stand out in his career and must be mentioned.

In the early years of the present century the vicar of Great Wyrley in Staffordshire was a Parsee named Edalji, who had married an Englishwoman. They had a son and daughter. The family was not popular in the neighbourhood, perhaps because the villagers felt that they could learn nothing about Christianity from a Parsee, and anonymous letters of a menacing and scurrilous nature constantly arrived at the vicarage. At the same time an epidemic of horse-maiming broke out in the district, and the authorities were violently criticised for not taking steps to catch the criminal. At length the police managed to link up the writer of anonymous letters with the maimer of horses, some references to the crimes having appeared in the letters, and in a manner peculiar to the police when they wish to silence criticism they managed to identify the writer and maimer with the vicar's son, George Edalji, who was arrested, tried, and condemned to seven years penal servitude in 1903. The case had been thoroughly 'cooked' by the police, and the verdict was so manifestly unjust that some folk protested and an agitation was kept going in *Truth*; but young Edalji would have finished his sentence and left prison a ruined man if Conan Doyle had not, in 1906, casually glanced through a paper called *The Umpire* and read the victim's statement of his own case, every word of which rang true.

Instantly putting everything else aside, Doyle gave his whole attention to the matter, studied the reports of the trial, interviewed the Edalji family, and examined the scene of the crimes. He discovered among other things that George Edalji, a law student who had written a book on Railway Law, held an unblemished record from his schooldays, that his employer, a Birmingham solicitor, had nothing but praise for him, that he had won the highest honours in his legal classes, that he was a total abstainer, had never shown the least sign of cruelty, was of a quiet, studious, rational disposition, and so blind that he could not recognise anyone six yards off. This last point was conclusive because, in order to commit the horrible crimes of which he had been accused, the young man would have had to cross a large expanse of railway lines, force several hedges, struggle through wires, and negotiate many other obstacles, all in the dark, to say nothing of leaving his bedroom which he shared with his father, who was a light sleeper, always locked the door, and had sworn that his son never left the room during the night.

Doyle wrote a series of articles on the case which were

published in the *Daily Telegraph* (January 1907) and caused
such a sensation that the Government appointed a committee
to examine the evidence. Committees are usually addle-headed
and this one was well up to form; it cleared Edalji of the
crimes, but as it stuck to the theory that he had written the
anonymous letters it refused him compensation on the ground
that he had contributed to the miscarriage of justice. Although
Edalji was instantly set free and the Law Society readmitted
him to the roll of solicitors, he never got a farthing's compensation for serving more than three years' imprisonment for
something he had not done, and with the £300 raised by the
Daily Telegraph he repaid an aunt who had financed his
defence.

As a result of his investigations Doyle was able to prove
conclusively that the letters had been written and the horses
maimed by a certain local man, an habitual criminal, and he
placed the evidence in the hands of the authorities. Whereupon the Home Secretary, Lord Gladstone, proved as conclusively that he was the head of a Government office by
refusing to accept the facts that were staring him in the face,
e.g. that the criminal had shown a horse-lancet to someone
with the remark that it had done the maiming, that he had
been trained in the slaughter-yard and was an expert at
butchery, that he had frequently written anonymous letters,
that his handwriting and his brother's corresponded with that
of the letters in the case, that he was periodically off his head,
that when he was away the letters and crimes ceased, beginning
again when he returned, whereas the outrages continued when
Edalji was in gaol; and so on. Doyle thought that the Home
Office bureaucrats were insane to ignore the evidence he had
placed in their hands; but in expecting reason and justice from
bureaucrats his own sanity was open to doubt.

Two years later he was involved in another mystery, but
this time he was up against not so much the stupidity as the
iniquity of the authorities. Having been successful in his
efforts on behalf of Edalji he was pestered with so many
requests to prove condemned men innocent that he went into
the Oscar Slater case with much reluctance, but at last, at the
instigation of several people, he studied it, and came to the
conclusion that it was a more monstrous perversion of justice
even than Edalji's.

On December 21st, 1908, a man entered the Glasgow flat

of an elderly woman, Miss Gilchrist, battered her head in with a blunt instrument, searched among some documents which he left scattered about, stole nothing except (possibly) a diamond brooch, and on emerging from the flat passed the murdered woman's servant, Helen Lambie, who had been out to buy a newspaper, and the occupant of the flat beneath, Mr. Adams, who had rushed up on hearing three knocks, a signal that Miss Gilchrist wanted his assistance.

Glasgow was agreeably horrified, and detectives set about the business of fixing the murderer. A German Jew named Oscar Slater, who was 'known to the police', left Glasgow for New York a few days after the crime. Suspicious, thought the police. He had actually embarked under an assumed name. Highly suspicious, thought the police. Before leaving he had pawned a diamond brooch. A clincher, thought the police. And even though they soon discovered that the brooch had belonged to Slater, they applied for extradition, and, after carefully coaching a number of witnesses, sent them to New York in order to identify Slater. Here we must note a few curious features. The police knew on December 26th that the pawned brooch was Slater's own, yet the cable to arrest him was not despatched until the 29th, and on arrival at New York he was searched for a diamond brooch pawn-ticket. At the outset therefore the police managed, by misrepresentation, to create an atmosphere of guilt around Slater. Of the three witnesses who might have identified Slater as the murderer, Adams was short-sighted and would not swear to anyone, Helen Lambie, after some hesitation and evasion, said that Slater was the man, and a girl of fourteen named Barrowman, who was in the street at the time and saw someone run out of the flat entry, declared at first that he was like Slater and at last that he *was* Slater, though she had only caught a fleeting glimpse of him under the lamplight. At the trial Lambie and Barrowman, who occupied the same cabin on their way to America, swore that they had never once discussed the object of their trip, a statement which should have cast some doubt on their reliability as witnesses.

Before the extradition proceedings were completed Slater announced his willingness to return, and his trial took place at Edinburgh in May 1909. The brooch clue having failed them, the police had to trump up another. Nothing easier. Slater had a tin-tack hammer. True there were no stains on it, nor on any of the man's suits, but after all the absence of stains merely proved the cunning and foresight of the criminal. Slater was able to prove an alibi, but one of the witnesses was his mistress, who of course was considered untrustworthy and whose mere existence emphasized his guilt in the eyes of the moral community. A witness named McBrayne, whose evidence would have been favourable to Slater, was suppressed by the police, who kept the Defence in the dark about him. The trial was a hopelessly one-sided affair. No attempt was made to prove that Slater had any connection with Miss Gilchrist or her maid; but the Defence made nothing of this and against Slater's advice failed to put him in the box. The Advocate-General, in a forensic frenzy, uttered innumerable statements that were quite untrue, but the Judge did not once pull him up, and the Jury decided against Slater, nine being for guilty, one for not guilty, and five for non-proven. He was condemned to death; but there was an immediate agitation for a reprieve, and two days before the execution his sentence was commuted to penal servitude for life.

Doyle's conviction of Slater's innocence, reinforced by the opinions of Sir Herbert Stephens and Sir E. Marshall Hall, both of whom said that there was not a *prima facie* case against him, resulted in a press campaign and a book, which forced the Government's hand, and in 1914 a Commissioner (Sheriff Miller) was appointed to go into the question. As the conduct of the police in framing up the charge was ruled out, and as no evidence was given on oath, the Commissioner was conveniently able to announce that there were no grounds for interfering with the sentence. But not wishing to lag behind the police in his attention to duty, Sheriff Miller managed to provide another scapegoat. A rising young Glasgow detective, Lieut. Trench, believed Slater to be innocent, and said that on the night of the murder Helen Lambie had mentioned another man as the criminal. He was bullied and sneered at by the Sheriff, who rejected his story, and shortly afterwards he was dismissed from the police force without a pension. Later he was arrested on a criminal but purely fictitious charge, which fortunately was dismissed with contempt by the Judge (Scott Dickson) before whom it came. The persecution to which Trench had been subjected shortened his life. But one important fact emerged while the Commissioner was sitting. It was stated at the trial that Slater had registered under a false name at a Liverpool hotel with the intention of covering his tracks. Now it was shown that he had signed his own name, although he had embarked under a different one in order, he confessed, to make a clean start in America.

After the Commissioner's report it looked as if the case were settled for good, but every new Secretary for Scotland was badgered by Doyle to examine it afresh. Nothing happened until Slater was released in 1927, having spent eighteen years at Peterhead prison. Stimulated anew by a book of the evidence compiled by a Glasgow journalist named William Park, who had steadily refused to accept the verdict against Slater, Doyle again agitated in the press for a re-trial. The Scottish Secretary, Sir John Gilmour, yielded to pressure, and the Court of Criminal Appeal, consisting of five judges, heard the case. By this time several new facts had come to light. Helen Lambie had confessed to the reporter of a newspaper that she had recognised the murderer, who was not Slater, and that she had been persuaded by the police to make her false statement, for which she had received £40. Also the woman Barrowman had admitted that she was never certain of Slater, that her statement was prompted by the officials, and that she had been coached in it fifteen times by the Procurator-Fiscal. Her reward was £100. On July 20th, 1928, Slater's sentence was quashed, and he was awarded £6000 compensation. Doyle saw him for the first time in the court-room during the hearing, leant across the benches, shook his hand, and said, 'Hullo, Slater!'

Unfortunately their communication did not stop there. The Government declined to contribute towards the costs of the trial, some of which were met by the Jewish fraternity; but Doyle, having engineered the appeal, had made himself legally responsible for the balance of some hundreds of pounds and considered that Slater should refund this out of the money he had received. Slater on the other hand thought that the Government was responsible, and as the Government thought otherwise there was considerable friction between Doyle and Slater as to which of them should pay the piper. 'It was a painful and sordid aftermath to such a story,' wrote Doyle. He was much hurt by the other's ingratitude, and when someone remarked, in mitigation of Slater's behaviour, that he had endured a great deal, Doyle replied, 'Yes, but he is passing it along.' Eventually Doyle carried his point.

One more of his controversies is worth recording because it shows him from a different angle and has a certain historical interest of its own. Just as he voiced the sporting instinct of the average man who rushes to the rescue of the defenceless, so did he share and express the emotions of the ordinary citizen who responds to the picturesque and sentimental appeal of tragic events. In the duel between himself and Bernard Shaw over the sinking of the *Titanic*, the two types of Irishmen are revealed to us: the one impulsive, serious, romantic, Catholic; the other logical, satirical, realistic, Protestant.

The White Star liner *Titanic* (46,328 tons) with 2201 persons on board left Southampton on Wednesday, April 10th, 1912, called at Cherbourg and Queenstown, and sailed from the latter during the afternoon of the 11th on her maiden voyage across the Atlantic. The managing director of the Company, Mr. Ismay, was on board, and the passage was made at high speed: about twenty-two and a half knots. In the course of Sunday the 14th four wireless messages were received from other boats reporting the existence of icebergs in the region through which the *Titanic* was travelling. None of these messages had the least effect on the navigation of the vessel, which was kept on its course without a reduction of speed. Herein the master, Captain Smith, was doing what many others had done. It was the general practice when in the vicinity of ice to keep the course, to maintain the speed, and to trust to a sharp look-out. The public expected quick passages; there was competition between the Transatlantic services; and up to date there had been no casualties. From 6 p.m. on Sunday evening the weather was fine and clear: the night was cloudless, moonless, star-lit. Just before 11.40 p.m. one of the look-outs in the crow's nest struck three blows on the gong and telephoned the bridge 'Iceberg right ahead'. Almost simultaneously the officer of the watch gave the order 'Hard-a-starboard' and telegraphed the engine-room 'Stop. Full speed astern'. But the iceberg was sighted at a distance of only 500 yards; and although the helm was already 'hard over' and the ship had fallen about two points to port, she struck the berg forward on the starboard side.

About midnight it was realised that she would sink, and the order was given to uncover the fourteen boats. Unfortunately there had been neither boat-muster nor boat-drill, and though members of the crew had received printed lists in which they could find the boats assigned to them, many of them had not troubled to look at the lists and did not know their boats. Consequently there were confusion and delay in getting them ready, made worse by the deafening screech of the escaping steam. Meanwhile stewards were rousing passengers, helping them to put on lifebelts, and getting them up to the boat deck. At about 12.30 the order was given to place the women and children in the boats. Many women refused to go, some because they would not leave their husbands; they did not realise that the danger was imminent and in any case they had heard that the *Carpathia* was on her way to the scene. Faulty organisation and panic resulted in many of the lifeboats leaving the ship less than half full, and though the sea was smooth few attempts were made by the crews of the lifeboats to save those struggling in the water after the ship had foundered. The Captain and four officers went down with the ship at 2.20 a.m., and only 711 persons were saved.

The English newspapers wrote up the story, and on May 14th, under the heading 'Some Unmentioned Morals', Bernard Shaw wrote down the English newspapers in the *Daily News and Leader*:

'Why is it that the effect of a sensational catastrophe on a modern nation is to cast it into transports, not of weeping, not of prayer, not of sympathy with the bereaved nor congratulation of the rescued, not of poetic expression of the soul purified by pity and terror, but of a wild defiance of inexorable Fate and undeniable Fact by an explosion of outrageous romantic lying?

'What is the first demand of romance in a shipwreck? It is the cry of Women and Children first. No male creature is to step into a boat as long as there is a woman or child on the doomed ship. How the boat is to be navigated and rowed by babies and women occupied in holding the babies is not mentioned. The likelihood that no sensible woman would trust either herself or her child in a boat unless there was a considerable percentage of men on board is not considered. Women and Children first: that is the romantic formula. And never did the chorus of solemn delight at the strict observance of this formula by the British heroes on board the *Titanic* rise to sublimer strains than in the papers containing the first account of the wreck by a surviving eye-witness, Lady Duff Gordon. She described how she escaped in the captain's boat

There was one other woman in it, and ten men: twelve all told. One woman for every five men. Chorus: "Not once or twice in our rough island story," etc. etc.

'Second romantic demand. Though all the men (except the foreigners, who must all be shot by stern British officers in attempting to rush the boats over the bodies of the women and children) must be heroes, the Captain must be a super-hero, a magnificent seaman, cool, brave, delighting in death and danger, and a living guarantee that the wreck was nobody's fault, but, on the contrary, a triumph of British navigation.

'Such a man Captain Smith was enthusiastically proclaimed on the day when it was reported (and actually believed, apparently) that he had shot himself on the bridge, or shot the first officer, or been shot by the first officer, or shot any-how to bring the curtain down effectively. Writers who had never heard of Captain Smith to that hour wrote of him as they would hardly write of Nelson. The one thing positively known was that Captain Smith had lost his ship by deliberately and knowingly steaming into an ice field at the highest speed he had coal for. He paid the penalty; so did most of those for whose lives he was responsible. Had he brought them and the ship safely to land, nobody would have taken the smallest notice of him.

'Third romantic demand. The officers must be calm, proud, steady, unmoved in the intervals of shooting the terrified foreigners. The verdict that they had surpassed all expecta-tions was unanimous. The actual evidence was that Mr. Ismay was told by the officer of his boat to go to hell, and that boats which were not full refused to go to the rescue of those who were struggling in the water in cork jackets. Reason frankly given: they were afraid. The fear was as natural as the officer's language to Mr. Ismay: who of us at home dare blame them or feel sure that we should have been any cooler or braver? But is it necessary to assure the world that only Englishmen could have behaved so heroically, and to compare their conduct with the hypothetic dastardliness which lascars or Italians or foreigners generally—say Nansen or Amundsen or the Duke of Abruzzi—would have shown in the same circumstances?

'Fourth romantic demand. Everybody must face death without a tremor; and the band, according to the *Birkenhead* precedent, must play "Nearer, my God, to Thee" as an

accompaniment to the invitation to Mr. Ismay to go to hell.
It was duly proclaimed that thus exactly it fell out. Actual
evidence: the Captain and officers were so afraid of a panic
that, though they knew the ship was sinking, they did not dare
to tell the passengers so—especially the third-class passengers
—and the band played Rag Times to reassure the passengers,
who, therefore, did not get into the boats, and did not realise
their situation until the boats were gone and the ship was
standing on her head before plunging to the bottom. What
happened then Lady Duff Gordon has related, and the
witnesses of the American enquiry could hardly bear to relate.
    'I ask, What is the use of all this ghastly, blasphemous,
inhuman, braggartly lying? Here is a calamity which might
well make the proudest man humble, and the wildest joker
serious. It makes us vainglorious, insolent and mendacious.
At all events, that is what our journalists assumed. Were they
right or wrong? Did the press really represent the public?
I am afraid it did. Churchmen and statesmen took much the
same tone. The effect on me was one of profound disgust,
almost of national dishonour. Am I mad? Possibly. At all
events, that is how I felt and how I feel about it. It seems to
me that when deeply moved men should speak the truth. The
English nation appears to take precisely the contrary view.
Again I am in the minority. What will be the end of it?—for
England, I mean. Suppose we came into conflict with a race
that had the courage to look facts in the face and the wisdom
to know itself for what it was. Fortunately for us, no such race
is in sight. Our wretched consolation must be that any other
nation would have behaved just as absurdly.'
    On May 15th Harold Spender came to the rescue of the
race, described Shaw as Mephistopheles, 'the spirit that
denies', and produced a journalistic gem: 'Put aside all the
stories of false pathos and ignoble action, and there still
remains a star! Throw out all the dross into the slag-heap, and
there still emerges a nugget of shining ore!' R. B. Cunninghame Graham thought Spender's letter unfair, and said so on
May 16th. Conan Doyle's protest appeared on May 20th:
    'Sir,—I have just been reading the article by Mr. Bernard
Shaw upon the loss of the *Titanic*, which appeared in your
issue of May 14th. It is written professedly in the interests of
truth, and accuses everyone around him of lying. Yet I can
never remember any production which contained so much

that was false within the same compass. How a man could write with such looseness and levity of such an event at such a time passes all comprehension. Let us take a few of the points. Mr. Shaw wishes—in order to support his perverse thesis, that there was no heroism—to quote figures to show that the women were not given priority in escape. He picks out, therefore, one single boat, the smallest of all, which was launched and directed under peculiar circumstances, which are now matter for enquiry. Because there were ten men and two women in this boat, therefore there was no heroism or chivalry; and all talk about it is affectation. Yet Mr. Shaw knows as well as I know that if he had taken the very next boat he would have been obliged to admit that there were 65 women out of 70 occupants, and that in nearly all the boats navigation was made difficult by the want of men to do the rowing. Therefore, in order to give a false impression, he has deliberately singled out one boat; although he could not but be aware that it entirely misrepresented the general situation. Is this decent controversy, and has the writer any cause to accuse his contemporaries of misstatement?

'His next paragraph is devoted to the attempt to besmirch the conduct of Capt. Smith. He does it by his favourite method of "Suggestio falsi"—the false suggestion being that the sympathy shown by the public for Capt. Smith took the shape of condoning Capt. Smith's navigation. Now everyone —including Mr. Bernard Shaw—knows perfectly well that no defence has ever been made of the risk which was run, and that the sympathy was at the spectacle of an old and honoured sailor who has made one terrible mistake, and who deliberately gave his life in reparation, discarding his lifebelt, working to the last for those whom he had unwillingly injured, and finally swimming with a child to a boat into which he himself refused to enter. This is the fact, and Mr. Shaw's assertion that the wreck was hailed as a "triumph of British navigation" only shows—what surely needed no showing—that a phrase stands for more than truth with Mr. Shaw. The same remark applies to his "wrote of him as they would hardly write of Nelson". If Mr. Shaw will show me the work of any responsible journalist in which Capt. Smith is written of in the terms of Nelson, I will gladly send £100 to the Fabian Society.

'Mr. Shaw's next suggestion—all the more poisonous because it is not put into so many words—is that the officers did not do their duty. If his vague words mean anything, they can only mean this. He quotes as if it were a crime the words of Lowe to Mr. Ismay when he interfered with his boat. I could not imagine a finer example of an officer doing his duty than that a subordinate should dare to speak thus to the managing director of the Line when he thought that he was impeding his life-saving work. The sixth officer went down with the Captain, so I presume that even Mr. Shaw could not ask him to do more. Of the other officers I have never heard or read any cause for criticism. Mr. Shaw finds some cause for offence in the fact that one of them discharged his revolver in order to intimidate some foreign emigrants who threatened to rush the boats. The fact and the assertion that these passengers were foreigners came from several eye-witnesses. Does Mr. Shaw think it should have been suppressed? If not what is he scolding about? Finally, Mr. Shaw tries to defile the beautiful incident of the band by alleging that it was the result of orders issued to avert panic. But if it were, how does that detract either from the wisdom of the orders or from the heroism of the musicians? It was right to avert panic, and it was wonderful that men could be found to do it in such a way.

'As to the general accusation that the occasion has been used for the glorification of British qualities, we should indeed be a lost people if we did not honour courage and discipline when we see it in its highest form. That our sympathies extend beyond ourselves is shown by the fact that the conduct of the American male passengers, and very particularly of the much-abused millionaires, has been as warmly eulogised as any single feature in the whole wonderful epic. But surely it is a pitiful sight to see a man of undoubted genius using his gifts in order to misrepresent and decry his own people, regardless of the fact that his words must add to the grief of those who have already had more than enough to bear.'

Shaw's reply was printed on May 22nd:

'Sir,—I hope to persuade my friend Sir Arthur Conan Doyle, now that he has got his romantic and warm-hearted protest off his chest, to read my article again three or four times, and give you his second thoughts on the matter; for it is really not possible for any sane man to disagree with a single word that I have written.

'I again submit that when news of a shipwreck arrives without particulars, and journalists immediately begin to invent particulars, they are lying. It is nothing to the point that authentic news may arrive later on, and may confirm a scrap or two of their more obvious surmises. The first narratives which reached us were those by an occupant of a boat in which there were ten men, two women, and plenty of room for more, and of an occupant of another boat which, like the first, refused to return to rescue the drowning because the people in it were avowedly afraid. It was in the face of that information, and of that alone, that columns of raving about women and children first were published. Sir Arthur says that I "picked out" these boats to prove my case. Of course I did. I wanted to prove my case. They did prove it. They do prove it. My case is that our journalists wrote without the slightest regard to the facts; that they were actually more enthusiastic in their praise of the *Titanic* heroes on the day when the only evidence to hand was evidence of conduct for which a soldier would be shot and a Navy sailor hanged than when later news came in of those officers and crews who did their best; and that it must be evident to every reasonable man that if there had not been a redeeming feature in the whole case, exactly the same "hogwash" (as Mr. Cunninghame Graham calls it in his righteous disgust) would have been lavished on the veriest dastards as upon a crew of Grace Darlings. The Captain positively lost popularity when the deliberate and calumnious lie that he had shot himself was dropped. May I ask what value real heroism has in a country which responds to these inept romances invented by people who can produce nothing after all but stories of sensational cowardice. Would Sir Arthur take a medal from the hands of the imbecile liars whom he is defending?

'Sir Arthur accuses me of lying; and I must say that he gives me no great encouragement to tell the truth. But he proceeds to tell, against himself, what I take to be the most thundering lie ever sent to a printer by a human author. He first says that I "quoted as if it were a crime" the words used by the officer who told Mr. Ismay to go to hell. I did not. I said the outburst was very natural, though not in my opinion admirable or heroic. If I am wrong, then I claim to be a hero myself; for it has occurred to me in trying circumstances to lose my head and temper and use the exact words attributed (by himself) to the officer in question. But Sir Arthur goes on to say: "I could not imagine a finer example of an officer doing his duty than that a subordinate should dare to speak thus to the managing director of the Line when he thought he was impeding his life-saving work." Yes you could, Sir Arthur; and many a page of heroic romance from your hand attests that you often have imagined much finer examples. Heroism has not quite come to that yet; nor has your imagination contracted or your brain softened to the bathos of seeing sublimity in a worried officer telling even a managing director (godlike being!) to go to hell. I would not hear your enemy libel you so. But now that you have chivalrously libelled yourself, don't lecture me for reckless mendacity; for you have captured the record in the amazing sentence I have just quoted.

'I will not accept Sir Arthur's offer of £100 to the Fabian Society for every hyper-Nelsonic eulogy of the late Captain Smith which stands in the newspapers of those first days to bear out my very moderate description of them. I want to see the Fabian Society solvent, but not at the cost of utter destitution to a friend. I should not have run the risk of adding to the distress of Captain Smith's family by adding one word to facts that speak only too plainly for themselves if others had been equally considerate. But if vociferous journalists will persist in glorifying the barrister whose clients are hanged, the physician whose patients die, the general who loses battles, and the captain whose ship goes to the bottom, such false coin must be nailed to the counter at any cost. There have been British captains who have brought their ships safely through icefields by doing their plain duty and carrying out their instructions. There have been British captains who have seen to it that their crews knew their boats and their places in their boats, and who, when it became necessary to take to those boats, have kept discipline in the face of death and not lost one life that could have been saved. And often enough nobody has said "Thank you" to them for it, because they have not done mischief enough to stir the emotions of our romantic journalists. These are the men whom I admire and with whom I prefer to sail.

'I do not wish to imply that I for a moment believe that the dead man actually uttered all the heartbreaking rubbish that has been put into his mouth by fools and liars; nor am I forgetting that a captain may not be able to make himself heard and felt everywhere in these huge floating (or sinking) hotels as he can in a cruiser, or rally a mob of waiters and dock labourers as he could a crew of trained seamen. But no excuse, however good, can turn a failure into a success. Sir Arthur cannot be ignorant of what would happen had the *Titanic* been a King's ship, or of what the court-martial would have said and done on the evidence of the last few days. Owing to the fact that a member of my family was engaged in the Atlantic service, and perhaps also that I happen to know by personal experience what it is like to be face to face with death in the sea, I know what the risk of ice means on a liner, and know also that there is no heroism in being drowned when you cannot help it. The Captain of the *Titanic* did not, as Sir Arthur thinks, make "a terrible mistake". He made no mistake. He knew perfectly well that ice is the only risk that is considered really deadly in his line of work, and, knowing it, he chanced it and lost the hazard. Sentimental idiots, with a break in the voice, tell me that "he went down to the depths": I tell them, with the impatient contempt they deserve, that so did the cat. Heroism is extraordinarily fine conduct resulting from extraordinarily high character. Extraordinary circumstances may call it forth and may heighten its dramatic effect by pity and terror, by death and destruction, by darkness and a waste of waters; but none of these accessories are the thing itself; and to pretend that they are is to debase the moral currency by substituting the conception of sensational misfortune for inspiring achievement.

'I am no more insensible to the pity of the catastrophe than anyone else; but I have been driven by an intolerable provocation of disgusting and dishonourable nonsense to recall our journalists to their senses by saying bluntly that the occasion has been disgraced by a callous outburst of romantic lying. To this I now wish to add that if, when I said this, I had read the evidence elicited by Lord Mersey's inquiry as to the *Californian* and the *Titanic's* emergency boat, I should probably have expressed myself much more strongly. I refrain now only because the facts are beating the hysterics without my help.'

It was no longer possible to extract much sentiment or romance from the stories of the survivors, so Doyle closed the discussion with quiet dignity on May 25th:

'Sir,—Without continuing a controversy which must be sterile, I would touch on only one point in Mr. Shaw's reply to my letter. He says that I accused him of lying. I have been guilty of no such breach of the amenities of the discussion. The worst I think or say of Mr. Shaw is that his many brilliant gifts do not include the power of weighing evidence; nor has he that quality—call it good taste, humanity, or what you will —which prevents a man from needlessly hurting the feelings of others.'

Apparently Doyle thought it unnecessary to reconcile his assertion that he had not accused Shaw of lying with his earlier statement that he could not 'remember any production which contained so much that was false within the same compass' as the letter that had provoked his outburst. The newspaper's readers did not mind, for ninety-nine per cent. of them would rather have been wrong with Conan Doyle than right with Bernard Shaw.

CHAPTER XI

THE MAN IN THE STREET

LIFE at Hindhead in the early years of the century continued to be agreeable, and Doyle's participation in public affairs did not interfere with his activities in the world of sport. He took a course of muscular development with Sandow, the strong man who used to lift an elephant as a normal person would lift a paper-weight and toss cannon balls about as his neighbour would toss tennis balls. Doyle's attempt to emulate Sandow was not wholly useless. He was driving a car, weighing over a ton, which 'ran up a high bank, threw me out on a gravel drive below, and then, turning over, fell upon the top of me. The steering-wheel projected slightly from the rest, and thus broke the impact and undoubtedly saved my life, but it gave way under the strain, and the weight of the car settled across my spine just below the neck, pinning my face down on the gravel, and pressing with such terrific force as to make it impossible to utter a sound. I felt the weight getting heavier moment by moment, and wondered how long my vertebrae could stand it. However, they did so long enough to enable a crowd to collect and the car to be levered off me. I should think there are few who can say that they have held up a ton weight across their spine and lived unparalysed to talk about it. It is an acrobatic feat which I have no desire to repeat.'

His other feats as a sportsman were less exhausting. At cricket he was a good bat, a useful bowler, and played for the M.C.C. in several first-class matches. It was a great moment when W. G. Grace's wicket fell to him, though he did not feel so cheerful when W. G. returned the compliment. Once he was bowled by A. P. Lucas in a very singular way. The ball rose to a height of over thirty feet and fell clean on top of the bails. The incident provoked him to write a yarn which he called 'The Story of Spedegue's Dropper'. He continued to play for Barrie's team, but seldom took part in the accompanying festivities. A. E. W. Mason told me that on one occasion they all spent the night at the Lygon Arms, Broadway, except Doyle, who remarked as he parted from them, 'I wonder what all the swells who live hereabouts think of the way you literary

fellows take up the place.' It almost seemed as if he did not
regard himself as a 'literary fellow'. The fact is that games
were for him something more than diversion, and he did not
like it when people played at playing. Thus he attained a
higher standard than is usual with an all-round man, and
though he never got below a handicap of ten at golf his pro-
ficiency at billiards enabled him to enter for the Amateur
Championship and to get into the third round.

He tried his hand at pretty well everything, and was even
anxious to drop from a balloon in a parachute, but satisfied
himself with the more normal procedure, ascending some
6000 feet from the Crystal Palace and descending near Seven-
oaks. 'The first time I went up in a balloon I was terribly
frightened,' he told P. G. Wodehouse, who interviewed him
in 1903 for a paper called *V.C.* 'It was pleasant enough at
first, with all the spectators cheering, and so on. But when
we had been rising some minutes, and were a mile from the
ground, and I looked over the side!—I was never in such a
miserable fright in my life. To see people running about,
looking the size of dogs, and to feel that there was only a sort
of strawberry-basket between me and *that*! It was a long time
before I would let go of the ropes. But after I had been up a
little while I became quite used to it, and I suppose that is
what happens to everyone.'

Doyle's simplicity is quaintly illustrated in two passages on
the same page of his autobiography. In the first he writes
against shooting for sport, because it blunts our better feelings,
hardens our sympathies and brutalises our natures. In the
second he writes in favour of fishing for sport, because the fish
is a cold-blooded creature which does not feel pain like a hare
or a deer. But the effect on our natures of unhooking a gasping
fish and leaving it to die by degrees must be more brutalising
than that of knocking a wounded pheasant on the head. As
for his suggestion that it is 'the sweet solitude of Nature, the
romantic quest, rather than the actual capture which appeals
to the fisherman', one can only reply that fishermen have been
seen on pier-heads and that real lovers of Nature would not
spoil their enjoyment of it by messing about with hooks and
lines.

Though he expended more energy in sport than most men
give to work, Doyle produced more work than those of his
contemporaries who had neither time nor inclination for sport.

He could write under any sort of condition. Sometimes he went to his study before the rest of the household was awake and wrote hard until breakfast-time. Sometimes he sat down immediately after a game of golf and worked until his brain gave out. He could detach himself completely from his surroundings and knock off a story while a crowd of people were talking and laughing in the same room, suddenly interjecting a remark which showed that he had followed the conversation while his pen had never ceased moving. Occasionally he slaved away as if his life depended on it. When he heard of the Congo atrocities he got all the first-hand accounts available and shut himself up in his study for a week, not once taking his slippers off to go out until he had written his pamphlet. Thus, in spite of his physical activities, his output was considerable, and in the first decade of the century the public were treated to more Holmes stories, more Gerard stories, more short stories about sport, warfare, and adventure, a volume of talk about his favourite books, *Through the Magic Door*, and another long historical novel, *Sir Nigel*, which describes the early life of Loring, hero of *The White Company*. If anything the later book is the better of the two, yet it never became so popular, much to the disappointment of the author, who did not perceive the cause. In the intervening fifteen years the public had vicariously enjoyed its bath of blood. Kitchener had obliged it with the battle of Omdurman, which had manured the desert with dervishes, the Matabeles had provided much food for powder, and the Boers had been even more accommodating. The age no longer panted for deeds of chivalry, and the idealistic pre-Quixote note of *Sir Nigel* found no echo in a country that had just concluded a series of campaigns for dividends.

But there was no falling off in the demand for Doyle's short stories, which whetted the popular appetite for sport, mystery, thrills and horror. He could not help giving the man in the street what he wanted because he himself was the man in the street; indeed so exactly did he represent the normal man that one might call him Everyman in the street. But the normal man is not the healthy innocent our newspapers would like us to think him. He is a mixture of strange desires, domestic sentiment, cruelty, kindness, and morbidity; and Doyle expressed his less pleasant characteristics as unerringly as his more presentable ones. The story in which the leper woman

infects Captain Sharkey; the episode of the jealous Turk who
persuades his wife's lover, an eminent surgeon, to remove her
lower lip while she lies drugged, her features hidden by a
yashmak; the torturing of the Marquise de Brinvilliers; these
and a dozen other yarns display Doyle as the medium for what
was barbarous in the ordinary man. 'I have myself, in my
complex nature, a hunger after all which is bizarre and fantastic,' says the teller of one of these tales. Doyle was simple
enough to think himself complex merely because he was not
all of one pattern. Sir Max Pemberton tells us that Doyle's
'bias towards the horrific' was apparent in his conversation as
well as in his stories: 'Upon one topic he was always delightful
[sic]. Why the Barbary pirates so attracted him it is difficult
to say. But if ever I desired to set him going with warmth I
had but to mention those corsairs of the Mediterranean, who
used to descend gaily upon the shores of the Midi and there
proceed to butcher and burn. Doyle himself thought chiefly
about the poor women thus carried to the harems of Barbary.
The tortures they must have suffered were for him a fascinating
study upon which he could always talk with eloquence and
with pity. Such pictures of the habits of good-looking corsairs
as the Decameron painted for us were not in Sir Arthur's
gallery. He did not tell of handsome youths wooing beautiful
maidens in the luxurious cabins of ships, where the wine
flowed and the fruit was luscious. Rather he spoke of fire and
torture in terms which caused the blood to freeze.'

Here we may pause to note that all unimaginative folk love
the fanciful, the horrible, and the uncanny, which for them
add a relish to life, just as people without sensitive palates love
curry. The imaginative ones do not require such stimulants,
finding the common round enough to stir their creative or
engage their contemplative faculties. Doyle, and many others,
mistook the fanciful for the imaginative, whereas the diagnostic
of the truly imaginative man is a sense of reality. The imagination wrestles with life and is intuitive; the fancy plays around
life and is inventive. Poetry, so called, is more often a flight
of the fancy than an effort of the imagination, which, because
it grapples with reality, expresses itself in humorous prose
more readily than in serious poetry; and so we find that Dr.
Johnson's greatest biographies are more imaginative than
Shelley's finest lyrics, Falstaff's speeches than Milton's sonnets.
The imaginative type, Shakespeare at its highest, deals with

everyday life and only occasionally with the bizarre. The
fanciful type, Dickens at its highest, revels in the weird and
only touches reality in flashes. Except for *The Merry Wives of
Windsor* (a 'command' performance which had to be written
on the spur of the moment) Shakespeare never even troubled
to invent a plot; while Dickens loved mystifying his readers
with plots that became more and more ingenious and involved,
and died before disentangling his last, which still exercises the
minds of fanciers. Perhaps the purest example of the man of
fancy in literature is Poe, who has been called the grand
master of imagination by people who do not know the difference. Had Shakespeare written short stories he might have
called them 'Tales of Reality and Imagination'. Poe should
have called his collection 'Tales of Mystery and Fancy'.

Doyle, in macabre vein, was a disciple of Poe. He was
brimful of fancy and restricted in imagination. But he was
too normal to get Poe's effects, and when he tried to outdo
Poe in horror he overdid it, giving the reader a physical shock
instead of a spiritual shudder. He had an adolescent ambition
to make the reader's flesh creep, and editors sometimes found
it necessary to make him tone down his work for publication.
One of his tales, 'The Curse of Eve', is a description of an
accouchement which, after a crisis, ends with the mother and
child doing well and the father in a state of rapture. But
Francis Gribble told me that he heard Doyle read it at the
Authors' Club before it appeared in Jerome's paper *The Idler*,
and that in the original version the wife died and the bereaved
father tried to kill the baby, shouting at it, 'You little beast,
you've murdered your mother!' Doyle saw life melodramati-
cally, like Dickens, his characters being as theatrical as those
of Dickens, though much less various.

Such sense of reality as Doyle possessed only functioned
when he described scenes of action. Here Scott was his master
in the longer romances, while his short tales (other than those
about Holmes and Gerard) have something in common with
the stories of Maupassant. Of course Maupassant, being
French, was obsessed with sex, while Doyle, being more
English than an Englishman, was obsessed with sport; but one
is not surprised to learn from Doyle that he and Maupassant
once hit on an identical theme: 'I had been travelling in
Switzerland and had visited, among other places, that Gemmi
Pass, where a huge cliff separates a French from a German

canton. On the summit of this cliff was a small inn, where we broke our journey. It was explained to us that, although the inn was inhabited all the year round, still for about three months in winter it was utterly isolated, because it could at any time only be approached by winding paths on the mountain-side, and when these became obliterated by snow it was impossible either to come up or to descend. They could see the lights in the valley beneath them, but were as lonely as if they lived in the moon. So curious a situation naturally appealed to one's imagination, and I speedily began to build up a short story in my own mind, depending upon a group of strong antagonistic characters being penned up in this inn, loathing each other and yet utterly unable to get away from each other's society, every day bringing them nearer to tragedy. For a week or so, as I travelled, I was turning over the idea. At the end of that time I returned through France. Having nothing to read I happened to buy a volume of Maupassant's Tales which I had never seen before. The first story was called *L'Auberge* (The Inn)—and as I ran my eye down the printed page I was amazed to see the two words "Kandersteg" and "Gemmi Pass". I settled down and read it with ever-growing amazement. The scene was laid in the inn I had visited. The plot depended on the isolation of a group of people through the snowfall. Everything that I imagined was there, save that Maupassant had brought in a savage hound.'

Not wholly unaware of the fact that there is no recommendation like self-dispraise, Doyle sometimes affected a humble attitude in estimating his fictional achievements: 'If we writers of stories have not great brains ourselves, we can at least provide something which will rest or distract the brains of others who work at more serious tasks than our own.' Yet he was far from indifferent to criticism, kept press-cuttings about his books, and once begged Lacon Watson to review his poems for *The Bookman*. This was a ticklish job, because the writing of poetry was not among Doyle's many gifts. He could write verse, of a sort, but not once throughout a volume of it is a deep emotion distilled by the imagination into perfect expression. His most successful effort combines his love of sport and Puritanism, the conflict between the two providing him with one of those excellent strokes of comedy which give vitality to all his best work. 'Bendy's Sermon' tells how Bendigo, the famous Nottingham prize-fighter, takes to

religion and preaches at revivalist meetings all over the country.
On one such occasion a crowd of fellow-bruisers turn up and
interrupt his prayers with ironical comments. He prays hard
for strength to endure the mockery, but at last he gives in—

> Then Bendy said, 'Good Lord, since first I left my sinful ways,
> Thou knowest that to Thee alone I've given up my days,
> But now, dear Lord'—and here he laid his Bible on the shelf—
> 'I'll take, with your permission, just five minutes for myself.'

He leaps from the pulpit and proceeds to knock hell out of
the sceptics—

> So that's the way that Bendy ran his mission in the slum,
> And preached the Holy Gospel to the fightin' men of Brum,
> 'The Lord,' said he, 'has given me His message from on high,
> And if you interrupt Him, I will know the reason why.'

Doyle's personal tastes are reflected in everything he wrote
and one has only to read his books in order to understand why
he was liked by nearly everyone who met him. He could
discuss religion or sport or literature or war or torture or
politics or science or murder with equal zest because he was
equally interested in all of them. 'He was one of the nicest
men I have ever met,' H. de Vere Stacpoole wrote to me,
'a grand man in every sense of the word'; and this was the
general verdict. He was always ready with advice, usually
helpful, and F. Anstey relates how, when *The Strand* was about
to serialise his novel *The Brass Bottle*, Doyle told him to ask
for ten guineas a thousand words, which he accordingly
demanded and received. Doyle also advised Anstey to turn
his story *The Man from Blankley's* into a play, which made a
small fortune for the author. But the man who attacked King
Leopold of Belgium and the police authorities of Great Britain
was not likely to keep quiet when a fellow-scribe misconducted
himself, and a famous writer of those days, Hall Caine, whose
novels sold by the hundred thousand, received a private rap
over the knuckles from Doyle when his methods of puffing
himself and his books became excessive. I quote from a copy
of the letter which Doyle left among his papers:

'DEAR HALL CAINE,

'Your letter and Massingham's arrived together by this
morning's post. I am very sorry if anything I say seems offen-
sive or is painful to you. I wish to make it as little so as possible
but on the other hand I am bound to say what I think.

'It was a common subject of remark at the time of the appearance of "The Manxman" that the book had had public attention drawn to it in an unusual fashion. Then came "The Christian" and again the same outcrop of preliminary paragraphs and notices. I am quite prepared to allow that this may have arisen to some extent from causes outside your own control, but you must allow that this involves injudicious and reckless trust in newspaper men with a carelessness as to what they may do or say which is not fitting in the case of one who stands as highly as you do. The explanation is only less serious than the alternative. It is your duty to see interviews in the proof, and as far as possible to check injudicious newspaper comments. Surely that is self-evident. I am convinced that you are wrong in thinking that my letter suggested any other articles or paragraphs which may have appeared to the same effect. I am sure that there was a general feeling that if this could pass there was an end to any attempt at professional etiquette in the future, and that each protest was independent of the other. It would be a real pleasure to me if I could conscientiously write such a sentence as you suggest and I would do it in an instant if I could, but though it is true that the letter was written in some haste, you make it plain that you took no steps to check it, and that you did not at once repudiate or contradict it, although you actually wrote a letter correcting one point in it.

'I don't think you have any solid grounds in any of your counter-attacks. In the medical profession to which I belong all public breaches of professional etiquette are corrected by public protests in the medical papers. I fancy it is the same in the law. I know of no other means of influencing professional opinion. As to impressions I was not commenting upon them but upon a concrete thing— an interview with a number of statements purporting to be from your own lips.

'Where also is the breach of etiquette in my protesting before the book appeared? Surely that was the right time to protest against injudicious preliminary comments. My protest had nothing to do with the book. I wished and wish it every success . . . but I want a high standard kept up in our noble profession and when you see me falling away from it I will thank you if you will remind me of it.

It is true that we are very much at the mercy of newspaper
men and publishers but we can keep them in some sort of
control if we wish. As I said before there is no reason why
I should pose as a purist, save that someone has to do
unpleasant and unthankful work—but I might say as a case
in point that I wrote this week to the magazine with which
I have been most identified, threatening to finally sever my
connection with them because they had an advertisement
praising a serial which I had written for them. It is for
critics not for authors or editors to praise or blame. But
the business men won't conform to this unless the Author
sets his foot down firmly. And the younger men won't
conform to any etiquette unless the leaders of the profession
—like yourself—give them a decided lead.

'I am sorry to seem so cantankerous.

'Yours faithfully,

'A. CONAN DOYLE'

The fact that Edinburgh University had bestowed the
degree of LL.D. on Doyle in 1905 may have encouraged him
to read this lesson to Hall Caine; but, as he grew older, preach-
ing took the place of fighting, just as it did with Bendigo,
Oliver Cromwell, and other pious souls.

His multifarious activities left him little time to enjoy the
quiet home life which, he once said, was the sort of existence
he would have chosen. (But one has heard this so often from
men of action.) Owing to the poor health of his wife he did
very little entertaining on a large scale at Hindhead, though
his daughter Mary recalls an occasion when he asked the
officers of the French navy to 'Undershaw'. The *Entente
Cordiale* between the two nations was then in its early and
hearty stage, the French fleet was at Portsmouth, and Doyle
invited every French-speaking person he knew to meet his
guests. 'My father had no interest whatever in social gatherings, as such, but only when they linked up with a big international idea,' Miss Conan Doyle informed me. In speaking
of their childhood on Hindhead, she said that her brother
Kingsley and herself were free to roam the countryside, and
used to spend their summer holidays at Seaview, near Ryde,
without supervision, but that they always had to be punctual
and scrupulously clean at meals. They were brought up in
Victorian fashion, their father a rather fearsome figure in the

background, held in reserve by nurses as a threat if they were naughty. 'If you aren't good I'll tell Daddy and you'll be punished,' was the usual admonition. Their mother, a permanent invalid, was utterly unselfish, never complained of her lot, and seemed to them a saint. As for Daddy, despite his severe moustache and reputation as a menace to ill-doers, he sometimes threw his cares to the winds and acted like a grown-up boy, bursting with high spirits, quite irresponsible, saying the oddest things and behaving in the oddest way. One such outburst has been recorded by a visitor. The family were sitting about the hall after dinner one night when a storm arose outside. 'Hullo!' exclaimed Doyle: 'rain! I should like to go for a stroll in this.' Accompanied by one of the younger members of the party he set out for a tramp over the hills, returning in an hour or so 'dripping at every angle' and thirsting for a game of billiards, at which he made a break of nearly three figures.

His wife died in 1906 and for some time he could not settle down to work. He visited Scotland, and while brooding in solitude at an inn near Dunbar he received an invitation to spend a week-end with Arthur James Balfour at Whittinghame. The house-party drew him out of himself and he talked nineteen to the dozen. Balfour was bubbling over with joy, having just won a gold medal at North Berwick, which gave him keener pleasure than any political success had done, and 'laughed heartily at small provocation'. He had been Prime Minister when the Russian fleet, *en route* for Japan, had fired at British trawlers on the Dogger Bank, and he spoke of the occurrence in a gentle voice and disinterested manner: 'I was very angry, really very angry about that affair. . . . Their Ambassador called that morning and gave complete assurances, or really I should have had to do something.' Doyle was much impressed by the ritual of family prayers at Whittinghame, the entire domestic staff being present. 'It was fine to hear groom and statesman praying humbly together that they be forgiven the sins of the day, and merging all earthly distinctions in the presence of that which is above us all.' If he had stayed for more than a week-end, the impression would have worn off.

The Edalji case, coming to his notice just then, helped him to forget his sorrows; and his marriage in September 1907 to Miss Jean Leckie, whose family he had known for some time, made a new man of him. To be near his wife's people, he sold

'Undershaw' and bought a house at Crowborough called 'Windlesham', which he gradually transformed. He also took a London flat, No. 15 Buckingham Palace Mansions. There were three children by his second marriage, Denis, Adrian, and Lena Jean (known in the family as 'Billy'). Their upbringing differed from that of Mary and Kingsley. Doyle's struggling days were over; no longer had he to take care of an invalid or to worry about a household. His second wife screened him from many troubles, managed his affairs, kept unwelcome visitors at bay, and generally speaking looked after him. Thus his cares dropped from him, and he became far more genial and expansive at home. 'My honeymoon began on the day I was wed, and will continue right through eternity,' he said to a friend not long before his death. But apart from the subduing influence of his second wife, the age was rapidly shedding the austerities of the nineteenth century, and Doyle, the medium of his age, slackened with it. The typical Victorian father became the typical Georgian father. The spiritual change was noticeable in his moustache, which from the stiff military one of Hindhead became the soft drooping one of Crowborough. Naturally the offspring of his second marriage benefited from the change, and they have nothing but happy memories of their childhood. Their parents adored one another and they adored their parents.

It was partly his romantic temperament but chiefly his need for money that inclined Doyle to the theatre the moment it became clear that he would have to bring up a second family. Already he had done well out of a drama on Sherlock Holmes, written by William Gillette, an American actor who played the leading character, and brought to the Lyceum Theatre, London, in the autumn of 1901, after a successful run in the States. Originally Doyle had written a five-act drama on Holmes. Gillette found it impracticable as it stood, but saw great possibilities in the character, and offered to write a play if he were given *carte blanche* in the selection of incidents and dialogue. On the advice of his agent, Doyle agreed, and scrapped his own drama. Gillette then steeped himself in the *Adventures* and *Memoirs* and struggled with his play, at last declaring that it was not possible to put Holmes on the stage. But his manager, Charles Frohman, encouraged him to go on trying, stopped his tour, and left him free to work on the play. In four weeks Gillette was delivered of his drama, wherein the first and last of the *Adventures* were ingeniously dovetailed and bits from several others appeared. A little later his single copy was burnt when the theatre in which he was playing at San Francisco was destroyed by fire. Again he shut himself up and reappeared in a fortnight with the play rewritten. It was a big success, and innumerable touring companies in England and America made a regular income for the creator of Holmes.

Doyle then decided to dramatise another of his popular characters, and a play on Brigadier Gerard, with Lewis Waller in the title-rôle, had a fair success at the Imperial Theatre early in 1906. The press notices were not wholly favourable, and on March 12th his mother sent him words of comfort. From her letter, which he preserved, we can see why he portrayed her as Lady Ermyntrude in *Sir Nigel*:

'God bless you and yours, my dearest, but never forget that you are His, who gave you to me for His glory and to do His holy will. . . . Don't trouble your dear heart with the critics . . . they have not really studied the dear Brigadier in the pages of his creator. I fear also that *many*, perhaps unconsciously, are irked by your successes. Above all, I should avoid the "gentle art of making enemies". I do not see that it does any good. We cannot supply brains, sense of beauty and fitness to others, and we should be sorry for them. The Conan arm is strong and his lance keen. He should be careful and reserve his powers for those (and they are but few nowadays) worthy of his steel.'

Some three years later Lewis Waller produced Doyle's play *The Fires of Fate*, a dramatisation of *The Tragedy of the Korosko*, at the Lyric Theatre, and had a moderate success with it. After which Doyle plunged head first into the theatrical whirlpool and was nearly drowned. He had written a stage version of *Rodney Stone*, which included the fights. As the cost of production would be at least £2000, no manager dared to risk it; so the author took the Adelphi Theatre on a six-months' lease at a rent which, with the salaries of the cast, came to about £600 a week, and *The House of Temperley*, as he called it, appeared in the spring of 1910. It failed for three reasons: the women stayed away, because in those days they were thought to be too gentle to watch even a fictitious prize-fight; there was a theatrical slump; and finally King

Edward VII died. Doyle was left with an expensive theatre on his hands at a moment when there were no bids for it. Holmes had saved him so often in the past that he banked on the detective to repeat the miracle, wrote steadily for a week, and was rehearsing *The Speckled Band* within a fortnight of the previous play's disappearance. H. A. Saintsbury, who had acted Holmes in Gillette's play over a thousand times on tour, was chosen for that part; and Lyn Harding, the finest all-round Shakespearian actor of his time, was cast for the villain, Dr. Grimesby Rylott ('Roylott' in the short story), and engaged to produce the play. There were heated arguments at rehearsals between author and producer. Doyle had pictured Rylott as an old-fashioned melodramatic villain in a frock coat; but Harding wanted to create a character and asked Doyle to write in lines that would bring out more boldly certain dramatic moments. Doyle, slow to see another point of view, refused, and sat stolidly in the stalls with the text in front of him, seldom looking up at the actors as they spoke their lines; while Harding, convinced that the character needed some extraneous decoration, set to work on his own account, building up the villain by degrees as a neurotic, now blinking an eye, now making a leg tremble, now pulling at a lock of hair on his forehead. Doyle never lost his temper, but he was displeased and told Harding in his calm way that he thought the part was being burlesqued. For a few days their relations, which had previously been pleasant, became strained. Harding was insistent and Doyle was upset. The date of production drawing near, and an agreement seeming farther away than ever, Doyle's manager suggested that James Barrie, a friend of both actor and author, should be invited to attend the next rehearsal. At the end of the second act Barrie turned to Doyle and said, 'Let Harding have his own way.' A sound piece of advice, for Dr. Rylott electrified the audience on the first night and received over a dozen 'calls'; after which the author walked across to the Grand Hotel and wrote to thank the actor for his wonderful characterisation.

Lyn Harding's thrilling performance made the success of the play and got Doyle out of his managerial difficulties. He showed his appreciation when the piece was revived in 1921 by Harding, who related the sequel to me: 'He came one night to see the play and asked if we were making a profit. When I told him we were just breaking even he said, "Don't send me any author's fees until you do make a profit," and he instructed his agents at once.'

Apart from the films, both silent and vocal, Holmes made one more appearance on the stage during his creator's lifetime, when Harold Terry and Arthur Rose wrote a drama round 'The Return', and Eille Norwood, who had made a reputation in the part on the screen, played Sherlock. Doyle did not attend the rehearsals, but he was in a box on the first night at the Princes Theatre. After the final curtain the audience shouted for him, and he took a call with Terry and Rose, saying, in response to cries for a speech: 'Ladies and Gentlemen, I am only the grandfather; these two are the parents.'

One theatrical gamble was enough for him, though he lost thousands in other business ventures. He passed on the lesson he had learnt to his friends. Horace Annesley Vachell sends me this: 'About the time when my play, *Quinneys*, was running gaily along at the Haymarket Theatre, he adjured me not to abandon substance, the writing of novels, for shadow. He spoke of the theatre as a land of shadows, a sort of fourth Dimension. "In the theatre," he said, "let another fellow back your brains, don't back them with your own cash." Sound advice.' Towards the close of his life Doyle confessed that 'If when I earned money I had dug a hole in the garden and buried it there I should be a much richer man to-day.' Gold-mines, coal-mines, machines for one thing or another, sunken treasure, island treasure; anything that had a spice of adventure about it appealed to him, and he usually paid heavily for the excitement. On the other hand he was a director of Raphael Tuck & Sons, Ltd., for thirty years, displaying 'sound common sense and business acumen'; he was chairman of Besson's brass instrument firm for a long period; and on account of his known qualities as a shrewd and diplomatic man he was chosen by Lord Northcliffe to unify the opposing factions that had resulted from the apathy of the British Committee for the Olympic Games. He was also quite capable of looking after his own interests, as the following letter to his play-agent, Arthur Hardy, shows:

'29 : 10 : 08

'DEAR MR. HARDY,

'I think that it would be better that I should take both "The Fires of Fate" and the Boxing Play back into my own hands.

'The arrangement between us was that you should have 5% if you placed the plays, but as a matter of fact it is I who have negociated entirely (bar your one interview) with Aubrey Smith, just as it was I who negociated with Vedrenne in the case of "Fires of Fate", and I foresee that it will be the same with the Boxing Play. I have found the openings, so why should I continue to use your agency? It really forms a needless complication. I may say that in the case of "Brigadier Gerard" also, it was I who approached Waller and managed the whole thing, so that I have always felt the payment of commission an unnecessary thing. However, Bright drew the agreement, embodying what I had arranged, and in that way it came about.

'I don't want to leave you with any sense of grievance, so if you will give me an idea of what any services you have rendered up to date come to I would write you a cheque for the amount.

'Yours very truly,

'A. CONAN DOYLE'

Incidentally Doyle lost about £8000 through leaving his theatrical affairs in the hands of Addison Bright, who made false returns, but got it back from the executors after Bright had committed suicide.

In 1912 Doyle broke fresh ground as a novelist, producing *The Lost World*, in which pterodactyls, dinosaurs, iguanodons, stegosauri, and such-like fauna crowd the landscape. It is the sort of thing that children are supposed to enjoy, and like all caterers for children, from the author of 'Bluebeard' to James Barrie and Walt Disney, Doyle had a pronounced streak of morbidity in his nature, due to an excess of fancy and an undeveloped imagination. The mysteries of the South American forests were sufficiently alarming before 1914, and even inspired a party of Americans to take a yacht and sail up the Amazon in search of Doyle's Lost World, the expedition being organised and equipped by the Pennsylvania University Museum; but since then we have discovered that nothing sub-human, super-human, pre-human or preter-human could possibly surpass in horror the primitive doings of ordinary humanity.

An amusing instance of the cleavage between Doyle's conventional opinions and his individual feelings is given in the character of Lord John Roxton. 'Like most men of action, he is laconic in speech, and sinks readily into his own thoughts,' says the writer, accepting the current view that strong men are silent. He then exhibits Roxton reeling off speeches by the yard, his instinct having prompted him to show the man of action as he always is in real life—a windbag.

What mainly concerns us in *The Lost World*, however, is the first appearance of Professor Challenger, 'a character who has always amused me more than any other which I have invented,' said the author, who believed that his model had been Professor Rutherford of Edinburgh University; but although he delineated Rutherford's physical characteristics, the originality, idiosyncracies, fiery energy and uncertain temper of the man are copied direct from his old friend Dr. Budd, who peeps out spasmodically from several of Doyle's heroes and villains, and plays the leading part in a tale called 'Crabbe's Practice', but who inspires Professor Challenger throughout. The most entertaining of all the Professor's outbursts occurs in *The Poison Belt* (1913), in which the inhabitants of the world are destroyed by something malignant in the atmosphere. Explaining the curious effect that the poison is having on himself and breaking it gently to his friends that something queer is happening to the universe, the Professor becomes pure Budd:

'You will the more easily condone any mental aberration upon your own part when you realise that even I have had moments when my balance has been disturbed. We have had for some years in this household a housekeeper—one Sarah, with whose second name I have never attempted to burden my memory. She is a woman of a severe and forbidding aspect, prim and demure in her bearing, very impassive in her nature, and never known within our experience to show signs of any emotion. As I sat alone at my breakfast—Mrs. Challenger is in the habit of keeping her room of a morning—it suddenly entered my head that it would be entertaining and instructive to see whether I could find any limits to this woman's imperturbability. I devised a simple but effective experiment. Having upset a small vase of flowers which stood in the centre of the cloth, I rang the bell and slipped under the table. She entered, and, seeing the room empty, imagined that I had withdrawn to the study. As I had expected, she approached and leaned over the table to replace the vase. I had a vision of a cotton stocking and an elastic-sided boot. Protruding my head, I sank my teeth into the calf of her leg. The experiment was successful beyond belief. For some moments she stood paralysed, staring down at my head. Then with a shriek she tore herself free and rushed from the room. I pursued her with some thoughts of an explanation, but she flew down the drive, and some minutes afterwards I was able to pick her out with my field-glasses travelling very rapidly in a south-westerly direction. I tell you the anecdote for what it is worth. I drop it into your brains and await its germination. Is it illuminative? Has it conveyed anything to your minds?'

Other influences besides Budd are traceable in Challenger, for Doyle had lately been studying theatrical effects in contemporary drama, witness the brief duologue between Challenger and his servant:

'Austin!' said his master.
'Yes, sir?'
'I thank you for your faithful service.'
A smile stole over the servant's gnarled face.
'I've done my duty, sir.'
'I'm expecting the end of the world to-day, Austin.'
'Yes, sir. What time, sir?'
'I can't say, Austin. Before evening.'
'Very good, sir.'
The taciturn Austin saluted and withdrew.

Doyle's boylike belief in the superiority of dons, to which allusion has been made in an earlier chapter, is again manifested when Professor Summerlee faces up to the crisis like a man: 'It was a brave, good speech, a speech from that staunch and strong spirit which lay behind all the acidities and angularities of the old zoologist.' Another brilliant Professor, Dr. Maupuis (in real life Dr. Geley), appears in *The Land of Mist* (1926), where Doyle's spiritualistic ardour surges over into fiction and Challenger is chosen to expose a medium and then to be converted. We can only feel profoundly thankful that their creator was fonder of Challenger than of Holmes.

Like the man in the street Doyle reverenced human encyclo-paedias, and he reacted to public events exactly like the man in the street. Describing the funeral of Queen Victoria for the *New York World* he called her 'the dead saint', and in his account of King Edward VII's obsequies for the *Daily Mail* he referred to 'the troop of Kings who escorted their dead peer, with the noble Kaiser riding at their head. England has lost something of her old kindliness if she does not take him back into her heart to-day'. This article was reissued as a pamphlet, and when he came across a copy some years later he placed a full stop after the word 'peer' and drew his pen through the rest. Until 1911 he had done his best to promote amicable relations between the English and German peoples; but in that year he took part in the International Road Competition organised by Prince Henry of Prussia, perceived from the behaviour of both British and German officers that war was inevitable, advised a firm in which he was interested to remove its money from Berlin, studied German war literature, and wrote articles warning his country of the dangers ahead. He was perhaps the first to realise that Great Britain could be beaten by the submarine, and he renewed his advocacy of a Channel Tunnel, strenuously urged the home growth of food, and said that the threat could be averted by the construction of submarine food-carriers.

In May 1914 he and his wife accepted an invitation from the Canadian Government to inspect the National Reserve at Jasper Park in the Northern Rockies. The Grand Trunk Railway placed a private car at their disposal, and in every way the trip was made costless and comfortable for them. While in New York he inspected The Tombs and Sing Sing prisons, walking round in a shamefaced way, 'for it makes you feel so when you encounter human suffering which you cannot relieve'; and of course he revisited his beloved Parkman country. Shortly after their return war broke out, and for the next four years his legs and pen were equally busy.

He described the 1914–18 war as 'the physical climax of my life as it must be of the life of every living man and woman'. To those of us who had something better to do than fool around with guns and buttons it was simply a tedious and insufferable interruption of life; but Doyle as usual spoke for the great majority. On the day that war was declared he held a meeting at Crowborough and initiated what eventually became the Volunteer Force (mostly composed of men above military age) which in time numbered some 200,000 up and down the country. He remained a private in the Crowborough Company for over four years, drilling, marching, signalling, camping, rifle-practising, and thoroughly enjoying it all.

Meantime he was making all sorts of suggestions in the news-papers, mostly of a life-saving nature. Body armour and shields for the soldiers was one of them (Dr. Budd first put the idea into his head), and though the War Office was impervious to the scheme its development in the form of steel helmets and tanks proved that it was not so mediaeval as it seemed. Because of his agitation for india-rubber collars, safety waistcoats, and collapsible boats, many men in the navy owed their lives to him; but, needless to say, he 'never received a word of acknow-ledgment or thanks from the Admiralty' for doing their thinking for them. He visited the British front and sometimes 'felt more emotional than befits a Briton in foreign parts'; he had a close shave on the Italian front when three shells burst about ten metres above the open car in which he was speeding; and he was most courteously received on the French front, where he noticed that the soldiers wore wound stripes, a human and consolatory touch which, as it could be appreciated without much mental effort, the British War Office copied when Doyle drew their attention to it.

While in France he was able to see his brother Innes (a general) and his son Kingsley, both of whom survived the war but died of pneumonia shortly after its conclusion. He was always the 'big brother' of Southsea days to Innes, who was afraid of opposing his anti-conscription views in person and with difficulty summoned up the courage to disagree with him on paper, as the following proves:

'22 Aug: 1915

'DEAR OLD BOY,

'I have written so many letters to you about compulsory service and torn them up that I can't remember what I have said and what I have not. I always feel like a rabbit in front of a boa constrictor when I try to put any opinions before you. I never dare to say to you that I don't agree at all and yet that is substantially the case about this. . . . I cannot understand you still saying that armies don't require preparing beforehand. You who led the crowd to prepare for the Olympic Games. . . .'

Innes helped him with hints and information for *The British Campaign in France and Flanders* (6 vols.), the writing of which occupied him all through the war and for some time after it. He corresponded with several generals during the campaign and talked with many junior officers who had taken part in the different actions. He even made notes of rumours heard in clubs. Among his papers I found these jottings, the first of which concerns the battle of Heligoland Bight:

'Gossip. Crimes Club. Nov. 9

'German sailors were convinced that the British meant to shoot them and were exceedingly grateful for kind treatment. One who had both forearms shot away waved his stumps and cried, "Hurrah for Nelson!"

'Troubridge made a bad bungle of the Goeben business.

'The two cashiered Colonels were in a village on the retreat from Mons. The Maire of the village begged them not to fight. They saw force coming. They sent out letter of surrender. Force proved to be the British Cavalry.'

His admiration of the Germans, whenever they put up a good fight, is revealed in another note:

'At this time Oct. 23 came the famous advance of the Ein-Jahrige, who carried the trenches of the Guards, West Surreys, and other famous regiments. It was a great exploit.'

Sometimes he wrote a series of such memoranda on the left of a foolscap sheet and sent it to a commanding officer for his comments:

'The British trenches were a mile and a quarter from river. The position appeared serious as there was a river and the Aisne Canal behind the troops, and no supports all the way to Paris.

'*Comment:* But be careful how you make use of this, as it was a tactical error, probably avoidable, but still we must not give away the Generalship.

'Confirms the demoralisation of the retreat from Mons. It was, if one may say so, a reasoned demoralisation, for it was essential to get on, and even rifles &c. had to be sacrificed to speed. The morale was all right and the army regathered. The British were angry at being placed in so exposed a situation. Germans finding the roads littered with rifles naturally thought the army destroyed and were annoyed when it came again.

'*Comment:* This is of course only "hearsay evidence".'

All of which shows how difficult it is to get at the facts while a war is in progress.

Naturally he was hindered by the War Office at every turn; and the commander-in-chief, Sir John French, hearing that he had communicated privately with officers, objected to a book containing information so gathered. Doyle wished to dedicate his first volume to French, who early in April 1915 expressed his approval, said that he would be only too delighted if it were published at once, but thought it would be advisable that the proofs should be submitted to him. On May 14th Sir Reginald Brade wrote from the War Office to say that objection was taken to the third and fourth chapters, and that, in the opinion of the General Staff, they should not be published yet. On May 20th Brinsley Fitzgerald, private secretary to Sir John French, informed Doyle that the Military Censor considered the appearance of the volume undesirable at the moment, adding that in any event Sir John 'would not wish the book if published to be dedicated to him as originally proposed'. On May 29th Brade returned chapters 4, 6, 7, 8 and 9, saying that the Headquarters Staff opposed their issue just then. And two years later (April 1917) Doyle was still being impeded by the authorities, for he heard that G.H.Q. 'cannot see their way to relax the censorship of your account of the Somme battle'. After the censor's blue pencil had done its worst, the work appeared, volume by volume, and Doyle described its failure to appeal to the public and critics as 'the greatest and most undeserved literary disappointment of my life'. It is, as might be expected, the most readable history of the campaign.

His private life during the war years was not very private. His wife started a home for Belgian refugees in Crowborough; a wing of his house was given over to the soldiers for their use and recreation; and once a week he entertained about a hundred Canadian officers to dinner, though by the way the members of his family (not the servants) had to live on three-quarters of their rations, the remaining quarter being their contribution to the national saving.

In April 1917 Doyle had breakfast alone with the Prime

Minister, Mr. Lloyd George, and on leaving Downing Street he went straight to the Berkeley Hotel, where he wrote a synopsis of their talk, which I reproduce verbatim. K stands for Kitchener, R for Rasputin:

'*L. G.*

'K. grew very arrogant (said L. G.). He had flashes of genius but was usually stupid. He could not see any use in munitions. He was against Tanks. He was against Welsh and Irish Divisions. He refused the flags which the ladies worked. He obstructed in all things and ruined the Dardanelles. But he was a great force in Recruiting. Miss Asquith said of him, "He is not a great man. He is a great Poster."

'L. G. had a row with him in the Cabinet and said to him, "Please remember that you are only one of 19."

'I told L. G. my experience with K. He was shocked.

'L. G. had sent a Welsh painter to do Mametz Wood. Listened with interest to my account of the action. Said it was a beautiful story.

'Was interested to hear how I did the history and said it was probably better done from human documents. Asked me whether I had picked out any particular man among all the generals. I said I had seen no genius but that they were all capable. He agreed. Wanted to know if I had met Bridges. Seemed to think most of him.

'Got on to armour and found him very keen. He said he had no doubt about it. Said the soldiers always obstructed. He had sent many devices but they were all shelved. I mentioned Watts of the 7th Division as open to armour. He said "Yes" and seemed to know all about Watts and admire him.

'Spoke about revolution in Russia. Guards had killed their officers. Czar weak. Czarina very like Marie Antoinette. Revolt was not pro-German. Czarina was. She had been much upset over death of R. Only one subaltern was left of the Guards. Byzantine.'

Doyle visited the Australians at the front in September 1918 and witnessed the beginning of the battle which finished the war. For us the interesting thing about his trip is the speech he made to some twelve hundred Australians. Standing on a mound in the pouring rain, he praised them for their splendid deeds, but 'ventured to remind them that 72 per cent. of the men engaged and 76 per cent. of the casualties were Englishmen of England'. In his opinion there had been 'a systematic depreciation of what the glorious English, apart from the British, soldiers did', and he had the pluck to tell a crowd of war-battered colonials, not notable for modesty concerning their own achievements, to keep a sense of proportion.

There spoke the English man in the street, whose voice would never have been heard but for this Scottish Irishman.

CHAPTER XII

THE LAST PHASE

THE biographer is concerned with this world, not the next, so there is no need for me to deal with Doyle's conversion to spiritualism except in so far as it was the inescapable outcome of his nature; for a man's beliefs are important to his biographer only as a revelation of himself.

Doyle's nature demanded a religion. The Jesuits had disgusted him with their hell-fire nonsense, and he was too rational to accept any of the ready-made creeds. He therefore began in his Southsea days to look about for something that would harmonise with his temperament and appeal to his reason. He took a long time to find it, attending innumerable séances, reading hundreds of books, investigating all sorts of phenomena, and experiencing those flashes of belief and black-outs of disbelief which are inseparable from such an enquiry. But when a man searches desperately for a faith he is bound to find what he is looking for sooner or later, and what he is looking for will be, for him, the Truth. Doyle wanted to believe in a future life, and he got what he wanted. His methods of examination, the object of his pursuit, and his resultant apostolate, throw light on his personality and must be touched upon here.

As with everything he undertook, from the writing of historical novels to the exposure of British justice, from the playing of golf to the handling of a rifle, he was very thorough, leaving no source of information untapped; and when his studies were completed he possessed one of the largest private libraries of spiritualist literature in the world. The more picturesque side of the investigations made a direct appeal to his fancy. Haunted houses, sepulchral voices, moving tables, automatic writing, materialisation of limbs, levitation of bodies, mysterious sounds, lights, and touches, dead silence and darkness and quivering apprehension; everything was there to stimulate and satisfy his love of the weird.

'Ghosts,' said William Blake, 'do not appear much to imaginative men, but only to common minds, who do not see the finer spirits. A ghost is a thing seen by the gross bodily eye; a vision, by the mental.' This remark of Blake's raises an interesting point which closely concerns the character of our subject. It is a misuse of terms to describe material phenomena as spiritual. The world of matter is the world we know by means of our five senses; the spirit-world cannot so be known, but is divined by our imagination, by the spirit within us. The phenomena observed at séances do not prove the existence of a spirit-world, which, if its existence could be proved by the five senses, would cease to be the world of the spirit: they merely prove that there are phenomena in the world of matter; which nobody has ever doubted. The true spiritualists are the great artists, and we enter the spirit-world through the medium of such miracles as Shakespeare's *King Lear* and Beethoven's Last Quartets and Salisbury Cathedral, not by the aid of such curiosities as a floating body or a mist of ectoplasm. Doyle believed in fairies, but did not think their presence was proved until someone had made a photograph of them; which is rather like believing that Wordsworth wrote his Ode on Immortality, but not feeling certain of it without a snapshot of him doing so.

People do not radically change their natures through life, and Doyle, who thought that he had been converted from materialism to spiritualism, had merely arrived at the inevitable faith of the materialist, the faith of one who can only believe on the evidence of his five senses, namely: that himself, Conan Doyle, the recognisable and conscious entity of this material world, went on for ever after death, presumably enjoying all the things that had made life so delightful at Crowborough. He thought that this faith removed the fear of death; but, as Bernard Shaw once pointed out, 'the man who has come to believe that there is no such thing as death, the change so called being merely the transition to an exquisitely happy and utterly careless life, has not overcome the fear of death: on the contrary, it has overcome him so completely that he refuses to die on any terms whatsoever'.

The reasons Doyle gave for a future life were as materialistic as his conception of it. 'If there is no after life,' said he, 'why should man strive to improve himself? It is a waste if all his efforts end in annihilation. . . . I am sure that the mass of mankind would argue that if there is only one life, and death ends all, our wisest course is to get as much pleasure as we may.' And again: 'The idea of punishment, of purifying chastisement, in fact of Purgatory, is justified by the reports from the other side. Without such punishment there could be no Justice in the Universe, for how impossible it would be to imagine that the fate of a Rasputin is the same as that of a Father Damien.' This is the old police-court view of God, a priest-created bogey who sits in judgment on his creatures and distributes rewards and penalties. To make people behave themselves by frightening them with what will happen if they don't is a form of morality that comes strangely from a 'spiritualist'.

Doyle's own notion of a materialist was a person who disbelieved in a life beyond the grave. Yet it could easily be shown that the most materialistic people are those who are so much in love with themselves, their power, their pleasure or their comfort in this world that they believe devoutly in a continuation of these blessings elsewhere; whereas the spiritual people are those who, having gladly sacrificed the material advantages of this life for its immaterial beauties, are not interested in the persistence of personality and face extinction without a qualm. It is usually the earthbound egotist who longs to be immortal.

Like all materialists Doyle felt impelled to make converts to his faith, and having convinced himself of what he wished to be convinced he started a crusade with all the vigour he had previously brought to the Congo atrocities, the cases of Edalji and Slater, the reform of divorce, the Olympic Games and tariff reform. Disbelief can be a dogma as much as belief, and the simple man who starts as a sceptic often ends as a fanatic. His friends noticed a curious outward change in Doyle. Hitherto they had known him as a burly sportsman, practical, prosaic, precise. Now he was either vague, with a dreamy far-away look in his eyes, or emphatically direct, with an angry flush in his cheeks. 'In a less practical man,' Arthur Rose wrote to me, 'his belief in spiritualism would have been fanatical. He carried it to extreme lengths, showing impatience with anyone who expressed the slightest doubt. Yet fanaticism is the last word I could attach to a man so solid. You would have judged him to have not the slightest spark of the mystic. Yet his eye would light with something like the mystic's when he spoke of the spiritland, and his devotion to the Cause was nothing less than a crusade, to which he sacrificed money and all other interests so far as I know.'

Another friend, Ernest Short, had this to say: 'My personal reaction was that the man took his spiritual experiences so seriously and was so profoundly convinced of their truth that argument or even discussion was impossible; one might just as well have argued with St. Theresa about her mystical experiences. Though with Doyle there would have been no difficulty at all in discussing lots of other matters. He was not in any sense unapproachable when he was interested.' Francis Gribble informed me that Doyle 'was very sensitive to any suggestion that any medium of his acquaintance was a fraudulent practitioner and once had a most violent row with Filson Young who exposed—or claimed to have exposed —some trickery at a séance at which he was present'. Sir Philip Gibbs had the same sort of experience with Doyle: 'Unfortunately he was much annoyed with me towards the end because of a book I wrote about a fake spiritualist to which he objected very strongly.' A. E. W. Mason also told me of a man who had exposed a medium, much to the annoyance of Doyle, who said that he was 'not a gentleman'. Hugh Kingsmill, sitting next to Doyle at lunch, happened to drop some remark about his theory of survival. 'It's *not* a theory,' growled Doyle in a manner that did not encourage further small-talk.

The 1914–18 war produced the new Doyle, who determined to spread the evangel, writing books and lecturing all over the country. He allowed nothing to interfere with his self-appointed duty, and when his son Kingsley was dying he refused to cancel an engagement to speak at Nottingham, replying, when urged to do so, 'No, under no circumstances would I break faith with the public. They have learned to trust me, and I must be worthy of that trust. Besides, Kingsley would wish it so.' His sense of humour was not always in abeyance. At Huddersfield he upset a bottle of water on the table in front of him, the reporters below getting the benefit of it, and after his speech he passed down a note to them: 'I may not have converted you, but at any rate I have baptised you.' He must have been amused, too, by a letter he received from a man who was serving a life sentence in Sing Sing prison, because he preserved it. 'I accept without questioning the opinions of two such master minds who have delved deep and often,' wrote the convict, who had been reading the works of Oliver Lodge and Conan Doyle. 'One obstacle in my path is lack of belief in life after death. If the grave ends all there can be no spirits.'

There was no hocus-pocus about Doyle, who was an absolutely honest man, convinced of the importance, the urgency, and the truth of his message. He sacrificed everything for it: money, prestige, and eventually his life. The most highly paid short-story writer of his time, he practically abandoned fiction at the age of sixty, devoted his pen to the furtherance of spiritualism, and began that exhausting platform propaganda which undermined his health and made him so unpopular in certain quarters that it cost him a peerage. Having delivered his message throughout Great Britain, he took his wife and family to Australia in 1920, to America in 1922, to America again in 1923, and to South Africa in 1928, speaking in many of the larger cities of those continents, and, after deducting the travelling and living expenses of his party, handing over the entire balance to the Cause. He wrote accounts of all his journeys, but as they are mostly concerned with the object of his travels we need not follow him. Several touches in his record are worth noting, however, because they reveal the man behind the missionary.

His arrival in Australia united the religious sects and the agnostics for the first time in history, and he was attacked by the clergy and the secularists with passionate unanimity at Melbourne, where he and his wife were invited by the British Empire League to lunch, at which the Federal Chancellor of the Exchequer, Sir Joseph Cook, made a speech, and Doyle uttered the truest word ever spoken in jest: 'In my reply I pulled the leg of my audience with some success, for I wound up by saying, very solemnly, that I was something greater than governments and the master of Cabinet Ministers. By the time I had finished my tremendous claims I am convinced that they expected some extravagant occult pretension, whereas I actually wound up with the words, "for I am the man in the street". There was a good deal of amusement caused.'

Naturally the crowds were more interested in the yarn-spinner than in the spookist, and during the tremendous welcome he received on the station platform at Sydney a digger was heard to ask, 'Who's that?' and an urchin to reply, 'The bloke that wrote Sherlock Holmes.' The pressmen wanted to know whether Holmes was irretrievably dead.

'Well,' said Doyle, 'you can say that a coroner has never sat upon him.' The storm of abuse at Brisbane did not lower his takings at the theatre, where the manager declared the business to be as good as 'comic opera in the season'.

Doyle got into conversation with the captain of the boat going from New Zealand to Australia and makes this characteristic comment: 'He had been torpedoed once, and had lost, on another occasion, nearly all his crew with plague, so that he had much that was interesting to talk about.' From which we infer that if the captain had also been tortured by the Chinese, tossed by an elephant, mauled by a tiger, rescued from the cannibals while being roasted, and the sole survivor of a family destroyed by fire, our materialistic spiritualist would have found him absorbing.

In spite of his preoccupation with the macabre, Doyle had much common sense, and he realised that the Australians, by discouraging immigration, were selling future security for present comfort.

While out there he heard of the death of his mother at the age of 83. She had joined the Church of England and had shown no sympathy with his psychic work. His brother-in-law, E. W. Hornung, also died, and Doyle returned just in time for his funeral at St. Jean de Luz.

Every lecturing record was broken by Doyle when he toured North America, but it is difficult to say whether this was due to the general interest in Sherlock Holmes or the next world. True he told his interviewers that they would all find themselves in Paradise after death, but being pressmen they felt dubious on the point. This is the sort of thing to which they subjected him:

'Well now, Mr. Doyle, say! Do they have golf in the next world?'

'No. I have no reason to say that.'

'You never heard them speak of golf?'

'No, I never have.'

'Well, you said they had amusements.'

'Yes, they say they have more than we.'

'Well, maybe golf is among them.'

'I never heard them say so.'

Next morning a newspaper headline ran: 'Doyle says they play golf in Heaven.' At every centre he had to accustom himself to such headlines as 'Do Spooks Marry?' and 'High Jinks in the Beyond'.

It is pleasant to find him still interested in his literary heroes: making a pilgrimage to the Mount Auburn cemetery at Boston in order to place flowers on the grave of 'one of my spiritual and literary godfathers, Oliver Wendell Holmes'; visiting the Parkman country again; leaving flowers on the grave at Indianopolis of Whitcomb Riley, a poet of his acquaintance who had written prettily about children while thoroughly disliking them; and looking for the little cottage at Fordham near New York where Edgar Allan Poe had spent his last years. 'If every man,' he wrote, 'who owed his inspiration to Poe was to contribute a tithe of his profits therefrom he would have a monument greater than the pyramids, and I for one would be among the builders. But his nature was sinister. A nature without humour is always sinister. But he had glamour to make amends—even as a youngster he had this glamour. Did ever schoolboy write such lines as those which speak of "the glory that was Greece, the splendour that was Rome"? They haunt the mind.' (They haunt it still more when not misquoted). People could not, however, count on Doyle's sustained interest in literature even when linked with spiritualism: 'I slept in the Vancouver boat that night, and was awakened by someone who had a clairaudient message for me from Charles Dickens. I wish I could suffer fools more gladly—but I apologised next morning.'

Doyle had always liked the Americans and their country, but several things did not meet with his approval. Pittsburg inspired him with the reflection: 'Personally I am of opinion that God sent a man into this world that he might improve in mind and in spirit, and not that he should make screws and rivets.' The Chicago gaol horrified him; there was no light or air in the building, which was loathsome. 'The architect who designed this ought to be in it!' he exclaimed. The treatment of the prisoners was mediaeval, and he came away 'sunk in deep melancholy' to write an article about it. From Los Angeles they visited Catalina Island, owned by Mr. Wrigley, the chewing-gum king. 'Venus would look vulgar if she chewed,' thought Doyle, 'and Shakespeare a lout. There was never so hopelessly undignified a custom. A man may drink and look a king among men, he may smoke and look a fine fellow and a sportsman, but the man, or, worse still, the woman, who chews becomes all animal at once.' (To be exact, all cow at once.) Their view of the Pacific Ocean on the way to the Mexican border was largely obscured by advertisements of Hot Dog and Frankfurter Sausage, while such queries as 'Why not a Kelly Car?' shut off the horizon. 'It is really shameful,' felt Doyle, 'that a few should for their personal gain ruin the aesthetic and artistic pleasure of the whole nation.' Yet, in spite of chewing-gum, advertisements, prisons, the press-gang, screws and rivets, in spite of the persecution to which mediums were subjected and the rampant materialism on every hand, Doyle hoped for and prophesied the eventual union of the English-speaking countries—the United States of Africa, America, Australia, Canada, England, Ireland, New Zealand, Scotland and Wales—each state retaining its own complete self-government, the predominant partner being the U.S.A.

His South African tour is mainly interesting because of the fighting spirit which still animated him at the age of seventy. His son Adrian told me that he was dissuaded with difficulty from physical combat with a man who suggested that he was using his eldest son's death as publicity for spiritualism. At Bloemfontein he was shown round by a Dutch journalist. Seeing the monument commemorating the 26,000 women and children who had died in Concentration Camps during the Boer War, he read the inscription, which appeared to place the blame upon the British. Such an assertion, he exclaimed, was disgraceful: the Concentration Camps were an act of clemency whereby the British fought the husbands and fed the wives. His protest was reported, and he was thoroughly abused by the Dutch press, one paper stating that he had gone out of his way to attack the monument as if the women and children had no right to one. He promptly called on the editor, who explained that he had misunderstood the inscription, which was in Afrikans, not Dutch. Then why had not the journalist apprised him of his error? he asked. That afternoon, before his explanatory letter could appear in the press, some hundreds of young men assembled outside his hotel with threats of violence. But he and his family were out on a motor trip, and when they returned the crowd had been dispersed by the police. They were advised to leave next day from the first station down the line; but Doyle flatly refused; and they were unmolested. Nothing seemed to frighten him, from armed gangsters to horned mammals, and I heard from Adrian Doyle that on their way back through East Africa his father suggested that the two brothers should take the flanks, himself the centre, when a rhinoceros was being driven towards them. It would naturally make straight for him; he would suddenly open his umbrella; and while it paused in surprise the boys could shoot at it. The beast did not take advantage of the arrangement, which Doyle seemed to think a perfectly reasonable one.

Not content with writing and speaking for his beliefs, Doyle did his best to make converts privately. The following quotations from letters I have received prove his proselytising zeal:

'I knew Conan Doyle, but not intimately. I admired and respected him greatly, but I could not believe as he did in the manifestations of spiritualism, and he knew it. I believe that all the manifestations are produced by the subconscious minds of the mediums, perhaps in connection with the subconscious minds of the sitters. One day when I was staying in the Grosvenor Hotel, London, I encountered Conan Doyle in the lift. I had recently published a novel called *Mrs. Maiden*, in which I had shown my disbelief in the manifestations of mediums being produced by visitations of the dead from the other world. Conan Doyle said to me, "My dear Hichens, you are on the side of the Philistines against the children of light." He then asked me to come to a lecture he was giving on the following Sunday. I went, heard an interesting and obviously sincere lecture, but was not converted. I believe Conan Doyle, in spite of his great talent and cleverness, was in error. But he was absolutely sincere. An admirable man and a fascinating writer.' (Robert Hichens.)

'Doyle was very sympathetic when I suffered a bereavement and gave me the name of a medium who startled me for the first time in connection with spiritualism. After two equally amazing further sittings with this medium, Doyle asked me what had happened, and, when I told him, immediately said that those results were not given me for my private consumption. He meant that I should make the matter public in either an article or lecture. The result was that he arranged for me to speak at the Aeolian Hall, which I did with the medium on the platform. It was my sole appearance in that part because, as a result of it, I was invited to attend séances which discouraged me by their futility and fatuity, not to mention their probable fake. I am not apt to scoff at occult things like séances. On the contrary, I am sure there are genuine phenomena worthy of scientific investigation.' (Arthur Rose.)

'In 1927, when my son was killed in a motoring accident, Doyle wrote to me urging that I should seek mitigation of my sorrow by recourse to the spiritualistic communications in which he so stoutly believed. That he should have troubled to do so I regard as an evidence of the man's warm kindliness.' (Rafael Sabatini.)

'He did his best to make a convert of me. I assisted at more than one séance and was challenged by my host to do anything I pleased to exclude fraud. None the less, what I saw and heard failed to convince me that communication between the quick and the dead had been established. Quite genially, he told me that I was too impatient, too eager for results; and he added, modestly enough, that patience had never failed him. I believe him to have been an absolutely honest man, incapable of countenancing any form of trickery.' (Horace Annesley Vachell.)

Doyle also started a Psychic Bookshop, where he was often to be seen supplying the curious with information about the exhibits. His arms struck at least one observer as being too small for his massive frame, and it was strange to watch him gesticulating his way round the room, talking in that rather muffled voice of his, and brushing aside every query, so sure of the truth himself that he would not argue whether a certain photo proved what he said it did: its bare existence was proof enough.

He was attacked from all sides: by Catholics, Protestants, Rationalists, and Scientists; by Freethinkers, Slavethinkers, and Nonthinkers; all of whom went for him with as wide a vocabulary of abuse as they could muster; but he usually gave something better than he got. One Roman Catholic convert[1] wrote to say that he was 'a disgusting beast', who ought to be horsewhipped for his 'filthy caricatures' of Jesus Christ, and to prophesy that his 'blasphemous ravings' would bring a 'dreadful judgment' on him. He replied: 'Sir, I was relieved to get your letter. It is only your approval

[1] Lord Alfred Douglas

which could in any way annoy me.' A laconic letter-
writer, he would often reply to a request for something with
a simple, 'Yes. A.C.D.' or 'No. A.C.D.' Once he sent a
note to P. G. Wodehouse, who forgot to answer it and in a
few days received this reminder on a post card: '? A.C.D.'

Doyle's home life was exceptionally happy. He and his wife
were lovers to the end. 'After twenty-three years of married
life,' she wrote, 'whenever I heard my husband's dear voice
in the distance, or he came into the room, a something radiant
seemed to enter and permeate the atmosphere.' He bought
her a picturesque old cottage in the New Forest called Bignell
Wood, and to this he would occasionally retreat in his later
years for peace and quiet. At Crowborough too it was sometimes necessary to get away from visitors as well as the children,
and there was a wooden hut in the garden where he and his
wife would have tea together, where he could work or meditate,
and close to which they now lie buried. To the children of
his second marriage he was more of a friend than a father.
In their earlier days he used to tell them stories of animals,
Red Indians, cricketers, pirates, and above all prize-fighters,
of whom he would say, 'I don't mind telling you, my dears,
that there have been times when it was not the words of good
and pious men, but it was the memory and example of those
old rascals, that have helped me over a rough patch of the
road.' Adrian Doyle can only recall one occasion when his
father did more than administer a reproof. At the age of
sixteen he happened to speak of a certain woman as ugly, upon
which his father boxed his ears and said, 'No woman is ugly.
Every woman is beautiful. But some are more beautiful than
others.' The sex, however, had less attractive qualities, and
when Adrian was a little older Sir Arthur advised him, if ever
he had much to do with women, not to forget that his father
was also a doctor.

Outside his home Doyle also aroused affection. Apart from
his love of sport, his genuine patriotism, and all the other
emotions which he shared with the average man, he was very
kind-hearted. He could probably have lived in comfort on
the money he gave away, and he could certainly have earned
a large income in the time he spent on other people's affairs.
His generosity manifested itself in all sorts of queer ways.
Returning from a game of golf one day, he met a tramp, who
displayed the holes in his footwear. Removing his own brand

new shoes, Doyle said, 'We take about the same size. Have these.' Another reason why people liked him so much was that he never spoke maliciously of anyone. 'During our long talks,' H. A. Vachell informed me, 'I never heard him say anything unkind about others.' He even criticised his idol Macaulay for writing so ruthlessly of Montgomery: 'One would have wished to think that Macaulay's heart was too kind, and his soul too gentle, to pen so bitter an attack. . . . One would think more highly of the man if he had not done that savage bit of work.'

In conversation Doyle was much more English than Irish. In the endless quarrels between the two nations he always took the English side, and he had both the bluntness and the reserve of the Englishman. In an unpublished article on Truth being stranger than Fiction he wrote: 'The most remarkable experiences in a man's life are those in which he feels most, and they are precisely the ones upon which he is least disposed to talk. All the really very serious things in my life, the things which have been stamped deep into me and left their impress for ever, are things which I could never bring myself to speak of.' He made up for this reserve concerning himself by passing on a great deal of information on other matters. He was always studying something—history, languages, archaeology, chemistry, astronomy, geology, zoology, and so forth—and as he had a good memory he was able to tell people, and enjoyed telling them, what they wanted to know about most things. In fact he could have been what he so much admired: a first-rate professor. On the other hand he was often too much absorbed in his thoughts to display the quickness of mind and observation expected of him. Two instances have been given me. 'I used to wear black Ascot stocks instead of collar and tie in those days,' wrote Arthur Rose, 'and I remember Doyle saying one day as he looked at me, "There's something sinister about you to-day." I recall my surprise that the author of Sherlock Holmes should not have known at once that he got that impression from the blackness of my neckwear. Any such impression was absent when my stock was of shantung, as it frequently was.' This Watsonish aspect came out even more definitely in a duologue with Hugh Kingsmill:

'Arnold Lunn is a son of Sir Henry Lunn, is he not?' asked Doyle.

'Yes.'

'And you are a brother of Arnold Lunn?'
'Yes.'
(After a minute's pause for reflection) 'Then you also are
a son of Sir Henry Lunn?'
'Yes.'

Doyle's personal popularity suffered when he embraced
spiritualism. His old friends became rather nervous of him,
and many of them he seldom met, their places being taken by
fellow-spiritualists. But he passed a day or two in the last
year of his life with one of the oldest, Sir James Barrie, who
used to take a large house near Cheltenham in order to enter-
tain during the summer months. In discussing Barrie's success
as a dramatist Doyle had once said to Lyn Harding: 'Yes,
Barrie is a rich man, but I think I am the happier.' Any
doubts he had entertained on the point must have been dis-
pelled when he found that his host's main occupation was the
flicking of moistened stamps, by means of a coin, on to the
library ceiling of Stanway Court. The members of the house-
party were a little apprehensive, on Barrie's account, that
Doyle would raise the subject of spiritualism. He did; but
the stamp-flicker bore it like a man, and the evening passed
off without a major crisis. From the notes Doyle made in his
bedroom that night, the conversation at dinner does not appear
to have been scintillating; but the fact that he thought it
worth recording has some bearing on his nature, so I print
the account exactly as he wrote it. The 'Douglas' referred to
was James Douglas, editor of *The Sunday Express*:

'Sir James Barrie's. Aug. 23–24/29.

'Present. J. M. B. Mr. Asquith. Lady Cynthia Asquith.
Two sons, one at Winchester. Younger one Simon. Mrs.
Davis, wife of Gunnery Lieut. in Navy, one boy. Mr. & Mrs.
Denis MacKail. Mrs. Thomas Hardy. Lady Lewis (widow
of Sir George).

Barrie said:

'Shaw gets up every morning and cries out, "Hurrah! I
am Shaw."
'Shaw's plays were about Town Councillors and Sanitation.
'Douglas—"The man who writes articles about 'If I were
God'."

'He (i.e. Barrie) had one psychic experience when some one kept pulling his arm back into bed. He rushed out of the room.

'He said he was out of touch and sympathy with the present generation of writers. They were too sexual. At the same time we had to stand aside and let us see what the youngsters could do. It was a pity women took the same line. He thought well of Lawrence, of a new man called Powys, and of Lacon Watson.

'Someone said that if Bacon did not write Shakespeare's plays, then he missed the chance of his life.'

Doyle's last work of fiction was *The Maracot Deep* (1929), in which Professor Maracot discovers the descendants of an ancient civilisation living on the floor of the Atlantic Ocean, and Professor Challenger discovers that the earth is sensitive by boring into its entrails. In describing the conditions of life in Atlantis just before the deluge, the author gives us a picture of England in the nineteen-twenties: 'There was no longer the quiet and simple family life, nor the cultivation of the mind, but we had a glimpse of a people who were restless and shallow, rushing from one pursuit to another, grasping ever at pleasure, for ever missing it, and yet imagining always that in some more complex and unnatural form it might still be found. There had arisen on the one hand an over-rich class who sought only sensual gratification, and on the other hand an over-poor residue whose whole function in life was to minister to the wants of their masters, however evil those wants might be.' Doyle's fears for England's future had already been expressed in 'The Last Galley', one of a series of episodes concerning which he wrote that 'if all my work were to be destroyed save only that one single section which I might elect to preserve, my choice would certainly be those historical pictures which come under the heading of *Tales of Long Ago*.' Each tale lifts the curtain on a moment in bygone history, and he was trying to do what Kipling had attempted in the *Puck* books; but neither Doyle nor Kipling made the past vivid because they were more anxious to teach history than to tell a story, to impart facts than to let their fancies rip. A. E. W. Mason showed how that kind of thing could be done convincingly in *Three Gentlemen*.

When he wrote the sentence quoted above Doyle was

probably thinking solely of his short stories, because he always spoke of his long romances as his best work and manifested keen satisfaction whenever they were mentioned. George Moore's high opinion of them, and Moore seldom praised any novels except his own, gave him great pleasure; and he was delighted when Hesketh Prichard wrote to him in March 1916: 'If it is of any interest to you I read *White Company* and *Nigel* when I was utterly fed up with all other books, having had 24 days in bed.' Prichard was ill with jaundice when he pencilled this note, after a long period spent in training 'snipers', during which he had 'walked down more front line trench than anyone in B.E.F.' A compliment by another author brought a look of gratitude to Doyle's face. At a lunch of the Dramatists Club shortly after the 1914–18 war Edgar Wallace remarked that people only thought of Doyle as the creator of Sherlock Holmes, but he was something more than that: he was the author of *The White Company*. After lunch Doyle took Wallace aside and had a long talk with him. One more incident in this connection. In 1929 the four long stories of Sherlock Holmes were issued in a single volume, and I reviewed them enthusiastically in *G. K.'s Weekly*, receiving a letter from Doyle which began: 'I must really send you a word of thanks for your kindly article upon Holmes.' But he went on to say that he sometimes hated Holmes and wished he had never created him, because his popularity had prevented a proper appreciation of *Sir Nigel* and the rest. A man gets a label, he complained, instancing Sullivan, whose popular work with Gilbert had hurt his reputation as a serious musician. Doyle added that Poe had influenced him, that Gaboriau had not, but that more than anyone else Joseph Bell had been responsible for Sherlock Holmes, in spite of whom, he admitted at the close of his letter, 'I have much to be thankful for and your kind article is the last example of it.'

Before leaving the subject we may concede that the pure action scenes in *Rodney Stone*, *The Refugees*, *The White Company* and *Sir Nigel*, are among the best in the language. Though he lacked the imagination of Sir Walter Scott, the charm of Stanley Weyman, the naturalism of Charles Reade, and the brilliance of Crosbie Garstin, no writer in English can capture and communicate the simple joy of physical energy and combat so infectiously as Doyle. Only Dumas can beat him at that game. But for one reader in the future who will turn to any of the four historical romances, a hundred will revel in the Holmes and Gerard sagas, which have a quality, at once amusing and exciting, peculiar to Doyle, and in which alone he has no rival.

Having delved into the past and probed into the future, having dived to the bottom of the sea and drilled into the bowels of the earth, there was nothing left for Doyle to write about, H. G. Wells having despoiled him of the other planets; so he bade farewell to fiction. But indeed the end was near. In October 1929 he set forth on his final lecturing tour, visiting The Hague, Copenhagen, Stockholm, and Oslo, and intending to visit every capital in Europe, even Rome, Athens, and Constantinople. But while at Copenhagen he awoke one night with a terrible pain in the chest; and although he was able to carry out his Scandinavian engagements, he did so with grave danger to himself, almost fainting with pain in the intervals between the meetings. He returned from Oslo a wreck, being carried ashore at Dover by two sailors and taken in a bath-chair from Victoria Station to his flat nearby. A specialist diagnosed *angina pectoris*, the result of over-strain, and ordered a complete rest. Doyle said that the following day, Armistice Sunday, he had promised to speak at the Albert Hall in the morning and at the Queen's Hall in the evening. 'Then you do so at the risk of your life, and I wash my hands of the consequence,' said the specialist. He took the risk, suffering from a violent attack in the cab on his way to the Albert Hall and receiving treatment in the waiting-room before he could appear. Somehow he survived his speeches at both meetings, though the effort was fatal. Henceforth the least exertion was forbidden, and he lived on the ground-floor at Windlesham.

In March 1930 he resigned from the Society for Psychical Research, having been a member for a period which he described as 'thirty-six years of patience', because it adopted a sceptical attitude towards certain séances in Millesimo Castle at which the medium was an Italian marquis. He censured the editor of the Society's journal for implying 'that an Italian nobleman, a member of the legislative body, had invited a circle of friends to his home to practise a succession of complicated frauds on them'. Doyle's worldliness and innocence are revealed in the sentence. Like the ordinary man, he was impressed by titles; and he never tumbled to the fact that the business of every legislative body in history has been to practise a succession of complicated frauds on the community.

Sir James Barrie heard of his condition and wrote early in April: 'I feel sad to think of you not being able to let yourself go as in the brave days of old, a phrase I could never recall without seeing you, as one may say, in the middle of it.' Barrie had been unable to follow him in his mission but had always admired his zeal and integrity: 'Candidly I cannot think of anyone for whom I have had more respect or who had a more gallant way with him of rushing to the help of the deserving who needed a leader.'

Once more he rushed to the help of the deserving. Owing to a law passed in the time of James I, mediums and those sitting with them could be punished with imprisonment; also spiritualist societies were not recognised by the law and could not benefit from legacies. On July 1st Doyle accompanied a deputation to the Home Secretary, Mr. J. R. Clynes, and made a speech urging the repeal of this antiquated statute and demanding legal protection for mediums. The strain was too much for him and he got back to Windlesham with difficulty. A day or two later a friend called to see him. 'I am quite serene and happy,' said he, 'quite prepared to go or stay; for I know that life and love go on for ever.' His wife was sitting behind him stroking his brow, and at one moment he turned to her and said, 'Jean, you are so good to me.' Pain kept him in his chair, and towards the end he could only signify his needs by moving his eyes. And so he died. But as, for him, death was merely the beginning of a new and wonderful adventure, let us say that he travelled on, starting the journey on July 7th, 1930, at half-past nine in the morning.

Eighteen years earlier he had written his own epitaph without intending it as such:

> I have wrought my simple plan
> If I give one hour of joy
> To the boy who's half a man,
> Or the man who's half a boy.

INDEX